RMB

"if you love Me . . ."

by

Clementine Lenta

240
LE
copy I

Sacred Heart Center
6026 West Harwood Ave.
Orlando, Florida 32811

NIHIL OBSTAT:

Rev. Patrick J. O'Carroll
Censor Librorum

IMPRIMATUR:

Most Reverend
† Thomas J. Grady
Bishop of Orlando

The nihil obstat and imprimatur are official declarations that a book or phamphlet is free of doctrinal and moral error. No implication is contained therein that those who have granted the nihil obstat and imprimatur agree with the opinions expressed.

Copyright © 1976 by Clementine Lenta

Sacred Heart Center
6026 West Harwood Avenue
Orlando, Florida 32811

Price per copy: $3.00
(discounts on quantity orders)

DEDICATION

Reverently dedicated to the Holy Trinity: to the Father Who created us; the Son Who redeemed us; and the Holy Spirit Who sanctifies us.

CONTENTS

CONTENTS

FOREWORD

Long ago Our Blessed Lord said: *"If you love Me, keep My commandments"*. (John: 14:15).

Down through the ages many have proved their love for Him by obeying His commands, often at great sacrifices, sometimes even at the cost of their lives. Many others have followed Christ rather indifferently and still others have turned completely away from Him.

The general failure of people and nations to understand and appreciate God's love for us, and our failure to give Him our love, prompted the Sacred Heart of Jesus to reveal Himself, on June 16, 1675, to St. Margaret Mary Alcoque, at the Visitation Convent in Paray-le-Monial. He told her, and us, *"Behold this heart which has so loved men. It has spared nothing . . . In return, I receive from most people only ingratitude by irreverence and sacrilege, by coldness, by contempt for Me and the Sacrament of My Love."* He pleaded for devotion to His Sacred Heart in reparation for our sins, for the renewal of our lives and the reconciling of sinners with God.

In 1917 at Fatima, Portugal, Our Blessed Mother pleaded for prayer, penance and the amendment of our lives, saying: *"People must stop offending God, Who is already too much offended."*

Closer to our own times, Pope John XXIII, Pope Paul VI and the Fathers of Vatican II called for reconciliation and renewal within the Church but, at the same time, stressing the need for personal, interior renewal.

Again, many have listened and obeyed, some have turned away, and some have remained indifferent, choosing to ignore the fact that genuine reconciliation and renewal must begin with self.

This book, *"if you love Me . . ."*, has been written to encourage each of us to take a candid look at self, at our relations with God, with His Church, and with our neighbor; and then, facing reality, to strive more earnestly to listen to, and obey, the requests of Our Savior, of Our Lady of Fatima, and the directives of the Second Vatican Council.

Shortly before his death, His Eminence, Richard Cardinal Cushing viewed the draft of *"if you love Me . . ."*, and wrote the following *Foreword:*

> "Conflicting voices come at us from all sides these days of *aggiornamento,* each proclaiming to point out the way to the authentic renewal urged by the Second Vatican Council. In the face of this confusion, there might come the temptation to decide that the safest course lies in doing nothing at all. One might argue that the work of renewal concerns the Church as a whole, or at least the hierarchy, the clergy and the religious. This, however, would be a mistaken conclusion to draw.

"For the fact is that the work of renewal concerns all of us and we must begin with ourselves. To help the individual layman in a sincere self-appraisal and self renewal is the aim of this volume, *"if you love Me . . ."*.

"The title is indeed a striking one. It grew out of many discussions the author had with dedicated men and women in one parish after another. 'What's wrong with our Faith?' was the question people kept asking, but it became obvious that they intended no criticism of the Faith itself: rather, their meaning was, 'Why are we slipping in its practice?'

"Mulling over these failings and searching into practical ways of doing something about them, the author came up with this intriguing coverage of nearly every facet of life. The book might very well be sub-titled: What we can do about prayer, purity, suffering, alcoholism, reparation, drug addiction, intolerance, apostolic action, relations between parents and children — and a host of other topics.

"What is unique about this volume is the variety of authoritative sources from which the author has drawn her material, the thought-provoking questions she asks, the appropriate prayers relating to the areas covered, and the practical advantages springing from the exhaustive listing of associations and literature available for the aroused reader.

"if you love Me . . ." should prove a valuable handbook for the countless members of the People of God who are seeking greater commitment to the cause of Christ."

The original manuscript has now been brought up to date and enlarged. I highly recommend it as a powerful and practical tool for genuine spiritual renewal of individuals, families, parishes and communities.

Francis Larkin, SS.CC.

Rev. Francis Larkin, SS.CC.
National Director of the Enthronement
of the Sacred Heart

"if you love Me . . ."

The place was Grand Rapids, Minnesota. The day was a warm, golden Sunday in October. The time was mid-afternoon.

We sat — thirty or so men and women — around a grouping of small tables in the auditorium of St. Joseph's Church. Our conversation was lively and friendly for this was the end of a coffee hour following a Carmelite meeting at which I had been the guest speaker. The topic was *Fatima and You and I.*

Out of one of those sudden pauses, a man said: "You know, it's just too bad. Our Blessed Mother took such special care at Fatima to warn the world about the necessity for prayer, sacrifice and the amendment of our lives and yet, by and large we remain so indifferent. Even now, when we have actually witnessed additional wars and other catastrophies about which Mary warned us."

"You're so right," said a frowning, pensive woman. "It is too bad. I wonder why this apathy is so widespread." She paused a few moments and then looking directly at me, she asked: "Could it be because the world we live in has become so materialsitic, so paganistic?"

"Could be," I answered, "but over and above this, there is another outstanding reason. More and more often these days Our Holy Father and many of our spiritual leaders remind us that a basic cause is our failure to actually realize that God loves us — each one, personally — and that He wants us to return His love. In fact, Our Blessed Lord even asked us to prove our love for Him: *"If you love Me,"* he said, *"keep my commandments."*

"That's it!" a man exclaimed. And his wife chimed in saying: "To really love God, we certainly need His help. Lucky for us, that we have the Mass, the Sacraments and other means of obtaining God's assistance!"

"We certainly should make better use of God's gifts," said another man, "especially the Mass. We all know that the Mass is the greatest of all prayers, the infinite sacrifice — Christ offered to God for us. And yet, we seem so indifferent about this tremendous gift. Our daily Masses are so little attended . . . why?"

The question set off a very animated session. And the discussion on the Mass then circled around to Holy Communion, Visits and Holy Hours.

Then someone, remarking about Benediction, stopped abruptly and looking at me, said: "I wish that you had jotted down the things that we had talked about. I think that it would be good to have the notes handy to read over once in awhile — to jolt us from getting too complacent or too indifferent about the practice of our Faith."

Later, on my way back home, I scribbled some notes about the session and slipped them into my brief case.

A few weeks afterwards, upon being invited to speak at a guild luncheon in another town, I remembered the Grand Rapids discussions and the notes. Thinking about them, I decided that if our Faith and its practices came into the conversation, I would take notes.

As things turned out, no one mentioned our Catholicity or any of its practices. So I, having noticed that this parish had an exceptionally fine set of Stations, remarked about their beauty and then said: "I suppose that with such inspiring Stations, you are all drawn to praying the Way of the Cross often."

Dead silence.

And then someone said: "I'm afraid not. I guess that I am guilty of leaving the Stations to Lent."

"Me, too," another voice said.

My next question, "Why?" brought a flurry of remarks and questions about the Stations. And then the conversation branched out into a thoughtful discussion about sin, sacrifice and reparation.

And so, I wrote another set of notes. Throughout the remainder of the year, I assembled quite a few more.

Here they are — along with supplemental notes written from additional information gleaned from numerous conversations and from extensive correspondence from people around the country.

Here now are the original and subsequent "jottings down to read once in awhile, to jolt us from getting too complacent or too indifferent".

Here now are you and I talking about some of our personal failings and about things which we could be doing to answer Christ's plea: *"If you love Me, keep my commandments."*[1]

The subjects discussed are presented in alphabetical order for quick and easy reference.

The Recommended Reading mentioned throughout the book consists mainly of popular pamphlets and paperbacks of Catholic information pertinent to daily living. These were chosen not only because of their inspirational and instructive merits but also because of their easy, quick-reading qualities.

[1]John 14:15

PRAYER

Let every creature give unending praise, honor, power and glory throughout all eternity to the most holy and undivided Trinity, the crucified humanity of our Lord Jesus Christ, the chaste motherhood of Mary, the ever glorious and blessed Virgin, and to the entire assembly of Saints, and may we be granted the forgiveness of all our sins. Amen.

ABORTION

A shocking announcement was nationally broadcast on the evening newscasts on Saturday, March 11, 1972. The statement, issued by John D. Rockefeller III, chairman of the Presidential Commission on Population Growth and the American Future, recommended a national policy of zero population growth based on a limit of two children per family. The commission's report also favored making contraceptives readily available for all single and married persons, voluntary sterilization, and liberalized abortion.

On that same evening a film, *The Last Child,* was presented on many stations over a national network. The program depicted a projection of possible coming events in which the government through its Population Control Center restricted the birth of children to one child per family. Any deviation from this law was punishable by arrest and by forced abortion. The center's regulations also forbade anyone over 65 years of age to seek medical assistance for any ailment and also prohibited physicians from providing such assistance.

The newscast and the film projected a horrifying situation, *one which could actually happen,* unless people — in large numbers keep alert, — pray, make proper protests to the president, senators and representatives, and persevere in pro-life efforts.

As a matter of fact, we already have a horrifying situation: the death of millions of innocent unborn infants, resulting from the United States Supreme Court's permissive decision of January 22, 1973 declaring that the states may not forbid women to have medical abortions during the first six months of pregnancy.

The vital questions therefore are: *are we concerned enough to protest this infamous ruling?*

Do we also care enough to object to the use of funds and the services of personnel of any government department, bureau or agency for the promotion of abortion?

But, we may ask: what good will an objection from me, just an ordinary citizen, do? Why should we send protesting letters to our officials?

First of all, because willful abortion — honestly defined — is murder: the deliberate destruction of the right to life.

Secondly, our expressed objections or approval of any measure become a part of public opinion which influences the decisions made by our lawmakers.

Thirdly, because the axiom, *all that is necessary for the triumph of evil is for good men to do nothing,* is still a positive fact.

Our spiritual leaders have repeatedly warned us about the evils of abortion. In fact, Pope Paul VI's encyclical, *Of Human Life,* dated July 25, 1968, reaffirms the Church's teaching that willful abortion is intrinsically evil and is therefore condemned. The American Bishops' collective Pastoral Letter, *Human Life in Our Day,* November 15, 1968, also condemns abortion.

And the *Declaration on Procured Abortion*[1] issued by the Vatican on November 24, 1974 again brands abortion intrinsically evil and urges action — including political action — "to combat its causes."

The anti-abortion document of almost 6,000 words, issued at Pope Paul VI's orders by the Vatican's Doctrinal Congregation, declared that no Christian may "conform" to an intrinsically immoral law.

"Nor can any Christian take part in a propaganda campaign in favor of such a law, or vote for it. Moreover, he may not collaborate in its application. It is, for instance, inadmissible that doctors or nurses should find themselves obliged to cooperate closely in abortions and have to choose between the Christian law and their professional situation."

All of these directives present a very clear condemnation of abortion and we are expected to co-operate by remaining firm with the Church's stand against this terrible evil. We should also be alert to the fallacies expressed by the proponents of legalized abortion. Their contentions are made to sound so reasonable, so humane, so necessary. We should, therefore, be sharply aware of their erroneous propaganda.

Many proponents, for example, declare that abortion is not murder because "the fetus is not a living humanism". This is a fallacious statement because world renowned geneticists and gynecologists of various backgrounds and various religions agree and publicly attest their conviction that life begins at the moment of conception; that genetically, everything that we will ever be becomes present at conception; that distinct heartbeats of a fetus can be heard at four weeks; that all organs are formed at six to seven weeks; and that a fetus of ten weeks is not essentially different from one of twenty or thirty weeks.

Therefore, willful abortion — at any stage — amounts to the destruction of human life. It *is* murder.

Other advocates of abortion claim that abortion is a private matter "entirely up to the pregnant women's rights over her own body". This is not the truth. Abortion is not just a private matter but, rather, it is a common matter because it does not involve the woman *alone* but also the rights of the man (father) along with the rights of another person, even though yet unborn. The destruction of this innocent, defenseless human being is therefore *not* any woman's right.

Some promoters of liberalized abortion spread the erroneous remark that objection to abortion is only the Catholic stand and that the Church has no right to impose its teachings on others.

This is a fallacy. Although it is true that the Catholic Church emphatically condemns abortion, still abortion has always been regarded as contrary to Judeo-Christian concepts. There are many ministers and rabbis who publicly condemn abortion and issue statements objecting to legalized abortion. Also, various local, state and national organizations engaged in combating abortion are comprised of people from all walks in life, of various beliefs. Therefore, to say that this is solely a Catholic issue is a fallacy and an insult to all these fine non-Catholic people. Actually, the abortion issue is not strictly a religious matter but a *human* issue, common to everyone, of every religious denomination.

The truth of the matter is that the Catholic Church cannot and will not impose its norms of morality on others but it has the duty to remind both people and government that the Natural Law and the Ten Commandments demand reverence for human life and its transmission, from the first moment of its conception to the last moment of its existence.

As for the government, it cannot and must not impose norms which could establish a state religion of immorality: *Secular Humanism* which requires support of programs which lead to the destruction of human life.

Actually, it is neither the function nor the purpose of government, at any level, to sponsor and/or promote programs which terminate life. In fact, it is the proper role of government to 1) protect the right of all its citizens to transmit life *without any contrary coercion, compulsion or propaganda* by government; and 2) to protect all life from the movement of conception until the time when *God — not the government* — decides to terminate life.

Proponents of abortion also encourage the use of contraceptive drugs and devices as abortifacients. The use of such means is absolutely immoral and therefore *not permissible* because abortion procured by the persons involved in the conception of life through the use of contraceptive drugs and devices causes the same murderous results as abortion by operative procedures.

Some advocates of legalized abortion laws state that the reason behind their stand is the question: do we want the underworld or the hospitals to control abortions? And still other proponents contend that liberalized laws are humane since they are sympathetic overatures to women who have been raped, women who are "too ill" to bear children, and to heartsick parents who worry about the birth of possibly defective children.

While it is to be deplored that illegal abortions are being performed by the underworld or by the unscrupulous, and while raped women, sick women, and defective children are certainly to be compassionated and assisted in their difficulties, still, these matters are *not* the true issue at stake.

The simple and honest point involved is that *willful abortion should not be permitted at all because it is the deliberate violation of man's most basic right: the right to life.*

This right even applies in cases where it is presumed that the birth of a defective infant is a possibility. In reality, every child — perfectly formed or defectively formed — has a right to life and a right to strive for the eternal happiness which God has destined for all who love and serve Him. The hardships endured by a handicapped person in this temporary life, however long it may be, is as nothing compared to the permanent joy of heaven.

Besides the immoral aspects regarding any willful abortion, there are both physical and psychological dangers involved. Even in legal abortions performed in modern, antiseptic hospitals, it is of record that serious complications and deaths do occur from infections, from perforations of the uterus, from poorly administrated salt injections, and from suction equipment failure causing the injection of air into the womb. The psychological damage which many aborted women experience is also extensive. Numerous responsible psychiatrists and clinicians attest to the disastrous and often permanent effects which these women suffer.

And so, we should all be alert to do whatever we can to assist efforts which promote life, rather than destroy it. There are many things which are open to our cooperation in this regard.

We could pray for the rescinding of pro-abortion laws; write protesting letters to local, state and national legislators, and to political candidates; express disapproval at PTA and other meetings; send alerting notices to parishioners; write open letters of protest to secular and diocesan periodicals; sign (and circulate) petitions apposing abortion; contact radio and TV stations, praising programs having a positive attitude toward life and protesting the negative ones; demand that speakers advocating the right to life be given equal time and opportunities on the airwaves and that they be allowed to speak at various meetings; write protesting notes to publishers and editors of periodicals which print abortion-referral advertisements; form and/or assist anti-abortion campaigns; and circulate pertinent leaflets and books.

Among the very useful, very popular of these items is the leaflet, *Murderous and Ghastly,* available from the Wanderer Press, 128 East Tenth Street, St. Paul, Minn. 55101; 25 for $1.00; and the unique, important digest, *Let's Save The Unborn!*, termed "a must" for anyone who cares; available from The Sacred Heart Center, 6026 West Harwood Ave., Orlando, Florida 32811; $1.25 postpaid (discounts on quantity orders). Among the films is a fifteen-minute film entitled *When Life Begins* (McGraw-Hill), a beautiful audio-visual showing the human cycle from fertilization through natural childbirth.

There are also a number of organizations, open to anyone or any interested group, which are engaged in endeavors aimed at protecting life. Here are brief mentions of four such groups, each examples of various efforts:

Apostolate to the Unborn: founded by Mrs. Julius (Mary) Seewaldt; specifically designed to spread knowledge of the fact that a fetus has a soul and must therefore be baptized. The importance of, and the necessity for, such baptisms are beyond estimation and so the apostolate offers free copies of the leaflets, *Baptism of a Fetus* and *Baptizing and Burial of Miscarriages* — as well as pertinent anti-abortion literature — to anyone interested. Requests should be mailed to the apostolate at Potter Road, (North Java) P.O. Varysburg, New York 14167, and should be accompanied by a stamped, self-addressed envelope.

Birthright: originated by Mrs. Louise Summerhill, 21 Donegal Drive, Toronto, 17, Ontario, Canada. It conducts continuous telephone service which offers distressed pregnant girls and women a "listening, compassionate ear", and then refers those who wish assistance to proper sources for counseling, medical, psychiatric or financial help, so that their babies may be born, *not aborted.* In the United States *Birthright* centers are located in many cities, large and small.

Civic Awareness of America, Ltd.: a non-profit venture open to people of all denominations. It stems from the efforts of Mrs. Alvin (Rose) Emmons and Mrs. Ray (Joanne) Kuffel and is headquartered at 1226 Sunset Ridge Drive, West Bend, Wisconsin 53095.

Among its projects of national importance is its filing of a civil suit against the U.S. Department of Health, Education and Welfare, the Planned Parenthood Association and the Planned Parenthood-World Population. This is a taxpayers' suit to enjoin HEW from making further grants to these associations and to enjoin it from using any existing allotments for programs of abortion counseling, vasectomy and artificial birth control.

The suit alleges that it does not seek to impose its moral beliefs upon others but does object, as taxpayers, to government financial support of the Planned Parenthood programs; and that government financing of these programs obliges plaintiffs to contribute to the support of acts which violate their consciences as believers in Judeo-Christian morality; that such programs open the door to cognate practices of various forms of elimination of human life, including euthanasia, and are therefore violation of the Civil Rights Act.

The suit also charges that government support of these Planned Parenthood programs aids in the establishment of a new religion: *Secular Humanism;* requires support of a program leading to the use of genetics and selective population control to achieve race superiority, as in Nazi Germany; and tends to destroy the American political philosophy that the inalienable right to life, including that of the unborn, is an endowment of the Creator, not of the state.

The organization invites the cooperation of anyone interested 1) by their prayers that God will bless its suit into a favorable judgment in its behalf; 2) by their signatures: that government officials may realize that there are countless citizens of all denominations, of all walks in life, who are absolutely opposed to government participation in programs which destroy human life (signature sheets and copies of the legal suit are available); 3) and by their contributions: to assist the organization in defraying its mounting costs of postage, stationery, printing and litigation expenses.

Save Our Unborn Lives: established by a nurse, Mrs. Edward (Jean) Neary and a teacher, Mrs. John (Miriam) McCue. Members are parents, professional people, young adults and college students. Its central address is 16 Doe Run Road, Holland, Pennsylvania 18966. Its endeavors consist in going, in pairs, to Planned Parenthood clinics on abortion-referral days, standing outside, and courteously giving girls and women entering these clinics pertinent literature, such as the folder, *This Is An Abortion: The Ultimate in Child Abuse,* which also contains the *Birthright* telephone number and the testimony of doctors regarding the dangers even in legal abortions.

Its efforts also include erecting large bill boards stating *Abortion Is Murder;* staging pro-life demonstrations; providing information and/or speakers for Catholic high schools; assisting nurses in their protest of the nurse's role in abortion; appearing on television and radio editorial and talk shows; printing an informative, pertinent newsletter; distributing *Abortion Is Murder* car bumper stickers; and placing advertisements in personal columns of newspapers, encouraging distressed pregnant girls and women to contact them or *Birthright.*

Along with these and other "action" efforts, we are also reminded that it is vitally important that we pray for the defeat of legalized abortion and that we offer reparation for those terrible sins. Many of our spiritual fathers are pleading for this reparation. Among these is the Rev. Francis Larkin, SS.CC., national director of the Enthronement of the Sacred Heart. In his message, *Massive Reparation for Massive Murders,* published in *Let's Save The Unborn!*[2], Father Larkin states:

"The death of innocent children murdered in their mothers' wombs continues to mount. This rapidly escalating and officially sanctioned violation of the commandment, *Thou Shalt Not Kill,* will certainly call down the just punishment of God on all those responsible, especially the "Christian" politicians who made it legally possible to kill babies.

"But the apathy of those who did nothing to fight these abortion bills when they were being debated, and who now are appalled at the ghastly murders being committed, will also be punished by God. In fact, all of us will suffer with the guilty, unless we offer adequate atonement.

"Let us offer many Masses, many private and public Holy Hours in atonement and let us pray many Rosaries beseeching our Blessed Mother to ask pardon of her Son for those misguided and often frightened girls and women who are having their babies killed by immoral physicians; that aborted babies will be baptized by Christian nurses before they are incinerated; and that Our Lady will obtain for many women the grace not to have an abortion when tempted or encouraged to do so."

Father Larkin also suggests that many more parishes and religious communities join with those which are already offering God a special *Program of Reparation and Apology.* This program was first introduced in 1971 in twenty-five parishes in Southern California. It consists of a meditated Rosary; a half-hour of Reparation and Apology, before the Blessed Sacrament exposed; Benediction of the Blessed Sacrament; and the Holy Sacrifice of the Mass, in which the parishioners are invited to receive Holy Communion in *reparation for the sins that so offend the Sacred Heart today.* For further information and a detailed outline, anyone interested may write to the Sacred Heart Center, 6026 West Harwood Ave., Orlando, Florida 32811.

The teachings of Christ and His Church regarding abortion are clear and emphatic. And so the vital question confronting each of us is: *what are we doing to protect the unborn?*

Of course, our private prayers, our public worship, and our various protesting efforts are a bit of a bother and they do require a little time and a little involvement, but then, what is the price for preventing the slaughter of innocents? — for, *candidly faced, willful abortion is exactly that.*

PRAYER FOR LIFE

O God, Giver of Life, help us to do our part to save unborn babies from death by abortion and aid pregnant mothers in distress.

Please strengthen us in our efforts to obtain an amendment to outlaw abortion in the United States.

AMEN

Recommended Reading:

The First Nine Months of Life by Geraldine Lux Flanagan. This is not a book about sex or abortion. Rather, it is the fascinating, scientific story of everybody's first nine months of life — from conception to birth. This positive approach shows that the unborn child is not just a piece of tissue, not just an appendage of the mother but a live human being, from the moment of conception. This classic is now available as a paperback at $2.00 per copy from the Committee of Ten Million, P.O. Box 10299, Glendale, California 91209.

[1]Copies are available from the Wanderer Press, 128 East 10th St., St. Paul, Minn. 55101; 35¢ per copy; discounts on quantity orders.

[2]This important paperback is available from the Sacred Heart Center, 6026 West Harwood Ave., Orlando, Florida 32811; $1.25 postpaid.

ALCOHOLISM

An unkempt man staggers along the street, stumbles a little and then in picking himself up, brushes against us. We look at him with open disgust and think, "the dirty, drunken bum!"

Dirty, yes. A drunken bum, maybe. But he is a man beloved of the merciful God, dear to someone or some family. Once, long ago, he was an ordinary, respectable person, even as you and I. A moment's prayer for this unfortunate one would have been more in keeping with the command of God — and His Church — that we love our neighbors as ourselves.

Even a drunk or an alcoholic? Even them. Especially them for they are so in need of understanding, prayer and assistance. Besides, how do we know that we will never become a drunk or an alcoholic? Impossible, we say. Not us.

Really? It is an outstanding fact that many a person who has thought, "It could never happen to me," has been sadly mistaken.

What then? Does this mean that it is wrong to drink anything alcoholic?

No. Though the Church recommends and praises total abstinence, it teaches that alcoholic beverages, of themselves, are not evil. Rather, it is their abuse — their immoderate use — which is evil and which must be avoided.

So, if we find that we are becoming problem drinkers, it is time — and past time — to change our drinking habits. The time to prevent the alcoholic habit, our counsellors warn, is *now* before actual alcoholism develops.

Maybe so, we think. But that does not apply to us. We are not problem drinkers.

Are we sure? Drink may be getting to be more necessary and more important to us than we realize.

Do we, for example, feel that we just must have a drink at definite times each day? Do we get the "shakes" if we don't have it? Must we drink *alone* as well as at social gatherings?

Does drink make us irritable? forgetful? moody? hard to get along with? Does it affect our peace of mind?

Is drink hurting our family? our reputation? our job or career? Is drink deadening our ambitions, our initiative? Is it making us cruel, careless or irresponsible?

These are some of the signposts warning us to check our alcoholic habits.

And what if, sad to say, we are not only problem drinkers, but already alcoholics — compulsive drinkers? Does this mean that we must condemn ourselves as hopeless cases? On the contrary.

There are thousands of alcoholics who have faced the fact that they are alcoholics and who have then, with the help of God and others, fought a valiant fight. They are now non-drinking, respected, successful people.

Among these are men and women from all walks in life, the famous and the unknown. Among the Catholic alcoholics was Matt Talbot who not only conquered alcoholism but rose to such sanctity that his process of beatification is now underway.

If they could conquer, so can we. How?

Much has been written and much has been said about this subject. Almost invariably, many authorities agree upon several points:

1. The alcoholic must face the fact that he or she is an alcoholic and must resolve to stop drinking, not merely give up the habit.

2. The alcoholic must face the fact that *without the help of God — without sincere prayer — there can be no lasting victory.*

3. The alcoholic must realize that he is in need of spiritual, physical or emotional help and must be willing to co-operate with such help: with his priest or minister, his doctor or psychiatrist; with *Alcoholics Anonymous* and, if a Catholic the *Calix Society.* Cooperating assistance is also available from *Al-Anon* groups whose members are spouses and children of alcoholics.

4. The alcoholic must never become careless or indifferent in his efforts to control alcoholic craving and *must avoid any and all drink, even a small glass of beer or wine.*

5. The alcoholic must understand that one of the best preventatives for "that jittery feeling" is food and proper relaxation and that he must make the proper use of these means as substitutes for drink.

6. The alcoholic must avoid needless tension and fatigue.

7. The alcoholic must tell himself, over and over again, that with the help of God, it can be done, it is being done, and he, too, will do it.

The plight of problem drinkers and alcoholics is very serious, affecting a great many people. It is reported that there are nine million adult American alcoholics and that one out of seven teens is a potential alcoholic. Each year thousands die from the proximate causes of alcoholism; about 100,000 divorces and 200,000 broken homes result; several hundred thousand children are traumatized by a childhood spent with alcoholic parents; about 75,000 serious crimes are committed by persons under the influence of alcohol; and around fifty billion dollars is lost to the economy as a result of the diminished productivity of both men and women who drink too much.

Couldn't we who — blessedly — are not directly affected have a greater compassion for these unfortunate ones? And couldn't we offer daily prayers in their behalf to the merciful Heart of Christ?

Prayer for Alcoholics

O Mary, my Queen and my Mother, mindful of that thirst which your Divine Son endured upon the Cross out of love for us, I ask your aid for all those who should totally abstain from alcoholic beverages this day. Mother of Divine Grace, beseech Him that they may not fail, and that our lives may ever be lived close to His Sacred Heart and your own Immaculate Heart.

Recommended Reading:

Dear Alcoholic ($1.25); this very special paperback offers hope and encouragement to potential alcoholics, alcoholics and their families; relates positive suggestions for gaining sobriety and achieving personal and family happiness; available from the Sacred Heart Center, 6026 West Harwood Avenue, Orlando, Florida 32811.

The Catholic Alcoholic (85¢); *When One is One Too Many* ($1.00); *A Word for the Problem Drinker* (10¢); published by the *Calix Society.*

The Life of Matt Talbot ($1.00) and *We knew Matt Talbot* ($1.50); both books published by the *Matt Talbot Legion.*

Apostolates relating to alcoholism are:

The Calix Society (7601 Wayzata Blvd., Minneapolis, Minn. 55416). Active membership is open to Catholic alcoholics who wish to overcome their problem and help others to do so. Auxiliary membership is open to non-alcoholics who wish to join in the Society's daily prayers.

The Matt Talbot Legion (c/o Carmel Retreat, 55 Demarest Avenue, Englewood, New Jersey, 07631). Membership is open to alcoholics and non-alcoholics who wish to unite in prayers in behalf of alcoholics and prayers for the canonization of Matt Talbot.

GOD grant me the
SERENITY
to accept the things
I cannot change;
COURAGE to change the
things I can;
and WISDOM to know the
difference.

THE ANGELS

The angels, we know, are pure spirits created by God to love Him, to adore Him and to serve Him. The beauty and power of these angels is tremendous and their concern and care of us is unlimited.

Among the angels whom we should particularly honor are St. Michael, the triumphant archangel who overthrew Satan: St. Gabriel, the glorious archangel who brought tidings of the Incarnation to the Blessed Virgin Mary; and St. Raphael, the great archangel of health, love, light and happy meetings.[1]

Among the thousands of angels who serve God and care for us are the Guardian Angels — one for each of us. This angel is our good friend and our life-long companion. Not until eternity will we realize the extent of his love and protection. From the day of our birth until the moment of our death, our Guardian Angel watches over us unceasingly. He prays for us, inspires us and presents our prayers and good works to God. He rescues us from spiritual and corporal dangers. And when we fall into sin he keeps urging us on to sorrow and to repentence.

But, we may wonder, what about the detracting statements being promoted these days, saying that belief in the existence of the Angels is superstitious folklore or lovely myths?

The existence of the Angels is an infallibly defined truth. Contrary opinions and statements are a distortion of truth, a Satanic fallacy designed to deprive us of the angelic assistance which God has provided for us. Such detractions are a piercing thrust against the revealed Word of God and the teachings of His Church.

Both the Old and the New Testaments depict countless incidents relating the existence of the Angels, their ministry towards God and their assistance — often in miraculous ways — to mankind. The Word of God also specifically mentions the names of three of the great archangels: Michael, Raphael and Gabriel.

Christ confirmed the existence of the Angels by assuring His worried followers that He could have a legion of Angels to assist Him, if He so desired their help. His Church, too, in its doctrine and liturgy, its music, art and literature clearly manifests belief in, and veneration of the Angels. Throughout the ages the Church has consistently taught that the Angels are a part of the Communion of Saints, pure spirits created to adore God, to minister to His commands, and to assist mankind. And in our modern times we note continued recognition of the Angels by the Church. In fact, Vatican II, in its *Dogmatic Constitution on the Church, No. 50,* repeats the importance of imploring their assistance.

Sacred Liturgy contains various feasts in honor of the Angels and the Church recommends that we practice devotion to them; that we observe their feast days; and that we pray to them daily. In fact the little prayer,

Angel of God, my guardian dear,
To whom God's love commits me here,

Ever this day be at my side
To light, to guard, to rule and guide

carries a plenary indulgence, at death, to those who say this prayer frequently during life.

We are also encouraged to participate in the endeavors of apostolates dedicated to increasing awareness of the Angels, to appreciate their ministry, and to encourage devotion to them. Among the apostolates is the *St. Michael League* headquartered at the Divine Word Seminary, Duxbury, Mass. 02344. Angel prayers, medals, leaflets and booklets are available from this organization at nominal prices. Among the recent books designed to help us know and love the Angels is *Angels in Religion and Art,* a delightful, interesting book authored by the Rev. Valentine Long, O.F.M. It explains how we know that the Angels exist, what they do, and how they are honored in religion, art, music and verse; $2.95 per copy; available from Franciscan Herald Press, 1435 West 51st Street, Chicago, Illinois 60609.

To think of the Angels is to think of the magnificence of God. And to think that God has favored each of us with a particular Guardian Angel is to think of His loving providence in granting us such faithful companions, ever alert to assist us in every need.

The saints loved the Angels, They rejoiced in their companionship. They honored them, prayed to them, and thanked them often. We could, too.

[1](St. Raphael's special powers are related in the *Old Testament* in the *Book of Tobias*)

ANGER

We are in a corner of the garden, transplanting some flowers. Out of the corner of our eyes, we notice our neighbor, Dan, coming towards us. Hastily, we turn our back, becoming very absorbed in the planting. So much so, that when Dan meekly, hesitantly says: "Good morning; its's a nice warm day, isn't it?", we pretend that we did not hear him. After a few seconds he goes slowly back into his own yard.

For an instant our conscience rebukes us and then bitter anger takes over. We know that it is wrong to give in to such anger but, after all, Dan did say some very cutting things to us when he blamed our boys for breaking his big front window . . . The nerve of him, the utter nerve . . . As far as we are concerned, Dan can just go jump . . .

Anger floods us again. Then conscience rises, saying: "Yes, but that happened over three months ago and Dan does seem sorry and willing to be friendly. Can't you forgive and forget?"

We can't, we think. It's too hard.

Yes, it is hard, especially since we have a temperament prone to anger, unbending when crossed. But does this mean that we may give in to anger whenever and wherever it strikes? Or that we may remain angry, sometimes for months at a time?

Hardly.

We are reminded that a long time ago when Peter asked Our Blessed Lord: "how often shall my brother offend against me, and I forgive him, until seven times"? Christ answered: "I say to you, not until seven times but until seventy times seven times."[1]

In other words: there should be no limit to forgiving.

Our Lord also stressed the necessity for reconciliation when He said: "If you are offering your gift at the altar and there remember that your brother has anything against you, leave your gift before the altar and go first to be reconciled with your brother, and then come and offer your gift."[2]

We are further reminded that the *Our Father,* the prayer which Our Lord taught to the apostles[3] — and us — contains the plea: *"forgive us our trespasses as we forgive those who trespass against us."*

But, we may say, I have a terrible temper and I can't help "flying off the handle" with sharp, angry, and even unkind remarks."

Can't we?

How hard have we tried to overcome this tendency? Are we *really* trying to check quick-anger by cultivating moments of silence to dispel hasty retorts? Do we try to combat lasting-anger by developing compassionate understanding of the viewpoints and feelings of others? And how often do we ask God to help us control our tempers and our tongues?

The gifts of the Holy Spirit, designed to assist us in growing in the love of God and neighbor, to help us overcome our faults, to strengthen us in temptation, and to encourage us in the practice of virtue, are available to us at any time. How often do we ask Him, in sincere, persevering prayer, for the gifts of humility, charity and forbearance?

We know that unrestrained, unjust and continued anger is wrong and that it often provokes other evil. Too often it lashes at our dear ones, causing hurts and quarrels; brings resentments and mistakes at school and at work; and starts trouble in social contacts. Sometimes, sad to say, it also becomes the opening wedge to physical violence, even to murder.

Why, then, must we always be right, always win the argument, always be so demanding, so righteously critical?

Why — especially when we know that the merciful Christ has told us to learn meekness and humility from Him, even though this means that we may have to "turn the other cheek"?

> Put on, as God's chosen ones, a heart of mercy, kindness, humility, meekness, and patience. Bear with one another and forgive one another, if anyone has a grievance against any other; even as the Lord has forgiven you, so also do you forgive.
> (St. Paul: Colossians 3:12-13)

> Whoever is angry with his brother, shall be in danger of the judgment . . . If you offer your gift at the altar and there remember that your brother has anything against you, leave your offering before the altar, and go first to be reconciled with your brother, and then coming you shall offer your gift.
> (St. Matthew 5:22-24)

[1]Matt. 18:21-22

[2]Matt. 5:23-24

[3]Matt. 6:9-13

APATHY

We are shocked when the news media reports incidents of apathy, sometimes as extreme as the witnessing of a murder by a number of people who cared so little that not even one bothered to phone the police for assistance.

The disturbing question arising from such incidents is: how would we have acted had we been there? Apathetic? Concerned? Involved?

We are shocked when we learn about deplorable conditions of poverty or injustice or maltreatment, sometimes as near as in our own community.

The question again arises: is there anything that we can do to change such situations? Are we in a position to offer financial help? Can we assist by the help of our minds and hands? Or do the circumstances need our involvement simply through reporting the matter, or by writing protesting notes to civil and/or other authorities?

We are shocked — or we should be shocked — at the terrible moral disasters confronting us. This is no small matter. Sad to say, our combined apathy has paved the way to many deplorable conditions. Too many of us have been too apathetic too long in too many situations. Now this widespread apathy is reaping devastating personal and public chaos.

But, we may think, isn't this conclusion an exaggeration?

Hardly.

The enormity of evil resulting from apathy is cogently summarized by Dr. James Brendan Smith in an article published by *The Maryfaithful*[1].

"Unless the overwhelming majority of our citizens have a change of heart, and the courage and strength to implement it, our once-Christian country will succumb to the final agony of moral death in which we find ourselves today. The greatest evil of our time is not in the vocal and widely publicized minority who openly defy the laws of God as well as those of our country, but the silent millions who, by their silence, permit these evils to be perpetrated. With all the sophisticated, scientific apparatus and innovations which have been designed to make life easier for us, we have indulged ourselves more than any other group in history, to the point where we have become a nation of conditioned laboratory animals that respond to the tinkle of a bell. A Paris designer says 'wear this' and we wear it; the movie reviewer says 'see this film' and we see it; the columnist recommends a certain erotic book, so we read it; the self-proclaimed theologian says, 'contraception under certain circumstances, is not wrong', so we practice it; the eminent physician says, 'Abortion in certain instances is morally right', so we go along with this erroneous thinking and are indifferent to the passage of laws permitting abortion; the educator says, 'teach the children about sex through sex education programs in schools,' so we allow our children to attend such classes without bothering to find out the composition of these programs, some of which are utterly despicable. Our goals are comfort, convenience and pleasure. Let someone else shoulder the responsibility, and let principles be damned.

"We have allowed ourselves to be so hopelessly mislead that we now condemn, ridicule, and penalize virtue, while rewarding evil. We have decided that our plan for the universe is better than God's so, while priding ourselves on the scientific achievements which prolong life, we suppress the natural forces that produce life. In our pitiable self-righteousness we abolish capital punishment for the arch-criminal convicted of horrible atrocities but we murder innocent, defenseless infants in their mother's wombs. We consigned the principles given to us by Almighty God Himself, on which our Church and our country were founded, to the most remote recesses of our minds . . ."

Again the penetrating question is: do we shrug off responsibility, leaving any personal or community correction "up to George"? Do we care enough to pray to God for enlightment and help? Do we offer Him reparation? Do we accompany our prayers with efforts towards the spiritual improvement of ourselves and our families? Do we care enough to stand up for principles pleasing to God, even though the issues involved are not popular and it may sometimes — especially at the start — cause us the price of "standing alone"?

Which do we prefer: apathy and indifference or courage and involvement?

[1] *The Maryfaithful* is published at Marian House, Powers Lake, North Dakota, 58773; subscriptions, $3.00 per year; single copies 25¢.

THE BREVIARY

Isn't it too bad that the *Breviary* in all its richness of liturgical prayer should be lost to so many of us? Why must this be so? Is it because we have never actually had a *Breviary*, never really looked at one, never tried to understand what it is?

The *Breviary* is a prayer book containing the *Divine Office* — the liturgical prayer of the Church. The *Divine Office* is the prayer of the Holy Spirit because it is essentially composed of portions of the Bible. And it is the prayer of Christ because He is present in the official prayers of the Church, common to all. Next to the Mass and the Sacraments, the *Divine Office* is the chief sanctifying power of the Church.

Although praying the *Breviary* is an obligation of the clergy and the religious, it is also the high privilege of the laity. The prayers of the *Breviary* prepare us for the Mass and they complete our Divine worship. And so, the *Missal* and the *Breviary*, together, make a complete plan of prayer.

When we pray the *Divine Office* we live each day and season as the Church presents it. And in the *Breviary's* psalms and prayers, we worship God in a prayer of perfection: we give God honor and glory; we thank Him for His great blessings; we beg pardon for our sins; and we bring Him our problems and our sufferings, begging His Divine assistance.

In the prayers of the *Divine Office* we praise God with all the beauty and grandeur of the world, as in the *Benedicte* when we pray (in part):

"Sun and moon, bless the Lord;
stars of heaven, bless the Lord,
Every shower and dew, bless the Lord;
all you winds, bless the Lord;
Fire and heat, bless the Lord;
cold and chill, bless the Lord;
Dew and rain, bless the Lord;
frost and cold, bless the Lord;
Ice and snow, bless the Lord;
nights and days, bless the Lord;
Light and darkness, bless the Lord;
lightnings and clouds, bless the Lord;
Let the earth bless the Lord;
praise and exalt Him above all forever."

At times in the prayers of the Breviary we cry out for God's mercy, saying:

"Incline your ear, O Lord; answer me,
for I am afflicted and poor.
Keep my life, for I am devoted to you;
save your servant who trusts in you.
You are my God; have pity on me, O Lord,

for to you I call all the day.
Gladden the soul of your servant,
for to you, O Lord, I lift up my soul;
For you, O Lord, are good and forgiving,
abounding in kindness to all who call upon you;
Hearken, O Lord, to my prayer
and attend to the sound of my pleading."

And at other times we pour out our thanks, praying;

"Give thanks to the Lord, for He is good,
for His mercy endures forever;
Give thanks to the God of gods,
for His mercy endures forever;
Give thanks to the Lord of lords,
for His mercy endures forever."

With the prayers of the *Divine Office* we gain in grace and inspiration. And we worship in union with thousands of priests and religious who daily praise and thank God, beg His pardon and seek His blessings. With the prayers of the *Divine Office* we become a part of a universal and unchanging prayer offered to God day and night throughout the world. And with the prayers of the *Divine Office* we are lead to meditation, to contemplation and to a fulness in our spiritual life.

For us, the laity, there is a special simplified English edition of the *Roman Breviary,* sometimes called the *Little Office* or the *Short Breviary,* available from various Religious Orders. It contains the psalms, readings from the Old Testament, liturgically related to each day; meditations from the Doctors and Fathers of the Church; scores of the Church's finest hymns; and various collects, antiphons and responsories from the Church's centuries of traditional prayer.

The *Breviary* is truly a magnificent prayerbook, containing Christ's prayers and ours. Our Holy Father has encouraged us to make use of the *Divine Office* and the Commentary tells us that "if we bring Christ completely into our prayer life and pray His prayer, we can expect that God will give us the grace to make the rest of our life conform to that of his Son. With the mind of Christ we shall live well and pray well. Our whole life will become a new song continuously giving glory to God."

THE BROWN SCAPULAR

Most of us received the Brown Scapular of Our Lady of Mt. Carmel and were enrolled in the *Scapular Confraternity* at the time of our Solemn Holy Communion. Maybe we understood and appreciated this great gift from Mary and have faithfully worn it. Maybe not. If not, we are losing a great deal.

Our Blessed Mother gave us the Brown Scapular on July 16, 1251. On that day, accompanied by a multitude of angels, she appeared to St. Simon Stock, the Carmelite Prior General. Holding the Scapular of the Carmelite Order, she gave it to him, saying: *"Receive, my beloved son, this Scapular. This will be to you and to all that whosoever dies in this Scapular shall not suffer eternal fire."*[1]

This "Scapular promise" is so wonderful that it seems almost unbelievable but there are three great proofs of its authenticity:

1) There are numerous historical documents quoting the above statement.
2) During the past 700 years the Church has encouraged this devotion and our pontiffs have placed numerous indulgences upon the devout use of the Scapular.
3) Scapular miracles and wonders, both spiritual and temporal, have been, and are, confirmed.

For the reward of our Blessed Mother's assurance of salvation, two conditions must be fulfilled:

1) One must be lawfully enrolled into the *Scapular Confraternity.* (Enrollment may be obtained through one's pastor)
2) One must be wearing the Scapular at the moment of death.

The Scapular must be worn so that it hangs over the shoulders, resting against the chest and back of the body. Strings may be of any color, of any material or of chains. After enrollment, replacement Scapulars need not be blessed.

There is another singular favor attached to the Brown Scapular Devotion: the *Sabbatine Privilege* — so entitled from the Latin word for Saturday. This privilege stems from Pope John XXII's disclosure of our Blessed Mother's revelation to him stating: ". . . I, the Mother of Grace, shall descend into Purgatory on the Saturday after their death and whomsoever I shall find in Purgatory, I shall free . . ."

This extraordinary favor is reported to have been recorded and promoted in a Papal Bull dated March 3, 1322. And a Decree by Pope Paul V, issued January 20, 1613, states:

"It is lawful for the Carmelite Fathers to preach that Christians may piously believe in the help promised to the souls of the brethern and the members of the Confraternity of the Blessed Virgin of Mount Carmel, namely, that the Blessed Virgin will assist by her continual intercession, suffrages and merits, and also by her special protection, particularly on the Saturday after death (which day has been consecrated to her by the

Church) the souls of the brothers and the members of the Confraternity departing this life in charity who shall have worn the habit, and shall have observed chastity according to their particular state of life, and also have recited the Little Office or, if unable to read, have kept the fasts of the Church and have also abstained from the use of meat on Wednesdays and Saturdays, unless the feast of the Nativity of Our Divine Lord should fall on one of those days."

The *Sabbatine Privilege* exists *independently* of the original Bull which granted it. Besides the many pontiffs who have spoken of this extraordinary privilege, there have been nine *official ratifications* pronounced by nine different popes. This validly established the privilege. In addition to this positive confirmation, at least three Doctors of the Church — St. Alphonsus Liguori, St. Theresa of Avila, and St. John of the Cross — specifically refer to it and extol its greatness.

The *Sabbatine Privilege* is therefore an outstanding favor, something highly worth striving for. It should be noted that the Rosary may be substituted for the Little Office, through application to any priest (all priests now have this special faculty) or through application sent to the Aylesford National Scapular Center at Cass Avenue North at Rt. 66, Westmont, Illinois, 60559.

There are also other rewards for the Brown Scapular devotion; many indulgences; a share in all the good works of the Carmelite Order and of the other Confraternity members throughout the world; and after death a continual remembrance in the daily prayers of the Carmelite Order, nine times a year in a Requiem Office and Mass, and once a year in the Solemn Commemoration of All Souls of the Carmelite Order.

But, we may ask, isn't the Brown Scapular now outmoded? Since the aggiornamento, aren't we supposed to drop such devotions?

Definitely not.

Speaking of devotions, Vatican II documents (CSL No. 13) clearly state: *"Popular devotions of Christian people are to be highly commended, provided that they accord with the laws and norms of the Church, above all, when they are ordered by the Apostolic See."*

Also, in March of 1965 Pope Paul VI repeated recommendation of approved devotions when he sent a message to the Marian Congress held in the Dominican Republic. The Holy Father quoted Article 67 of the Dogmatic Constitution of the Church: *"Let the faithful hold in high esteem the practices and devotions to the Blessed Virgin approved by the teaching authority of the Church in the course of the centuries."* And then he continued, saying: "It is our conviction that the Rosary of Mary and the Scapular of Carmel are among these recommended practices . . . the Scapular is a practice of piety, which by its very simplicity, is suited to everyone, and has spread widely among the faithful to their spiritual profit."

Wearing the Brown Scapular is an expression of love and confidence in our blessed Mother — just as wearing our mother's picture in a locket or wallet would be a sign of devotedness to our own mother. It is a constant reminder calling us to imitate Mary's faith and hope, her humility and purity, her obedience and charity — so that striving to follow her example, and imploring her kind help, we may be formed into the likeness of Christ. The chief end of this devotion is to make holy those who practice it and experience confirms that the Scapular devotion sanctifies, often being the means of conversions from evil.

In her final apparition at Fatima on October 13, 1917 Mary appeared as Our Lady of Mt. Carmel, holding the Brown Scapular.

Couldn't we accept Mary's gracious Scapular gift? It's ours, if we want it.

PRAYER to
OUR LADY OF MT. CARMEL

Most Blessed and Immaculate Virgin, Ornament and Splendor of Carmel, you who regard with an eye of special kindness those who wear your blessed habit, look down in kindness on me and cover me with the mantle of your special protection.

Strengthen my weakness with your power; enlighten the darkness of my mind with your wisdom; increase in me faith, hope and charity. Adorn my soul with such graces and virtues as will ever be pleasing to your Divine Son and to you.

Assist me in life and console me in death, with your most amiable presence, and present me to the Most Holy Trinity as your devoted servant and child; that I may eternally bless and praise you in heaven. Amen.

Recommended Reading:

Sign of Her Heart by John M. Haffert (Ave Maria Institute, Washington, New Jersey 07882; $.85 per copy). This book, a best-seller of over 100,000 copies, explains the Promise of Salvation. Bishop Sheen, in its preface, calls it masterly.

Our Lady's Promise (about the Brown Scapular) and *Our Lady's Promises* (about the Brown Scapular and Fatima) leaflets obtainable at 5¢ each from the *Scapular Apostolate,* 329 East 28th St., New York, New York 10016.

[1]Most Rev. John Grossi, Historian and Superior General of the Carmelite Order, 1345-1437; (Viridarium Ordinis Virginis Mariae de Monte Carmelo, reproduced in the Analecta Ordinis Carmelitarum, VIII (1932, Rome).

CATECHETICAL PROGRAMS

We know that some of the catechetical programs in use in some of our parishes are simply not adequately presenting the authentic doctrines of our Faith to children and teens.

What about this?

We are reminded by the Second Vatican Council, in its *Declaration on Christian Education,* that parents have the *primary* responsibility for educating their children. And we are further encouraged by many zealous pastors to assume this responsibility. Among such forthright statements is that of the Rev. Robert J. Fox, a distinguished pastor, author and lecturer:

"*Parents, you are the first educators of your children in the Catholic Faith.* You do not have to follow blindly pseudo-educators who camouflage the true Faith from your children. You must teach them at home and you ought to be able to cooperate with parish and diocesan programs of religious education. But you have the *right and duty to demand* that all auxiliary helpers in our schools and CCD programs are working in loyalty to Mother Church, faithful to the Magisterium of the Church. You must not become discouraged to the point of giving up when you meet opposition in some areas.

"*You are the primary educators* and with your Catholic sense of what is the true Faith you can save the day for the future of the Catholic Church in America. It is your *right* and your *serious* duty."[1]

The question therefore arises: are the catechetical texts being used in our parish those which adhere to the authentic teachings of the Church? If the series are those which contain distortions, confusions and omissions, do we voice our objections and respectfully demand the use of orthodox texts?

If such is the case and we must confront pastors, school superintendents, directors of CCD programs, principals and teachers about this matter, we need not rely upon our own judgments. There are also a number of comprehensive, clear evaluations compiled by esteemed theologians and competent professors and educators. Among these publications are:

Grade and High School Religion Series Evaluations, a book authored by the late, distinguished Monsignor Rudolph G. Bandas, PH.D., S.T.D., member of the Roman Pontifical Academy of Theology and an official advisor at the Second Vatican Council. It examines and evaluates the Kalt & Wilkins series and those of Sadlier, Allyn and Bacon, Benziger and others. The book, $2.50 per copy, is distributed by the E. M. Lohmann Company, 413 Sibley Street, St. Paul, Minnesota 55101.

Our New Catechisms ($1.00) a definitive study of the Allyn & Bacon Benziger, Paulist and Sadlier series; *The New Catechisms vs The Credo of the People of God* ($1.90) an analysis of catechetical materials compared with the truths of Pope Paul's *Credo of the People of God; Examining the Evaluation Instrument* ($1.00) a critical study of the USCC Dept. of Education's *Instrument for the Evaluation of Religion Textbooks; Catechesis Without Dogma* (50¢) and examination of the 7th grade texts in Allyn & Bacon's *Bible, Life and Worship* series; and *Hi Time's Secular Gospel* (35¢) a critical analysis of the *Hi Time* series; each available from Catholics United for the Faith, Inc., 222 North Avenue, New Rochelle, New York 10801. Various other evaluations are published by CREDO, P.O. Box 66601, Houston, Texas 77006.

Also of very practical value in assisting priests, religious, parents and lay teachers to realize that something can be done, *should be done,* to produce truly effective religious education for the youth of today is the interesting paperback, *Religious Education: Its Effects, Its Challenges Today,* authored by the Rev. Robert J. Fox. The book, 95¢ per copy, is available from the Daughters of St. Paul Press, 50 St. Paul, Boston, Mass. 02130.

To help parents determine whether or not their children are learning the basics of the Catholic Faith, Father Fox also compiled the following quiz which provides parents with a simple, at-home method of checking their children's knowledge of our Faith:

BASIC RELIGIOUS QUIZ

1. Who is God?
2. What are angels?
3. What do you mean by your soul?
4. Why did God make you?
5. What is original sin?
6. What has happened because of the disobedience of Adam and Eve?
7. What is the difference between mortal and venial sin?
8. What kind of a sin is it to miss Mass on Sunday through one's own fault?
9. What three things are necessary to make a sin mortal?
10. Why do we honor Mary so greatly?
11. What is meant by the Redemption of Jesus Christ?
12. What must we do to gain the happiness of heaven?
13. What is the Catholic Church?
14. Why do we believe the Catholic Church is the true Church?
15. Did Jesus Christ give special authority to one of the apostles?
16. Who is the successor of St. Peter?
17. What is a sacrament? What are the seven sacraments and what does each of them do?
18. What happens at the Sacrifice of the Mass? (He should make reference to the Sacrifice of the Cross).

19. Do you receive bread in Holy Communion? (The child should be able to answer that it is *not* bread, but only the appearances and that we actually receive the *living* Body, Blood, Soul and Divinity of Jesus Christ).
20. How do we receive the Sacrament of Penance (Confession) worthily?
21. What are the 10 Commandments and briefly what does each one command or forbid?
22. What are the chief laws of the Church?
23. How do you say the Rosary? On what do we meditate when we say the Rosary?
24. Recite the Apostles' Creed, the Our Father, the Hail Mary, the Glory Be . . . an Act of Contrition.
25. Does it matter which church you may belong to? (The child should be aware of the *fullness* of true faith to be found in the Roman Catholic Church).

Many parents have used this quiz and as a result, have adopted the practice of weekly, one-hour family-catechism sessions. Series which present authentic Catholicity are used and the sessions not only "teach catechism" but deepen family love and unity.

It is encouraging to note that on April 11, 1971 the Religious Instruction Committee of the Holy See's Congregation of the Clergy issued a General Catechetical Directory,[2] under the leadership of Cardinal John Wright. It is approved by Pope Paul VI and it sets forth guidelines for the proper instruction of Catholics in the teachings of the Church.

It will necessarily take time to implement corrections in erroneous catechetical texts but in the meantime — now and in the future — *it remains the primary duty of parents to see to it that their children receive adequate training in the orthodox, official teachings of the Church.*

Among the series which *do* present authentic Catholicity are the following, here listed in alphabetical order: *Divine Master Series* (The Daughters of St. Paul Press, Boston, Mass.); *Faith of Our Fathers Series* (E. M. Lohmann Company, St. Paul, Minn.); *Know, Love and Serve Series* (Prow Publications, Kenosha, Wisconsin); *My Way to God Series* (Our Sunday Visitor Press, Huntington, Indiana); *New St. Joseph's Baltimore Catechisms* (Catholic Book Publishing Company, New York City); and the *Way, Truth and Life Series* (The Daughters of St. Paul Press).

These series present to youth the Faith that they are looking for — not watered-down versions of the teachings of Christ and His Church but, rather, the love and mercy of Christ, not separated from the Cross.

Each series combines traditional teaching with new presentations; are written with Christ's law of charity as the keynote; and clearly explain the truths of our Faith. The books are geared to the various age and class levels, are beautifully illustrated, and attractively presented.

Also recommended are the following texts, here listed in alphabetical order: *An Illustrated Catholic Family Catechism* (The Remnant, 2539 Morrison Avenue, St. Paul, Minn.); *The Catholic Faith: A First Book for Small Children* (Msgr. Eugene Kevane, c/o Notre Dame Pontifical Institute of Studies, Middleburg, Virginia); *The Children's Bible* (Golden Press, 1220 Mound Avenue, Racine, Wisconsin); *My Bible History* (My Mission House, 1324 52nd St., Kenosha, Wisconsin); *The Penny Catechism* (Prow Publications, Kenosha, Wisconsin); *St. Peter's Catechism of Catholic Doctrine* (Lumen Christi Press, Houston, Texas); and *This Is Our Catholic Faith* (St. Basil Church, P.O. Box 8086, St. Paul, Minn.).

With the availability of so many fine catechetical publications, the question naturally arises: *why should series and/or texts be used which undermine the Faith by complete omissions or distortion of true concepts or by misplaced emphasis?*

Many concerned parents have wondered what they could do to correct situations in which "defective" catechisms are being used. In such cases parents are advised to get together, meet with their pastor, and calmly and respectfully voice their objections, and ask for corrective measures. If no co-operation is received, a committee should present the matter to their bishop through their chancery.

In some localities parents have felt it necessary to provide catechetical classes for their own children and any others who wish to attend. Among the most successful of these projects are the *St. Thomas Aquinas School of Religion,* P.O. Box 6161, San Rafael, California; the *Holy Innocents School* at Mountain Lakes, New Jersey 07046, and the *Morning Star Academy* at the Holy Family Monastery Center in West Hartford, Conn. 06107.

These and other such endeavors entail time and sacrifice but the sponsoring parents willingly assume the effort involved, for in doing so they are safeguarding their two most valuable treasures: their Catholic Faith and their beloved Children.

[1]Excerpt from the article, *Who Are the Basic Teachers of Your Children?,* originally published in Our Sunday Visitor, June 18, 1972. (Reprinted by permission)

[2]The major requirements contained in the *General Catholic Directory* and in the document, *Basic Teachings of Catholic Religious Education* are presented in the leaflet, *Parents, Pastors, Teachers: Do Your Children's Religion Books Teach What the Church Teaches?* A free sample copy is available from *Catholics United For The Faith* 222 North Avenue, New Rochelle, New York 10801; 10 copies for $1.00; 25% discount on orders of 50 or more.

COMMUNISM

Communism is the publicly avowed enemy of God. Christ taught love; communism teaches hatred. Christ preached truth; communism teaches deceit. Christ's commands bring freedom and goodness; communism brings oppression and evil. Christ's way brings joy and peace; the communist way brings despair and war.

Since communism is such a formidable enemy of Christ, it is also the enemy of all Christians. What, then, can we do to protect ourselves against this destructive menace?

Our Church leaders and many governmental officials have strongly urged that we alert ourselves to the dangers of communism and that we learn its purposes, methods and tactics. They point out that reading and study will help the cause of Christ and of our country against communism.

A great many pamphlets and books have been written for this purpose. Among the "musts" are the Papal Encyclicals, *Atheistic Communism and Quadragesimo Anno,* available from the Daughters of St. Paul Press, Boston, Mass. 02130; 25¢ per copy; *Questions and Answers on Communism,* an excellent book about the nature of communism, the communist line and the secret of Soviet success in the United States, written by the late Cardinal Richard Cushing, available from the Daughters of St. Paul Press, Boston, Mass. 02130; paperback, 50¢ per copy; *Masters of Deceit,* the enlightening, forceful book written by J. Edgar Hoover, the late director of the F.B.I., written, as he states in the book's Foreword, "because every citizen has a duty to learn more about the menace that threatens his future, his home, his children, the peace of the world . . . the time is too late not to recognize this ism for what it is: a threat to humanity and to each of us;" *Brainwashing: From Pavlov to Powers,* written by Edward Hunter — a factual account of the horrible machinations of communist brainwashing endeavors; and various other books written by, or about, people who have endured incredible cruelty under communism's tyrannical rule and its mock trials, false imprisonment and terrible punishments. Among these is the deeply moving *Memoirs* (Josef Cardinal Mindszenty). This extraordinary book was written, as the Cardinal said, "so that the world may see what fate communism has in store for mankind." And he reminds us that "we must never act opportunistically . . . disregarding religious interests"; and that we must work for Church and country, for the family, for Catholic institutions, and for freedom of the individual. Every Christian, he tells us, has the duty to make use of his rights as a citizen; and above all, to remain confident for "prayer can intensify physical and spiritual forces; it is a power that can even overcome the laws of nature." *Memoirs* is available from the Cardinal Minszenty Foundation, P.O. Box 11321, St. Louis, Missouri 63105; $10 per copy.

Also recommended is the booklist, *Inside the Communist Conspiracy* (25¢ per copy) presented by the Cardinal Mindszenty Foundation. The preface of this pamphlet states that it "includes books which the Communists have desperately tried to prevent us from reading. If we are to save our country from the fate which has overtaken more than twenty other nations, Americans must read these books and make them available to the many high school and college students who have been victims of the paper curtain.

"*Inside the Communist Conspiracy* is the only reading list which gives proper prominence to the official government documents on communism. These reports have been called 'the most secret government documents in America today' because they are so often given the silent treatment by book review journals, they are rarely stocked by bookstores, and they are seldom displayed or catalogued by libraries. Yet these government reports are the best source of information for the average American citizen. When they are out of print, they should still be available from any library. Insist that your local library stock these vital documents and catalogue them in such a way that they are obtainable by local citizens."

We are also encouraged to exercise our patriotism by being loyal to American principles; by being careful to vote intelligently; and by becoming interested in local, state and national political affairs; and by writing to newspapers and government officials, protesting Communist subversion or measures which aid Communism; and withholding support from organizations, magazines, advertisers, movies, etc. which support Communism.

Also effective is action encouraging others to learn the truth about communism, particularly by arranging for lectures in our parish and community. Among the organizations especially designed for this purpose is the *Cardinal Mindszenty Foundation* (P.O. Box 11321, St. Louis, Missouri, 63105). This is a non-profit educational association formed to combat Communism through knowledge and fact. It provides informational material to individuals, schools, colleges, service clubs and other groups to help more persons understand the nature, theory and practice of Communism. It assists in the formation of Catholic and non-sectarian study groups and conducts seminars on Communism. It also presents an award winning radio program, *Dangers of Apathy* and publishes a monthly *Mindszenty Report* and a bi-weekly newspaper column, *The Red Line,* which analyzes the current Communist line in the national and international Communist press.

Another alerting means is the displaying of the thought-provoking *Exhibit of the Martyr Church* in parishes and communities. This authoritative exhibit, prepared by the Pontifical Biblical Institute, was originally presented in Rome at the time of the Second Vatican Council. It portrays the betrayal of the Captive Nations and emphasizes the need for personal involvement in spiritual and educational programs to save America from the lot of the Captive Nations. Detailed information for displaying this exhibit (films, slides, photographs and books) may be obtained from Cross Publications at Kenosha, Wisconsin 53104.

Also available is the publication, *Captive Nations,* compiled by the editors of *The Immaculata* magazine in collaboration with John Cross. The purpose of this 60 page, well illustrated issue is to break the silence surrounding the persecution of our brothers and sisters in Christ — a tragedy which is staggering in terms of both human suffering and eternal implications. The publication contains articles written by people who have expert knowledge of Communism and conditions in the Captive Countries. Among these authors are several priests and a Lutheran minister who endured frightful tortures under Communist imprisonment. Of special interest is an account about Father Werenfried Van Straaten, the "bacon priest", whose untiring work to alleviate the poverty and suffering of people in the Captive Nations is tremendous.

Copies of *Captive Nations* may be obtained from the Franciscan-Marytown Press at 8000 39th Avenue, Kenosha, Wisconsin, 53141; (50¢ each; 10 or more to one address, 40¢ each; 100 or more to one address, 30¢ each; all postpaid).

Particularly helpful in teaching youth about Communism is *The Truth About Communism:* a highly recommended, thoroughly documented series designed to help immunize our youth against revolutionary, communistic infection; presented in complete high school and grade school units with study guides; compiled by the Rev. Cletus Healy, S.J.; available from The Truth, Inc., 3400 West Michigan Street, Milwaukee, Wisconsin 53208.

Our church leaders and our government officials have repeatedly tried to alert us to the dangers of Communism. So did Our Lady of Fatima. In fact, back in 1917 at Fatima, Portugal when Russia was just a "little" nation and Communism just budding Russian Politics, Our Blessed Mother warned us of coming dangers. She told us that wars are a punishment permitted by God because of sin. And to offset sin, Our Lady asked for the amendment of our lives, for the daily Rosary, for consecration to Her Immaculate Heart and for penance and reparation.

In fact, She stated: "If my requests are granted, Russia will be converted and there will be peace. If not, she will scatter her errors throughout the world, provoking wars and persecutions of the Church; the good will be martyred; the Holy Father will suffer much; and various nations will be destroyed."

Evidently too many of us have not listened to Our Blessed Mother and have not answered her requests, for we have been the unhappy recipients of World War II, the Korean War, the Viet Nam War, conflicts in the Middle East and various other regional uprisings. And Communism has become a world power, sweeping nations before it and threatening a devastating nuclear World War III.

The all-important question therefore is: are we answering — and getting others to answer — Our Lady's requests? If not, why not?[1]

Is it because we are not as familiar with the message of Fatima as we could be? If so, we could increase our understanding by such reading as *This Apocalyptic Age* ($1) and *More About Fatima* ($1), both available from Fatima International Box 647 M.P.O. Hamilton, Ontario, Canada, L8N 3K7; *Fatima or Moscow?,* a very interesting, "different" Fatima booklet which presents a timely, candid look at Our Blessed Mother's message in relation to self;(50¢ per copy) available from the Sacred Heart Center, 6026 West Harwood Avenue, Orlando, Florida 32811; and *Meet the Witnesses,* photos and detailed statements of people of various ages and backgrounds who were present during the "miracle of the sun"; ($3.00) from Ave Maria Institute, Washington, New Jersey 07882.

Such reading emphasizes the point that no matter what human means — political, military, scientific, social economic — that we may use to halt confusion, atheistic communism or war, the fact remains that *nothing will succeed unless — and until — we fulfill Our Blessed Mother's requests at Fatima, for in truth, Mary asked only what God expects of each one of us.*

If we wish, we could use these and other Fatima publications in our personal correspondence; place them on literature stands; use them as Marian projects of our school or parish clubs; and supply quantities to retreat houses, information centers, hospitals, and other institutions.

We could also join the *Blue Army of Our Lady of Fatima,* an offically approved international apostolate. Members pledge themselves to fulfill Our Blessed Mother's requests. The pledge is a sincere intention, not binding under pain of sin. Members also encourage others to do so, acting personally or through efforts of local *Blue Army* Cells. Further information regarding membership, about the *Blue Army Cadets* for youth, and about the *Blue Army School of Apostolic Information* for adults (young and older) is available from the apostolate's center at the Ave Maria Institute, Washington, New Jersey 07882. Also available are Fatima leaflets, books, tapes, films, telecasts and and lecture services.

Priests who wish to do so may become members of the *Apostolate of Our Lady of Fatima for Priests.* This apostolate, founded on the occasion of the 50th anniversary of our Blessed Mother's apparitions at Fatima, is especially designed to encourage priests to do all in their power to assist in spreading the Fatima message; and thereby to inspire the laity to pray and sacrifice for priests and for priestly vocations. Further information is available from the *Reparation Society of the Immaculate Heart of Mary,* 100 East 20th Street, Baltimore, Maryland 21218.

The Church's approval of the acceptance of the apparitions and the message of Fatima is an established fact. The message is important; it is directed to all mankind; and it is for the good of all. Not only has it been repeatedly approved by such distinguished popes as Pius XII, John XXIII and Paul VI, but each of them has earnestly recommended our belief in, and our adherence to, the message of Fatima. Added to this, is the obvious approval of God as indicated by the authenticated miracles that take place at the Fatima shrine, many of which occur at the time when sick are blessed by Our Lord in His Eucharistic Presence.

Shall we, therefore, follow the inspiring lead of Christ's Vicars on earth and accept the message of Fatima, using it as a means of personal sanctification and as an effective instrument towards a just and lasting peace? Or, do we prefer to remain among the unconcerned and the unbelievers?

The choice is ours.

The time is now.

Recommended Reading:

Our American Catholic Heritage by Rev. Albert J. Nevins, M.M. This book presents a full, proud history of America written with warmth of feeling. It is an epic narrative from the days of the Norsemen to the Apollo 9 Mission. It relates the triumphs and martyrdoms of the early missionaries, the heroic Catholic heroes of the Revolution, and many events of human interest. The book, containing 479 illustrations, photos, maps and charts, is available from the Book Dept. of Our Sunday Visitor, Huntington, Indiana 46750; deluxe edition, $12.00; paperback, $5.95.

[1]See chapter on The Fatima Message

CONFESSION

We kneel in the confessional, telling our sins to God through His representative, the priest.

Then the priest asks if we are sorry for our sins and if we have resolved to amend our lives (and where necessary, to make restitution.) He speaks a few words of advice or encouragement, assigns a penance, and then imparts God's forgiveness:

"May Our Lord, Jesus Christ, absolve you and by His authority I absolve you from your sins in the name of the Father, and of the Son, and of the Holy Spirit. Amen."

Then the priest says; "God bless you! Go in peace."

And we go from the confessional — in peace.

The sacrament of Penance is a consolation not only in the peace that it imparts but also in its assurance of true forgiveness. Our Blessed Lord, knowing our weakness and our tendency to doubts or to scrupulousness, gave us a confessional method of *absolute certainty.*

Confession is truly a gift of many facets. Not only does it forgive our sins and restore us to the friendship of God, but it also gives graces which strengthen us against future onslaughts from the world, the flesh and the devil.

So if we are in the habit of going to Confession just when necessary or rarely, then we are not very wise. We are losing many helpful graces. In fact, our spiritual advisers recommend bi-weekly Confession as a general practice, even though we may be guilty of only very slight imperfections.

But, we may question, in these modern times isn't the practice of frequent Confession officially regarded as of little importance?

Decidely not.

Vatican II directives contain various statements alluding to the importance and the value of frequent Confession: the *Dogmatic Constitution on the Church, No. 42; Decree on the Bishops' Pastoral Office in the Church, No.* 30; *Decree on the Ministry and Life of Priests,* Nos. 5, 12, 18; etc. And the Council's teachings clearly reflect statements from the encyclicals, notably from the *Sacred Liturgy* and the *Mystical Body,* including the following:

"Tragic ruin would follow from the opinion of those who assert that little importance should be given to the frequent confession of venial sins. Let those who make light of or weaken esteem for frequent Confession realize that what they are doing is foreign to the Spirit of Christ and disastrous for the Mystical Body of Our Savior."

And so, it is clearly evident that the Church still earnestly advocates the practice of frequent Confession.

Perhaps we may have been staying away from the sacrament of Penance because we are ashamed of confessing serious sins. If so, we are certainly most unwise. There is actually no reason to be afraid. God already knows our sins. We can't hide them from Him. And as far as the priest is concerned, we can't shock him. He has been trained to understand souls and sins. Naturally, he is saddened to hear our grave sins but at the same time, he rejoices at our repentance, and thanks God for it. There is, therefore, no reason for being afraid of Confession.

Not only does a good Confession forgive our sins but it also acts as a defense mechanism guarding us against presumption or despair. Against presumption, for we know that the sacrament forgives *only* when we confess all of our mortal sins, humbly, contritely and sincerely, with a true purpose of amendment. Against despair, for we know that God is loving and merciful, that He is anxious and willing and ready to firgive sin — even the most heinous.

God gave us proof of His infinite mercy when, upon the cross, He forgave the repentant sinner: *"This day thou shalt be with Me in Paradise,"*[1] and when He forgave His executioners — and us — saying: *"Father, forgive them for they know not what they do."*[2]

He also gave us a positive means of continuing forgiveness: on the day of His Resurrection, the most glorious day of His earthly life, He appeared to His apostles and said: *"Peace be to you . . . whose sins you shall forgive, they are forgiven; and whose sins you shall retain, they are retained."*[3]

And so, we are most privileged to have Our Savior's magnificent gift of the sacrament of Penance: mercy, forgiveness, love, joy and peace.

PRAYER on GOING TO CONFESSION[4]

O my Jesus, I beg special blessings
and graces for all people going to
Confession today;
For all who are afraid to be completely
honest in the confessional;
For all who are overly scrupulous;
For all, heavy with mortal sin, who
need special help;
For all who turn away from Confession;
and
For all priests hearing Confessions today.

Recommended Reading:

The Good God (This book portrays the loving compassion, kindness, gentleness and mercy of God towards everyone, especially towards sinners); available from the Marian Fathers Press, Stockbridge, Mass., 01262; cloth edition, $3.00; paperback, $2.25.

[1]St. Luke, 23:43
[2]St. Luke, 23:34
[3]St. John, 20:23
[4]Reprinted by permission from *Restoration.*

CONFESSIONS (CHILDHOOD)

Some people, these days, are promoting the opinion that Confession for children should be deferred until the age of nine, ten, or older.

This recommendation raises a penetrating, vital question; would the proposed deferment actually *bring good* to children or would it *deprive them of good?*

A very holy pope, Pius X — who became Saint Pius X — dealt with this same problem, emphatically stating that it is neither just, wise nor sound to advocate different ages for First Confession and First Communion. His mandate, *Quam Singularli,* issued on August 8, 1910, reaffirmed the decree of the Lateran Council: that the *same* age, the age of discretion — usually seven years — be observed for the reception of *both* sacraments; and that "the custom of not admitting children to Confession or not giving them absolution when they have attained the use of reason must be entirely abandoned."

Since that time this has been the practice approved by subsequent pontiffs. But, some people question, is this recommendation current? Have we had any recent official directives concerning this matter?

Yes. On April 11, 1971 the Religious Instruction Committee of the Sacred Congregation for the Clergy issued, with the approval of Pope Paul VI, a *General Catechetical Directory* whose *Addendum* clearly indicates that it reaffirms the value of the traditional practice of First Confession at the time of First Communion, stating: ". . . the Holy See judges it expedient that the now-flourishing custom of putting Confession before First Communion should be preserved."

It also cautions against any arbitrary change in this traditional practice, stating: "The Holy See does not overlook the special needs and circumstances of different regions but it urges the Bishops not to depart from the established custom in this serious matter without prior consultation with herself, in the spirit of hierarchial communion. Nor should they in any way permit parish priests or teachers or religious institutions to abandon the established usage or to go on ignoring it."

These directives were strengthened on May 24, 1973 when the Sacred Congregation for the Discipline of the Sacraments and the Sacred Congregation for the Clergy issued an official document, approved by Pope Paul VI, and signed by their respective Prefects, Antonio Cardinal Samore and John Cardinal Wright. The declaration stated that First Confession *must* precede the reception of First Communion. It also stated that all experiments regarding First Communion before First Confession must be halted by the end of the 1972-1973 scholastic year.

In spite of these clear directives, proponents of deferring First Confession contend that early Confession causes tensions and anxieties.

What about this?

If this be so, from where does the difficulty stem? Is it *really* because Confession is approached too soon or is it because Confession *has not been properly presented and explained* to children?

Life is filled with incidents which are anxiety-related, both in childhood and adulthood. Unfortunately, we can't just skip over them or pretend that they do not exist. If we do, then we really do subject ourselves to tensions and traumas. If we are wise, we try to face difficulties, cope with them, and take them in our stride.

A child's life has many perplexing situations and ordinarily we anticipate the child's fears and prepare him to meet them by explaining the reason for the problem and the good that will result from it. We reassure him by telling him that we, too, have experienced similar difficulties and we give him our loving companionship. In this way, we face the problem along with the child. We do not allow him to run from it or pretend that is does not exist or defer it until later on.

For example: going to a dentist or a doctor may be a rather fearful, anxious problem for a child — especially if he is not properly prepared for it — but even so, we do not put it off until he or she is ten years old, or older, on the grounds that he will be better able to "take it" when he is older!

Going to kindergarten at five or six years may be a nervous experience for a child — especially if he is not properly prepared for it — but even so, we do not defer his schooling until he or she is nine or ten years old, on the grounds that when the child is older, he will adjust more readily!

Going to Confession may be a little difficult for a child — if he is not properly prepared for it — but does postponing Confession until he is ten or older really help him? And what about God's role in the matter? Doesn't He assist the child with sufficient graces?

Confession is a tremendous gift of love and mercy given to us all by our Divine Savior. It is not a sacrament to be feared by anyone — child or adult. Rather, it is a gift to be appreciated and treasured. A gift which brings us closer to God and gives us joy and serenity.

Where is the fear, for a child, if he is taught that although we love God and should show Him our love by obeying His commands, still we are all rather imperfect people and at times we think and say and do things which do not please Him. And when we have done so and then are sorry for these failures — called sins — we have the marvelous opportunity to go and tell Our Lord about them; to say that we are sorry; to tell Him that we will try to do better; and to ask Him to forgive us and bless us.

We call this, we tell the child, going to Confession, and we all make our Confessions to Father John who represents God in our parish, and to whom God has given the power to administer the Sacrament of Penance which takes away sin.

A simple explanation, such as this, eliminates anxiety and tension. It is easily understood by any normal seven year old child — especially since he has already experienced occasions when he has been disobedient or quarrelsome and has then tearfully told his Dad (or Mom): "I'm sorry,

Daddy; I didn't mean to do that; I won't do it again." And having received his father's loving forgiveness, the child runs — happily and peacefully — off to play.

Assistance in explaining First Confession-Communion is available in numerous publications including the popular paperback, *Jesus-The Bread of Life,* published by the Daughters of St. Paul, 50 St. Paul's Avenue, Boston, Massachusetts 02130; 50¢ per copy; its companion Activity Book, 20¢ each; and its Parents-Teachers Manual at $1.50 per copy.

And if a cassette or reel is preferred, there is the excellent, *Let's Prepare to Receive Jesus,* which presents remote and immediate preparation for First Confession and Holy Communion. The cassette, a one-hour recording, is priced at $5 and the reel at $6. Available from POPE Publications, Box 6161, San Rafael, California 94903.

Fear of Confession is also eliminated by the example and the companionship of a child's parents and/or brothers and sisters. Going to Confession along with his loved ones, gives a child a sense of security and a feeling of rightness.

Another point: of the millions of Catholics who have gone before us and the millions living today, how many can *truthfully* attribute emotional or nervous troubles to going to Confession at an early age?

Granted that there have been — and there still are — some people who are afflicted by scrupulosity or anxiety, but these most assuredly are the exception rather than the rule. And, again, doesn't their problem stem from personality defects and/or lack of proper parental or priestly guidance?

Surely, the merciful, loving Heart of Christ did not give us the Sacrament of Penance — or any other Sacrament — to bring us difficulties! Rather, properly received, they bring joy and peace of soul.

In deferring Confession to the age of ten or older (excepting for exceptional cases) there is also the serious danger that a child may habitually brush off the malice of such "little" sins as lying, quarreling, unkindness, selfishness, disobedience and the like as being of no consequence — thus, establishing patterns of thought, extending into the future, that "anything goes" as long as it is not such terrible evil as murder, suicide, adultery or armed robbery!

Although Confession primarily brings us God's forgiveness, it also gives us His blessing and many graces, including strength and courage to withstand future temptations. That is why it is our great privilege — child or adult — to receive the sacrament not only when mortal sin makes it necessary but also frequently, even when we are guilty of only slight imperfections.

Confession also give us an opportunity of receiving the confessor's counselling and helps us — children and adults — to form a right conscience. In fact, this can be an invaluable aid to children since a confessor's kindly directives can be a helpful means of developing virtuous habits during a child's early years — before the age of ten or so when habits, good or bad, are already quite well defined. Even little children have a sense of moral values and very often Confession is just what they need to soothe their childhood sense of guilt.

This is the judgment not only of saints, popes and holy confessors, but also of many eminent psychologists and psychiatrists, a judgment clearly stated in various publications, such as the following:

"The child's admission of guilt and attempts to make amends are steps toward self control. The child gains peace of mind through confessing his misdeeds and receiving forgiveness." (*Patterns of Child Rearing* by Sears, Maccaby and Levin; Harper & Row, pp. 377-379).

And so, we reach the penetrating, vital conclusion: for these and other reasons — as well as in obedience to the official directives of the Church *— we actually do not have the right to defer childhood Confessions until the age of ten or so.*

CONSECRATION TO OUR BLESSED MOTHER

We know that total consecration to Our Blessed Mother is highly recommended as an effective way to personal holiness and happiness but still we hesitate about following through. Perhaps we have heard sermons or lectures about this consecration or we may have read St. Louis de Montfort's great classic, *True Devotion to the Blessed Virgin Mary,* but somehow the consecration seems too involved, too difficult.

Actually, it is not too difficult.

St. Louis explains total consecration by telling us that it means a complete giving of oneself to Mary, and through Mary to Jesus. Nothing is held in reserve so that all that we are, all that we have, all that we hope to be is given to Our Blessed Mother: our life and the end of our life; our hearts, souls, minds and bodies; our prayers, works, joys and sorrows. Everything is thereby given to Mary in order that she may, in as nearly perfect a manner as possible, give all to Jesus for His greatest glory and the welfare of souls.

But, we may ask, why should we make such a consecration?

Because the paramount aim of our lives should be to reach Christ and total consecration to Mary provides a solid foundation for true devotion to Our Lord and an easy and secure means of finding Him and serving Him faithfully.

But, we may question, what about the objection, voiced by some people, to approaching God through Mary "because the Bible says that Christ is our only mediator"?

This reference — the words of St. Paul (1 Tim. 2:5-6), "there is one mediator between God and men, the Man Jesus Christ, Who gave Himself a Redemption for all" — applies to Christ's unique role as *Mediator of the Redemption.*

Actually, in the Bible we note that Abraham, Moses and the Prophets often acted as *mediators of intercession* between God and the People. Of all such mediators,. Mary — the masterpiece of God's creation, the mother of Christ, and the spiritual mother of us all — is certainly the most powerful. She is truly the *Mediatrix of All Graces.*

But, we may ask, how are we to apply this method of total consecration to our work-a-day world? How do we apply the principle of living in, for, with, and by Mary to the common events of our daily life?

St. Louis points out that we are to live our total consecration to Mary by trying daily to live in her presence: by having Mary with us as a silent partner so that we ask her advice; we seek her help; we try to say, do, and think only whatever she would do, or not do, in order to please and serve God.

For example: when invited to a movie, party, dance or whatever — are these things all right? Would Mary go to them? If not, then we are to choose another movie, leave the party, turn down the date. Or, is this book a good one? Would Mary read it? Again, would Mary be saying or doing what I am about to say or do — at home, at school, at work, in entertainments, on vacations?

But, if we give everything to Mary, does this mean that we can't pray for ourselves or for others?

On the contrary. St. Louis says that this consecration does not hinder us from such prayers, whether for the living or dead, although the application of our prayers and good works depends on the will of Our Blessed Mother. In fact, "it is this very thing which will lead us to pray with more confidence . . . Our Blessed Lord and Our Lady will never let themselves be outdone in generosity and gratitude."[1]

But, we may wonder, if we give everything to Our Blessed Mother, what if someday we may be in Purgatory and in need of prayers?

St. Louis answers this question by assuring us that this complete surrender of our prayers and works to Mary obtains special assistance for us in Purgatory.

"A fervent soul," he writes, "who gives God all that he has, without reserve, so that he can do no more, a soul who makes an entire sacrifice of himself to Christ and His Holy Mother, will this generous soul be more punished in the other world because it has been more generous and more disinterested in self than others? Far, indeed, will that be from the truth! Rather, it is toward that soul that Our Lord and His Holy Mother are the most liberal in this world and in the other."[2]

How important, we may ask, is this total consecration?

Very important. Because by this devotion, St. Louis says, "we give to Jesus, in the most perfect manner, inasmuch as it is by Mary's hands, all that we can give Him, and far more than any other devotion, because here everything is given and consecrated to Him, even the right of disposing of our interior goods and of the satisfactions which we gain by our good works, day after day."[3]

And what are the rewards for those who give themselves to Mary through total consecration of self?

The rewards are immeasurable: "The most Holy Virgin, who is a mother of sweetness and mercy, never lets herself be outdone in love and liberality. Seeing that we give ourselves to her, to honor and serve her, she meets us in the same spirit . . . In a word, as the consecrated person is all Mary's, so Mary is all his."[4]

As the best of all mothers, Mary loves her faithful children. She furnishes them with everything that they may need, both for soul and body. She directs them, according to the Will of her Divine Son. She protects and defends them against their enemies. She helps them carry their crosses with more ease, more merit and more glory. She keeps them close to the Heart of Christ.

ACT OF CONSECRATION TO THE IMMACULATE HEART OF MARY[5]

I, (Name), a faithless sinner, renew and ratify today in your hands, O Immaculate Mother, the vows of my Baptism; I renounce forever Satan, his pomps and works; and I give myself entirely to Jesus Christ, the Incarnate Wisdom, to carry my cross after Him all the days of my life, and to be more faithful to Him than I have ever been before.

In the presence of all the heavenly court, I choose you this day, for my Mother. I deliver and consecrate to you my body and soul, my goods, both interior and exterior, and even the value of all my good actions, past, present and future; leaving to you the entire and full right of disposing of me, and all that belongs to me, without exception, according to your good pleasure, for the greater glory of God, in time and in eternity. Amen.

Recommended Reading:

True Devotion to the Blessed Virgin Mary (St. Louis de Montfort's classic) paperback, $1.50
True Devotion to Mary (a popular, modern version of the St. Louis classic written by Eddie Doherty) paperback, $1.00.
Leading the Little Ones (designed to teach children how to think about, and love, Our Blessed Mother) paperback, $1.00.
The Secret of Mary Simply Explained (pamphlet) 25¢.
Unconditional Surrender to Christ Through Mary (record album) $7.00; all available from Montfort Publications, 40 South Saxon Avenue, Bay Shore, New York, 11706.

[1]*True Devotion to the Blessed Virgin Mary,* part 2, Chap. 1, No. 132
[2]*True Devotion to the Blessed Virgin Mary,* part 2, Chap. 1, No. 133
[3]Ibid., part 2, Chap. 1, No. 123
[4]Ibid., part 2 Chap. 2, No. 144
[5]As compiled by St. Louis de Montfort and approved by the Church.
A holy card, bearing this act of consecration, is available from the Montfort Fathers at 40 South Saxon Avenue, Bay Shore, New York 11706. For a free copy, send request with a stamped, self-addressed envelope.

CONTRACEPTION

Time was when discussion about birth control was considered a delicate matter, its mention quiet and restrained. Today reticence is gone and the subject is openly debated and widely publicized via the tongue, the pen and the airwaves.

The resulting arguments and confusion led to a thorough study of the subject which culminated in the issuing on July 25, 1968 of a papal encyclical, *Humanae Vitae — of Human Life.*[1]

Pope Paul's directive, banning the use of mechanical and chemical methods of birth control, reaffirms the Church's teaching that such practices are intrinsically evil: that they are directly opposed to the divine and natural laws — a desecration of the Sacrament of Matrimony.

To some, the encyclical is a bitter disappointment. To others, it is a heroic document. As Cardinal John Wright has stated; "The pressures on Pope Paul to speak on contraception other than he did have been massive. They have been pressures of human respect, politics, prestigious opinion, emotional torment, threats that Church unity might be destroyed or ecumenical hopes dimmed.

"In the face of such pressures, the Holy Father's pronouncement must be seen as truly magnanimous and the Pope himself takes on heroic stature as a courageous teacher, prophetic in the Old Testament sense, evangelical in the richest sense of the New.

"The professionals have been fully consulted and patiently heard; the leader has spoken as only he could and should do . . .

"What Pope Paul has done, what he had to do, is recall to a generation that does not like the word, the fact that sin exists; that artificial contraception is objectively sinful; that those who impose it, foster it, counsel it, whether they be governments, experts, or — God forgive them! — spiritual directors, impose, foster and counsel objective sin."

But, we may object, this ruling is too hard.

Is it?

Hard, yes. But not too hard. God gives His special help to the fulfillment of this law, as well as to all His commands.

A mature, honest look at the marriage vocation and at other vocations puts the problems of marriage in proper perspective. The truth is that all vocations bring joys as well as difficulties, responsibilities as well as pleasures. None are too easy or free from the necessity of self-sacrifice and self-discipline.

But then, God did not promise anyone a carefree life in this world. Rather, He pointed out that the troubles and sorrows of these temporary years — however hard they may be — are insignificant in relation to the unending joys of the life to come with Him. Christ warned us all — religious, married or single — that there is a price to pay for a ticket to heaven: *"If any man will come after Me, let him deny himself, take up his cross and follow Me."*

Self-sacrifice, daily prayer and the frequent reception of the sacraments help anyone carry his cross and meet the difficulties encountered in his particular vocation. God gives His blessings to anyone who believes in Him, who asks for His help.

But, we may protest, we can't afford any more children.

Really?

Here again, the honest point is: how much does pleasing God mean to us?

Of course, if we just must have wall-to-wall carpeting, color TV, the finest stereo, the best cameras, the most modern furniture, a new car every year or so, clothes from the most fashionable shops, etc., then there may, indeed, be no funds left for bearing and raising children.

But if we love God enough to sacrifice — if the sacrifice means that we will never have a fur coat or a car that is new; if our clothes and household items must come from rummage sales; if we must learn to sew, bake our own bread, etc., if at times, we must even swallow our pride and ask for financial help from relatives or charitable sources, then there will be funds for the babies which God wishes to give us.

But, we may object, the encyclical is not an infallible document so isn't the matter of birth control up to our own conscience?

The encyclical has come to Catholic people, and to all people, from the Supreme Teacher of the Church. No conscience is a right conscience, or even a well guided conscience, if it does not take this into account. In fact, Vatican II clearly and emphatically reminds us of this obligation. In the Dogmatic Constitution on the Church *(Lumen Gentium)* 25, the Council Fathers state:

"This religious submission of *will* and of *mind* must be shown in a special way to the authentic teaching authority of the Roman Pontiff, even when he is *not speaking ex cathedra.* That is, it must be shown in such a way that his supreme magisterium is acknowledged with reverence, the judgments made by him *are sincerely adhered to,* according to his manifest mind and will. His mind and will in the matter may be known chiefly either from the character of the documents, from his frequent repetition of the same doctrine, or from his manner of speaking."

We, therefore, have a serious and imperative obligation to form a *correct* conscience, according to the Holy Father's directive — *not according to our own likes or our own wishes.*

Although it is true that man must always follow his conscience if he would avoid sin, still it must be a *correct* conscience. This Pope Paul and many other authorities have repeatedly declared. Man's conscience can only be correct when it conforms to God's Will, and God's Will can only be known with absolute certainty through the Church of which the Pope is the authentic interpretor.

The Church's teaching is that if one errs through invincible ignorance, he is justified in following his erroneous conscience. However, he must correct it as soon as he discovers his error. In the case of birth control, since Pope Paul has precisely and clearly declared that the use of contraceptives is gravely sinful, no Catholic can honestly claim that he does not know, or cannot learn, what the Church teaches in this matter.

Not only is this point proclaimed in the encyclical, *Humanae Vitae,* but it is also clearly emphasized in the documents of the Council of Vatican II (Pastoral Constitution on the Church in the Modern World, *Gaudium et Spes,* 50, 51, which states: "... sons of the Church may not undertake methods of regulating procreation which are found blameworthy by the teaching authority of the Church in its unfolding of the Divine Law."

And so, we cannot take the matter of contraception lightly. We cannot just "take it or leave it", especially since it concerns a very serious moral matter.

But, we may ask, why are we Catholics forbidden to use the pill and other contraceptives while people of other religions are free from such regulations?

This question is off center.

It is not the Catholic religion which forbids such birth control but the will of God through divine and natural laws. From earliest times, birth control has been acknowledged to be a terrible evil. In fact, the Bible — Genesis 38:8,9,10 — states that God punished it by death because it is "a detestable thing."

But what about responsible parenthood? Does the Catholic Church ever approve of couples spacing or limiting themselves to a few children?

Yes. Catholic couples may limit the number of their children if that is their prudent judgment and if they fulfill the proper conditions.

These conditions are that they must have a serious reason, for example, illness of the wife; the decision to limit the family size must be mutual; the danger of committing sexual sins must be remote; they must abstain from their marital rights for a space of months or years, or periodically during fertile days each month; and they must exclude contraception by either party, whether it be mechanical or chemical, withdrawl, sodomy, sterilization or abortion.

This teaching is moral, reasonable and practical. Contrary to some opinion, chastity in marriage is indeed possible and is being observed by countless couples. Unselfish love, mutual respect and the blessings of God bring peace and joy to the observance of continency.

It is noteworthy that there is now an apostolate, the *Couple to Couple League,* which is encouraging couples to live in obedience to God's own laws of love and life. It teaches a natural family planning method that works and is in harmony with authentic Catholic faith and morals. It also reminds physicians that they "can do a great favor to their patients by helping them to live within the Church's marital doctrine which allows natural family planning."

This non-profit organization (also open to non-Catholics) was inaugurated in 1971 by John and Shelia Kippley. Its headquarters are at Cincinnati, Ohio (mailing address: P.O. Box 11084) from which local chapters may obtain teacher training and adequate teaching materials so that both biological data and the values involved in the natural methods only decision are presented. Also available is their book, *The Art of Natural Family Planning.*

Some people ask: What about medications required in the treatment of disease which might result in the prevention of conception? May these be used?

The encyclical reaffirms the Church's teaching that the use of therapeutic means which are truly necessary to cure diseases of organisms, even if an impediment to procreation should result therefrom, are permissible provided that such an impediment is not directly willed.

Speaking of medications, besides the immoral aspects involved in the use of the pill for birth prevention, there is also a medical element. Contrary to popular promotion of the pill, many physicians — including prominent gynecologists — are decidedly against its use. Their judgment is that it disturbs natural process and balance and could cause serious, dangerous after-effects. In fact, some cite the rising incidents of embolism in women who use the pill.

What about abortion and sterilization? May these be used?

No. The encyclical repeats the declaration of the Church that the direct interruption of the generative process already begun (abortion) directly willed and procured, even if it be for therapeutic reasons, is absolutely to be excluded. Why? Because abortion, honestly defined, is murder: the deliberate destruction of the right to life.

Regarding sterilization, direct sterilization — whether permanent or temporary, whether of the man or of the woman — is also absolutely forbidden because it is the willful abuse of the body and the deliberate prevention of fertility. Indirect sterilization — as that caused by imperative surgery removing diseased organisms — is permissible because it is absolutely necessary medical treatment for the cure of an illness; it is *not* the deliberate prevention of fertility.

But, we may wonder, what about the population explosion? If artificial birth control is not practiced, what will happen to the needy?

The antidote to the population explosion is not birth prevention. To use something evil to correct a situation — real or anticipated — is not the right answer to any problem.

In this situation, doesn't the remedy lie in promoting positive, helpful means of providing for the welfare of mankind? In developing better agricultural methods and products, irrigation systems, and the use of more adequate equipment which will vastly increase harvests? Doesn't the remedy lie in a more equitable distribution of wealth between the haves and the have-nots; in governmental and educational procedures which will correct conditions for poverty stricken peoples and areas; in the developing and use of the immense tracts of wilderness still uninhibited?

In fact, recent improvements in agricultural methods and products have been so effective that fears of a future worldwide famine are now judged to be without basis. Among the internationally famed nutrition experts who attest to this fact is Dr. Jean Mayer, Professor of Nutrition at Harvard University and Director of the White House Conference on Food and Nutrition. It is his contention that within the next twenty to thirty years "food will be removed altogether as a limiting factor to population" and that increased food production and international organizations will make large-scale famines, such as those that have occurred in India and China, a thing of the past.

As to the use of land, it is an irrefutable fact that there are still vast sections of undeveloped wilderness which could be utilized and made productive. As the Most Rev. John R. Quinn clearly indicated in his analysis, *Population Explosion: Peril or Panic?*, dated February 15, 1972, released by NC News:

". . . Little emphasis is given to the fact that seventy percent of the people in the United States live on two percent of the land. The Amazon Basin in Brazil is 1/20th of the land surface of the earth and is still virgin soil. There are 180 million acres of some of the world's most fertile soil lying unused in Ethiopia. Huge land areas such as Mindanao in the Philippines are still uncultivated. In America, our government has retired at least 22.5 million acres into the soil bank. Idaho, Montana, Nevada, Wyoming, North and South Dakota each have a population of less than a million people. In California almost half of its twenty million people live in only four counties.

"Dr. Colin Clark, one of the world's great economists and author of the book, *Population Growth and Land Use,* states that it is his contention that if we take world resources of arable land at four billion acres, this would feed at maximum American standards forty-seven billion people.

"It is well known that statistics on population are imperfect and by no means scientifically accurate . . . Philip Houser of the University of Chicago, for example, is quoted as saying: 'Projections of future populations are admittedly fictions. No one can actually predict future population and anyone who claims that he can is either a fool or a charlatan.'

". . . The real problem lies in the improper and unjust distribution of wealth and resources, the overcrowding of great numbers in small areas, and the careless, unplanned consumption of goods and commodities. Solutions can be found. The Israelies, for example, have dramatized what can be done through the combination of technology and hard work by turning a desert into a dwelling . . ."

It is significant that Pope Paul VI told participants at the World Food Conference, held in Rome in November, 1974, that the global food crisis stems from unwillingness to correct maldistribution of the world's resources and from the overconfidence which nations place in industrialization. Among the forthright statements in his eight-page address, the Holy Father stated: "It is inadmissible that those who have control of the wealth and resources of mankind should try to resolve the problem of hunger by forbidding the poor to be born or by leaving to die of hunger children whose parents do not fit into the framework of theoretical plans based on pure hypotheses about the future of mankind."

From these and other authoritative statements, it can readily be seen that the argument for promoting contraception because of the lack of land space and the lack of food is actually a fallacy.

But some people ask, what about the arguments, advanced by the proponents of birth prevention, stating that because of ecological dangers birth control is imperative?

Although it is true that problems relating to pollution of the land, the air and the water are indeed extensive, still the remedy does not consist in promoting programs which immorally prevent life but rather in undertaking constructive programs to correct the environmental conditions which cause pollution.

The truth, therefore, is that immoral birth prevention is not the answer to individual, community, national or world problems because something that is morally wrong can never be right. No amount of arguing, excusing or rationalizing can ever justify the deliberate violation of the divine and natural laws.

Whether or not we obey God's laws and the teachings of His Church is up to each of us. The problem reduces itself to: *how much do we love God and how much do we value our own souls and the souls of others?*

Eternity has no ending.

PRAYER
AGAINST THE FORCES OF ANTI-LIFE[2]

St. Gerard, powerful protector of the mother and the unborn child, beg God, we beseech you, to conquer the horrible forces of anti-life, and to enlighten those in error that they may understand the deadly malice of their sin and return to the observance of His holy law. Pray, too, for mothers that they may highly cherish their wonderful prerogative of motherhood and bring up their children in the holy love and fear of God for the salvation of their own souls, and to the eternal praise and glory of His Name, through Christ, Our Lord. Amen.

Recommended Reading:

Humanae Vitae, A Sign of Contradiction by Dr. Dietrich von Hildebrand; Franciscan Herald Press, 1434 West 51st St., Chicago, Illinois 60609; paperback, $1.50.

In Defense of Human Life by the Rev. Msgr. John F. McCarthy; Lumen Christi Press, P.O. Box 13176, Houston, Texas 77019; paperback, 75¢.

The First Nine Months of Life by Geraldine Lux Flanagan. This is not a book about sex or abortion. Rather, it is the fascinating, scientific story of everybody's first nine months of life — from conception to birth. This positive approach shows that the unborn child is not just a piece of tissue, not just an appendage of the mother but a live human being, from the moment of conception. This classic is now available as a paperback at $2.00 per copy from the Committee of Ten Million, P.O. Box 10299, Glendale, California 91209.

[1]This encyclical is available in pamphlet form at 25¢ per copy (discount for quantity orders) from *Our Sunday Visitor,* Huntington, Indiana 46750.

[2]This is the official prayer of the *League of St. Gerard,* an approved apostolate designed to combat by prayer the forces of anti-life and to spread devotion to St. Gerard, the "mother's saint". Beautiful slides depicting the saint's life, loaned free of charge to any parish or institution, are available from the league's center, c/o the Redemptorist Fathers at Liguori, Missouri 63057.

Units of the *League of St. Gerard* may be organized in any parish. Membership is open to both the laity and religious. Annual dues are just one dollar and are used to provide free distribution of St. Gerard medals, leaflets and pamphlets to individuals and to Catholic hospitals.

CONTRIBUTIONS

We have so many appeals for donations — to our church, our school, the Community Fund, etc. It seems that "every time we turn around someone is asking for money for something." And so we begin to feel pressured and annoyed. We already have so many expenses. There are the mortgage payments, the car payments, medical bills, the children's schooling, etc. All of a sudden, everything seems just too much.

True, true. But isn't this reaction the result of how we look at giving?

If we stop to think that we are living in the most prosperous country in the world and that our standard of living, compared to the needy in countless slum villages throughout the world, makes each of us "millionaires", then we really are not very generous, are we?

Of course, every nation and its people may live according to the standard with which God has blessed them. But with our prosperity there comes the obligation of sharing our blessings and our luxuries with the poor of the world.

Divine law has ordained that "sheaves were to be left in the field, olives on the trees and grapes on the vine for the poor and the fatherless."

In our modern world we, personally, may not have wheat, olives and grapes to give to the poor and the homeless but most of us do have an abundance of food, clothing and material possessions.

Are we justified, then, in cramming our refrigerators and freezers with luxury food items and in wasting so much food — it is estimated that the average American housewife dumps 400 pounds of edible food into the garbage every year — when 300 to 500 million people are hungry and one billion people suffer from varying degrees of malnutrition?

Are we justified in spending so much for clothes — many times unnecessary or too extravagant — when there are hundreds of thousands of women who tear paper off billboards to make clothes for their children?

Are we justified in spending so much for permanents, cosmetics, hair tonics and other items designed to beautify when many of the world's fifteen million lepers are denied the disease-arresting sulfone drugs which not only eliminate suffering but also prevent terrible disfigurements?

Are we justified in spending so much money for too many and too expensive toys for our children when millions of children sit listlessly staring into space — too weak and ill to smile, let alone play?

Are we justified in spending so much for liquor when thousands of people must stand wearily in line, anxiously waiting their turns to receive a small keg of precious water, just enough for absolute necessities?

Are we justified in redecorating our homes too often and in buying unnecessary new furniture and appliances when billions of people live in crumbly shelters, in paper shacks or just on the streets?

Are we justified in buying bigger and better cars too often when so many of the starving and the sick cannot even walk?

Actually, are we too poor to help the poor? Is giving to the missions once a year on Mission Sunday enough? Couldn't we be doing something more for others?

Couldn't we, for example, have a family coin bank for the orphans? And at Christmas time, at least, couldn't we ransom a pagan baby in honor of the Christ Child?

In many places people are so poor that they are unable to support their children. And so, these little ones are often neglected and abandoned. In many cases pagan parents are willing to give or sell their children to missionaries or to native Christians. Those who contribute the ransom price — five dollars — have the privilege of becoming the "rescued" child's spiritual sponsor of Baptism and may supply a Christian name for the baby. Contributions for the ransom are handled through the *Pontifical Association of the Holy Childhood* at 800 Allegheny Avenue, Pittsburgh, Pa., 15233, and also through various Orders such as the Capuchin Fathers, the Society of the Divine Word, etc.

When we buy a new home, car or appliance, even though it be on contract, could we make an offering for those who have no homes or who must live in make-shift shelters?

When we take a vacation could we make an offering for those who are shut-ins?

Could we sew our own clothes or buy less clothes or watch the sales and then give the saving to those who need clothes?

Could we walk to work now and then, "do" our own hair, drop one of our secular magazines or book subscriptions, cut down on our cigarettes, malted milks and martinis? The lepers are waiting for the drugs which this saving could buy for them.

Among the apostolates specificially engaged in assisting the victims of leprosy is the *Damien-Dutton Society* whose headquarters are at P.O. Box 1222, New Brunswick, New Jersey, 08903.

These — and other methods of saving and giving — are a sharing of our blessings with the unfortunate and with God, for Christ identified Himself with the poor and the suffering.

DEATH

Death is the opening door to heaven — to God and eternal happiness. Even so, we would rather not think about death. Not now, anyway. Besides, right now we are too busy with college and all its activities, or we are engrossed in getting started with our careers, or we are working hard to get the mortgage paid off and our children's schooling set up. Death, we think, is a long way off.

Is it? Others have thought the same thing but have been surprised by a sudden death. This may happen to us, too. How do we know that we are going to live to be 60, 70, or 80?

What then? Shall we go about our affairs depressed and fearful?

On the contrary. Our Lord told us what to do about death: to be prepared for death so that it does not come upon us "as a thief in the night."

How shall we be prepared? Actually, we know the answer. We have heard sermons on the subject of death so many times. Our spiritual teachers have tried so often to impress upon us the fact that the best preparation for a holy death is holy daily living — to live each day as though it were to be our last day on earth. We hear and we know yet somehow we tend to feel that the advice is for "the other guy".

Sometimes, sad to say, we are presumptuous about death — especially if we are living in habits of serious sin which we do not want to break. God, we then think, is good. He will not let us die in sin. He will not let us go to hell.

Really?

Such reasoning is way off center. The point is not that God "lets" but that we — each of us — must make a choice. We merit heaven if we obey the commandments and fulfill the duties of our state in life. We place ourselves in hell by turning away from God and His Will — deliberately preferring ourselves and our own will, living contrary to God's commands, in effect saying: "I will not serve!" The choice is ours.

God is, indeed, good. He is Goodness, itself — kind, merciful and forgiving towards any repentant sinner, no matter how great or numerous the sins may be. But God is also perfectly just. And being just, He cannot give unrepentant, obstinate sinners the same reward that He gives to His faithful servants.

Our Blessed Lord emphasized this truth when He told us about the Last Judgment (Matt.25:31-46): that the angels would separate the good from the bad and that the good would enter with Him into the everlasting joys of heaven but the wicked would be cast into the eternal fires of hell, where there would be weeping and gnashing of teeth.

Knowing this, to be negligent or rash about preparing for our death is most unwise.

Rather, our spiritual fathers remind us that we should live in a continuous state of grace; also, that daily we should pray, especially to Our Blessed Mother and to St. Joseph, patron of the dying, for the grace of a holy death and for God's blessing upon all who are to die this day and night; and that we should be anxious and willing to receive the Last Sacraments. When death comes towards our dear ones, we should assist them in receiving the Sacrament of the Sick (Extreme Unction) not fearfully, at the last possible moment, but while they are still conscious so that they may be ready to go to God and so that the beautiful, forgiving words of the Sacrament and of the prayers for the dying may encourage and console them.

A very helpful means of helping our ill and dying non-Catholic relatives or friends, is the use of a prayer-card, *My Daily Prayer,* especially designed for this purpose. It offers a perfect act of faith, hope, love, contrition, and a desire for Baptism. If the patient is too ill to read, the prayer may be said for and with him. A free sample is available from the *Markham Prayer-Card Apostolate,* 60 Compton Road, Cincinnati, Ohio 45215. (Quantity orders are nominal in price, set just to cover costs.)

We could also assist the dying by becoming members of the *Apostolate in Honor of St. Joseph for Dying Sinners,* 110 West Madison Street, Chicago, Illinois 60602. Through this enrollment, special prayers are offered daily for them. No dues or meetings are required. The apostolate provides a special *Manual of Devotions* (50¢) which contains many prayers for the dying, the *Heroic Act for the Dying,* information regarding the *Priest's Sick call,* the *Layman's Sick Call, How to Baptize infants, How to Baptize Adult non-Catholics.*

Not only should we prepare for death by living a holy life and by daily prayers for a holy death but we should also be alert to recognize and protest current efforts advocating euthanasia (legalized "mercy killing"). Various states are now considering legislation which would allow the patient and his doctor to decide, together, the time and manner of death. *Death and Dying* lectures, seminars, classes and panel discussions — all too often presenting the purely human and psychological aspects in a manner contrary to the teachings of God and His Church — are becoming more and more popular. And it is common knowledge that the *Alethea Center on Death and Dying* (State Tower Bldg., Syracuse, New York 13202) has a ten-year plan, begun in 1974, for imposing euthanasia on the United States by 1983. Its 42-page report entitled *"A Social Invention"*[1] clearly describes its strategy and tactics, year by year, aimed at achieving euthanasia laws at federal, state and local levels of government. This well organized, well financed, sophisticated scheme could indeed lead to the destruction of the old and infirm. The hope of stopping the pressure for death-on-demand by the Alethea organization, and similar groups, lies in vigilance, prayer, courage, action and persistence.

Are we listening? Are we praying?

PRAYER FOR THE DYING

O Saint Joseph, Foster-father of our Lord Jesus Christ and true Spouse of the Virgin Mary, pray for us and the dying of this day (this night.) Amen

O most Merciful Jesus, Lover of souls, I pray You by the agony of Your most Sacred Heart and by the sorrows of Your Immaculate Mother, cleanse in Your Blood the sinners of the whole world who are now in their agony and are to die this day. Amen.

O Agonizing Heart of Jesus, have mercy on the dying!

Recommended Reading:
Do Not Weep (a book of sympathy and comfort especially intended to console the bereaved) available from the Rev. J. Walter Stocklosa, A.M., 36 Trull Lane, Lowell, Mass. 01852; $3.00 per copy.

[1]Copies of the document may be obtained for $1.00 from Charles R. Pulver, 4918 Bethel Road, Cazenovia, New York 13035.

DRIVING

A screeching ambulance whizzes past us. Another accident. Poor people, we think. And we wonder how the accident happened. Maybe the driver was drunk . . . Well, we say to ourselves, that is one thing we will never do — mix drinking and driving.

No? Perhaps not. But how careful are we of other dangerous driving habits and practices? Angry driving, for example. This causes so many accidents. Are we among those who are guilty of this?

Do we jump into the car, tearing out of a driveway when we have had a quarrel at home, a stormy session with the boss, etc.? If so, our attention can't be on what we are doing and so we are prone to accidents.

Does following a slow-poke driver make us so angry that we risk passing, even on a hill, a curve or a slippery stretch of road?

Do we become so annoyed at someone who has taken "our" right-of-way or a parking space which we were aiming at, that we give the gas pedal a sudden, fierce jab . . . wham!

Calmness, patience, kindness, thoughtfulness would have eliminated the resulting accidents.

Perhaps we may not be drunken drivers or angry drivers but what about other immoral driving practices?

Do we drive without a license or while a license is under revocation or suspension?

Do we drive without the insurance protection for others, required in most states?

Do we violate restrictions against excessive speed, reckless driving through stop signs, red lights, etc.?

Are we show-off drivers? Do we play driving games? Do we dare others — or accept dares — to drag-race on streets or roads not designated for racing?

Do we drive, knowing that our eyesight is poor, not adequate for the vision normally required for safe driving?

Do we "take chances" — driving cars with faulty brakes, worn out tires or other mechanical defects?

Do we permit minors or other unauthorized drivers to use our car or truck?

Do we bribe or attempt to bribe enforcement officers or licensing agents?

Are we a party to fraudulent or excessive accident claims against insurance companies? Do we commit perjury in accident litigation matters?

Under the natural law and the civil law, we are morally responsible for our own safety, for the lives of our passengers, for others — driving or walking — and for the property of others. Therefore, if we drive in such a manner that it endangers lives or property, then we are violating the commandments: *Thou shalt not kill and Thou shalt not steal.*

Our statuettes of the Sacred Heart[1] or of Our Lady placed on dashboards are not to be superstitiously regarded as guaranteed protection against accidents. Rather, these sacramentals are intended to remind us to offer a prayer for our own safety and for that of others — to remind us that we are morally bound to be kind, considerate, careful drivers.

THE DRIVER'S PRAYER[2]

Grant me, O Sacred Heart, a steady hand and watchful eye.
That no one shall be hurt as I pass by.
You gave life, I pray no act of mine,
May take away or mar that gift of Thine.
Shelter those, dear Lord, who bear me company,
From the evils of fire and all calamity.
Teach me to use my car for others need;
Nor miss through love of undue speed.
The beauty of the world; that thus I may,
With joy and courtesy go on my way.
O Sacred Heart of Jesus, Have mercy on us.

[1]Sacred Heart satuettes and a copy of the *Driver's Prayer* may be obtained from the Sacred Heart Auto League, c/o Sacred Heart Southern Missions, Walls, Mississippi, 38680. (This apostolate was formed to promote careful, prayerful driving and to encourage us to offer our driving time in reparation to the Sacred Heart.)

[2]This is the official prayer of the Sacred Heart Auto League; copies are available from it at nominal prices; address: c/o Sacred Heart Southern Missions, Walls, Mississippi 38680.

DRUGS

It is a beautiful, spring day, just fine for house cleaning, so we start in our teen-age son's room.

The closet. Might as well begin at the top shelf. Swiftly, we remove a conglamoration of items: a camera, a flashlight, a pair of sun glasses, two pairs of gloves, an old cribbage board, a small box.

The box slides from our fingers to the floor. We stoop to pick it up and it jerks open at our touch. We stare unbelievingly at its contents: hypodermic needles, a syringe, an empty vial . . . We are stunned. This just can't be.

Numbly, we drop into a chair, looking at, but not seeing, the telltale evidence of drugs . . .

Moments pass into minutes and we are finally able to accept the fact that everything adds up: Bill's deep moods of sulleness and aloofness and then his sudden, wildly gay spirits — drugs.

What shall we do? Oh, what shall we do? To whom shall we turn? Who will listen and help us? . . . Why, Father Joseph, our pastor . . . Of course!

Quickly, we leave the house and head for the rectory. Fortunately, Father is in and free to see us.

From him we learn that the situation calls for the following:

1. That we must pray, pray and pray;

2. That we must confront Bill in kindness, not with yelling, bitter recriminations;

3. That we must assure Bill that we will assist him in overcoming his problem; that the situation is not hopeless; that with God's blessing and Bill's own co-operation, he can conquer the habit;

4. That we must explain to Bill that although the abuse of drugs is a serious sin because it destroys the most noble part of man — his personality — and because it so often leads to other sins, still, drug addiction is also an illness, and so medical assistance and/or psychiatric help and personal or family counselling may be necessary;

5. That Bill and we, too, must face the fact that for him, drugs are definitely out — even the smallest dosage or the mildest in form; that just as the alcoholic must acknowledge the fact that he cannot tolerate any liquor, anytime, not even a few swallows of beer, so too, the drug addict must completely give up the use of drugs — however painful this may be;

6. That we must find out the reason why Bill has the drug habit. Did he start taking drugs just for "kicks" or to get along with the gang? Or is it because he has a problem, real or fancied?

7. That sometimes in order to give full assistance, extraordinary measures may be necessary; for example: we may have to allow the addict to leave high school (which he hates and with which he cannot cope) and go to a trade school where he can learn work suitable and satisfying to him. Because of his or our sensitiveness to the problem or because the ad-

dict does not have the stamina to withstand the pressures of his peers or other local drug solicitation, it may even be expedient for us to move to another section of town or to the country or to another city.

The Bureau of Narcotics and Dangerous Drugs advises parents to teach children respect for drugs of all kinds, even aspirin which can cause death by overdose. Parents are also advised to discuss the subject with their children, stressing the fact that anyone can feel good, feel acceptable, feel sociable without depending on drugs. Children should also be reminded of the penalties under law and that the abuse of drugs leads to loss of reputation, success in school, future careers, health and even death.

Many clergymen, psychiatrists, and law enforcement officials warn parents that their personal habits can help induce children into experimenting with drugs. Why? Because if parents appear incapable of breaking smoking or drinking habits or constantly resort to pills to remedy minor discomforts, an acceptable attitude of dependence on possibly harmful things is presented. Research findings indicate a definite link between parents' drinking and pill-taking habits and the use of alcohol or other drugs by children.

Parents are also advised to show real concern for their children, their schooling, interests and companions. Discipline and authority, but not tyranny, are important to children. In fact, some young persons who become addicted to drugs say that they think that they would not have done so if their parents had really been concerned about them and had imposed strict standards.

There are various useful booklets intended for parents and others who are concerned about drug abuse. One of these is *Our Drugged Youth,* authored by Rev. Jess L. Pedigo, a distinguished Protestant clergyman; available at 50¢ per copy from the Christian Crusade, Box 977, Tulsa, Oklahoma 74102.

However, parents are also cautioned about books and films that are supposedly intended to stop drug abuse but are more likely to encourage drug experimentation and abuse. Sometimes they present a soft approach which minimizes the dangers, and some even portray youths who are on LSD, walking around in a daze, exclaiming: "How wonderful! How beautiful!" Thus, far from warning the young viewer, this could easily suggest a desire for a similar experience. And so, parents should be alert to the type of books and films on this subject which may inadvertently be in use in schools, workshops, etc.

Another point to be noticed, is the fact that many youths — and adults — smoke marijuana on the assumption that "it is only a weak drug and does no harm". Many distinguished scientists attest otherwise. In fact, on May 9, 1974 the Senate Subcommittee on Internal Security, chaired by Senator James O. Eastland, conducted a series of hearings on the marijuana-hashish epidemic and its impact on our national security. All of the scientists who testified stated that they considered marijuana to be a very dangerous drug which accumulates in the brain and may result in irreversible brain damage. They further stated that this was the consensus at several international conferences of marijuana-hashish researchers.

To obtain a copy of this report, we may write for the Congressional Record of July 24, 1974 on the Senate Drug Hearings to Senator James O. Eastland, Senate Office Building, Washington, D.C. 20510. We could also tell others about the existence of this congressional record.

Many law enforcement officials emphatically state that if more stringent anti-drug laws were to be passed and upheld — the drug problem would be drastically curtailed. And so they repeatedly recommend that parents voice their concerns to legislators, encourage others to do so, and promote measures on the local, state and national level aimed at the passage of stricter, more binding anti-drug laws.

The saddest aspect of the current widespread abuse of drugs (including alcohol) is that its victims now include children ten-years old; that children and teens often become drug peddlers in order to support their own terrible habit; that many obtain the necessary money by theft and prostitution; and that many run away from home and live on-the-streets. The resultant hardships cause untold suffering, often ending in premature, violent deaths.

Our youth are conditioned to the use of drugs by rock music, shows, the underground press and other media. The understanding and assistance of pastors, parents, and teachers is urgently needed to assist both potential and actual users.

Whatever the sacrifice in time, effort and expense, whatever the cost in heartbreaking struggles, disappointments, setbacks and more struggles, the fact remains that with prayer, family love and co-operation, counselling medical, psychiatric or social service help, drug addicts can be assisted in facing their problem, in learning to live with it and above it — thus becoming a credit to themselves and their dear ones, and a joy to the merciful Heart of Christ.

THE ENTHRONEMENT OF THE SACRED HEART

Most of us — especially when we read the Bible or the Life of Our Lord, or when we hear a moving sermon — think about how wonderful it must have been to have lived in Palestine during the time when Our Lord lived there.

We think how happy we would have been to welcome Him to our city, to bring our children and suffering ones to Him for His Blessing. Perhaps we might even have invited Him to come and rest awhile at our home — to have dinner with us, too.

We think how fortunate Lazarus, Mary and Martha were to have been such special friends of Our Blessed Lord. How favored they were to be able to offer Him the hospitality of their home at Bethany.

We did not have this privilege. But we do have the privilege of making our homes other Bethanys — places where the Sacred Heart of Jesus is the King and Center of our lives; places where He is welcomed as the hidden, honored Guest; places where He is so loved that the family instinctively turns to Him in all its problems, joys and sorrows. We can do so through an official act of the Church known as the *Enthronement of the Sacred Heart.*

It began through the insights and zeal of two men of God: a pope and a priest. The pope — later canonized a saint — was Pope Pius X and the priest was the great apostle of the Sacred Heart, the Rev. Mateo Crawley-Boevey, SS.CC., of Valparaiso, Chile.

At the time, 1907, secular modernism was already gaining a strong hold in the family and in civic, social, intellectual and political circles. Pope Pius X, keenly aware of the engulfing dangers, repeatedly warned of the grave necessity for a return of people and nations to Christ and His teachings. He had chosen as his motto: *To Restore All Things in Christ.*

In the meantime, Father Mateo, also concerned about the widespread deterioration of the home and of society, made a pilgrimage to Paray-le-monial, France, to the chapel where Our Lord had so often appeared to St. Margaret Mary, repeatedly asking for devotion and reparation to His Sacred Heart and promising great blessings to all who would comply with His entreaties.

There, while kneeling in prayer before the Blessed Sacrament, Father Mateo was miraculously cured of a serious illness. At the same time, he received the extraordinary grace of understanding what he must do for the spiritual regeneration of families. He was inspired to clarify Our Lord's promise: *"I will bless every dwelling in which the image of My Heart shall be exposed and honored."*

On his knees that very night — August 24, 1907 — he formulated his crusade to "reconquer the world for Christ, the King", family by family and, thus, from the family to the community, to the nation, and throughout the world.

Soon afterwards, Father Mateo developed his idea into an official Enthronement Ceremony authorized with the blessing, *and by the command,* of Pope (Saint) Pius X.

From the Vatican, Father Mateo went to the Holy Land where he spent long hours, especially at Nazareth and Bethany, meditating on Our Lord's love for family life.

Upon his return to South America via the United States, he preached in a Spanish church in New York City and inaugurated his crusade for the *Enthronement of the Sacred Heart in the Home.* Zealous laymen prepared the families and then, accompanied by the parish priest, Father Mateo went from home to home, enthroning the Sacred Heart in the place of honor.

The results were astounding. Terrible sinners, including enemies of the Church, were converted. Fallen-aways returned to the sacraments and the spiritual life of the entire parish changed — so much so that many called it a new Pentecost. As the crusade spread, always with the same startling results, it became quite evident that this was indeed the work of the Sacred Heart, not of men.

Until his death in 1960 the saintly priest traveled around the world in sickness and in health, in hardships from inclement climate, in complications caused by foreign languages and customs, in obstacles from cruel hostilities, and in other personal dangers — always preaching Christ's love and mercy, and locally starting the *Enthronement of the Sacred Heart* in homes.

In the meantime succeeding pontiffs all approved, blessed and encouraged the movement. In fact, in 1967, the Enthronement's 60th anniversary, Pope Paul VI imparted to all the promoters of the *Enthronement* and to all families consecrated to Jesus Christ, the King of Love, his apostolic blessing. The *Enthronement Movement* continues now through national centers. In the United States headquarters are at 3 Adams Street, Fairhaven, Mass 02719, with the Rev. Francis Larkin, SS.CC., serving as the national director. Assisting with *Enthronment* endeavors are the *Men of the Sacred Heart,* a national apostolate headquartered at 6026 Harwood Ave., Orlando, Florida 32811.

The *Enthronement Ceremony* is the installation, by the head of the family, of an image of the Sacred Heart in a place of honor in the home, along with an act of consecration of the family to the Sacred Heart. But it is a great deal more. In fact, it is the official and social recognition of the Kingship of the Sacred Heart of Jesus over the Christian family. It is a ceremony through which the family says, in effect: *"Jesus, we want You to rule over our family; we adore You as our King of Love; we accept You as our loving Friend, always occupying the first place in our hearts and in our home."* Thus, the *Enthronement* is a family covenant with Jesus.

This positive recognition of the Kingship of Christ makes hearts and homes loving shrines of the Sacred Heart so that family prayer, devotion to the Holy Eucharist, obedience to the commandments, and the practice of virtue bring the true spirit of the Gospel to the family, and from the family into society. This is due to two things: 1) the fidelity of the family to their commitment to pray together and 2) the fidelity of Jesus to His promises to bless, protect and help families in all of their needs.

Millions of families throughout the world have consecrated themselves to the Sacred Heart through the *Enthronement Ceremony* and their dedication has brought — and is bringing — them many family blessings and joys,[1] as well as special graces of strength and courage during times of sufferings and trials.

Various books and rituals designed to help us effectively enthrone the Sacred Heart in our homes are available from the national center. Among these are the *Enthronment of the Sacred Heart* by the Rev. Francis Larkin, SS.CC., ($3.00); *Jesus, King of Love* by the Rev. Mateo Crawley-Boevey, SS.CC., ($3.00); *The Firebrand* (autobiography of Father Mateo) ($4.00); *Understanding the Heart* by Father Larkin, ($1.00); *Honestly, Have You Tried Everything?* (a popular paperback depicting the love and mercy of the Sacred Heart as an antidote to today's family problems; ($1.25); and the autobiographies of St. Margaret Mary and Blessed Claude, each a 50¢ paperback. Also available are an *Enthronement Recording* ($3.50); a beautiful sound-color film, *The Sacred Heart Enthroned,* which may be purchased or rented at reasonable rates; a *Do-It-Yourself Enthronement Ritual* which enables the family to have the ceremony without the necessity of having a priest in attendance; various tapes of key lectures on the Sacred Heart, originally presented at national meetings of the *Enthronement Movement;* the ritual for the *Business Covenant Ceremony* (Enthronement of the Sacred Heart in business and professional establishments.)

The *Enthronement of the Sacred Heart* is intended not only for homes but for schools, convents, institutions, parishes, dioceses and even for cities, states and nations. For in accepting Christ's Kingship and in trying to live in His presence, the family, the community, the nation, the world are restored to Christ.

During His earthly life Our Blessed Lord sought consolation and refuge from the persecution and the hatred of His enemies in the homes of His friends, especially in the home of Lazarus, Mary and Martha. Now, as then, He seeks other Bethanys where He will be made the intimate confidant of the family. His Sacred Heart, filled with love and mercy, is anxious to come and give His infinite treasures to those who love and honor Him.[1]

[1]See index regarding Promises of the Sacred Heart.

ERA: THE EQUAL RIGHTS AMENDMENT

The Equal Rights Amendment (ERA) has a very appealing title. It is also a very misleading one. In fact, if the amendment were to become law, rather than being beneficial, it would be very detrimental and destructive.

One of the first and most ardent opponents of this bill is the distinguished Mrs. Phyllis Schlafly. When the amendment was first introduced, she studied the measure and its ramifications very thoroughly and she was appalled at its hidden evil. Mrs. Schlafly has since written and lectured extensively on this subject. Here are her findings, briefly stated:

"The Equal Rights Amendment pretends to be an advance for women, whereas actually it will not do anything at all *for* women. It will not give women 'equal pay for equal work' or any new employment advantages.ERA does not even apply to private industry, and there is no way it can extend the rights already guaranteed by the Equal Employment Opportunity Act of 1972. Under this Act, women have already won multi-million dollar back-pay settlements against the largest companies in our land.

"The Education Amendments of 1972 have already given women full equal rights in education at every level, from kindergarten to graduate school. The Equal Credit Opportunity Act of 1974 has already ended all past discrimination in credit.

"On the other hand, ERA will take away many rights and advantages women now have. It will take away a young girl's exemption from the draft. When the draft is resumed for the next war, ERA will require the military to assign women to combat duty equally with men. Congress could draft women now if the American people wanted this to happen; but if ERA is ratified, Congress will no longer have the power to *exempt* women.

"ERA will have a devastating effect on present preferential rights of wives and widows — rights which are justified in recognition of the obvious fact that women have babies and men do not. All family support laws will have to be rewritten to be absolutely equal between husband and wife. Thus, ERA will invalidate all the state laws that obligate a husband to support his wife, to provide her with a home, and to be the primary support of his minor children.

"The elimination of the husband's primary obligation will also wipe out the right of the wife not employed outside the home to get credit in her husband's name and to draw Social Security benefits based on her husband's earnings.

"Section 2 of ERA is a grab for power at the Federal level. It will take out of the hands of the states, and send down to Washington, D.C., enormous areas of law including marriage, family property law, divorce, child custody, prison regulations, insurance rates, and protective labor legislation. Why give Washington, D.C. more power over our lives when the Federal Government can't cope with the problems it has now?

"ERA will create endless mischief in other areas. ERA will wipe out our right to have single-sex schools and colleges, because they 'discriminate' on the basis of sex. ERA will mandate coed sports in all schools and colleges, including football and wrestling, as has already been ordered by Pennsylvania's highest court under its State ERA.

"ERA will grant homosexuals and lesbians the right to get marriage licenses because it will forbid treating the sexes differently. ERA will give the radicals the constitutional basis on which they can litigate to force churches and synagogues to ordain women, since not to do so would be an unconstitutional denial of an equal right.

"Reasonable men and women do want reasonable differences of treatment between men and women in regard to the draft, combat, family support, factory work, police forces, and prison regulations. We do not want the 'gender free' society promoted by the women's lib movement.

"In 1975, 16 state legislatures rejected ERA while only one state ratified it. Many states which hurriedly ratified several years ago are now considering motions to rescind their previous ratification, and two states have already rescinded, namely, Nebraska and Tennessee."

It is a fact that some states which have approved ERA did so in a hurry and without much serious debate. Contrary to widespread misconceptions, such approvals can still be rejected. But some proponents are loudly contending that once a state has approved ERA, it cannot rescind it. However, this is not the case. Among those who disagree is the eminent constitutional authority, Professor Charles L. Black, Jr., of Yale's Law School, who has stated:

> "Clearly a State can change its mind either way before the amendment is officially declared to be ratified . . . Parading precedents is a fallacy. The Supreme Court has reversed itself sometimes and it is Congress' responsibility to do the rational thing. The States may freely withdraw their ratification at any time before an amendment is officially declared to be part of the Constitution. It would be very dangerous to have any State corralled into approving it." (Put into the *Congressional Record* on May 8, 1975.)

Time is of the essence with ERA proponents and they are making an all-out effort to obtain success. An all-out effort by opponents is therefore crucial. Among those who warn us of the need for opposing action is the distinguished author and lecturer, the Rev. Robert E. Burns, C.S.P. In a recent column, Father Burns stated:

> "Presently the ERA juggernaut is stalled. It must not be allowed to start up and move again. Pressure must be put on State legislators to oppose ERA. Some of these people need to be informed so the facts must be laid on the table. As Phyllis Schlafly

says, 'ERA will give women no rights they do not now possess, but it will deprive them of many rights and protections they now have by law.'

"Women are today protected by (1) the Fifth and Fourteenth Amendments; (2) the Equal Pay Act of 1963; (3) the Education Amendments of 1972; (4) the Health Manpower Training Act of 1964; (5) the Equal Employment Opportunity Act of 1972; (6) Title VII of the Civil Rights Act of 1964; and (7) the Fair Labor Standards Act.

"Women are guaranteed equality in educational opportunities, admissions, and employment by the following: (1) Executive Order 11246 as amended by 11375; (2) Title VII of the Civil Rights Act of 1964; (3) Equal Pay Act of 1963 as amended by the Education Amendments of 1972; (4) Title VII and Title VIII of the Public Health Services Act.

"Let's face it, our society has downgraded women instead of uplifting them. Women have been reduced to a sex symbol. What do abortion, promiscuity, and free sex do to elevate women? It simply degrades them. It's about time we reversed the trend and worked to uplift women and restore them to their rightful place of dignity and respect. The defeat of the ERA will be a giant step in that direction. The voters in New York and New Jersey who rejected ERA in November, 1975, have given us renewed courage and confidence for this fight."

It is therefore obvious to any right-thinking person that the Equal Rights Amendment would certainly not guarantee equal rights.

It is also obvious that this matter concerns everyone. Our prayers are needed. Our cooperation in alerting others to the dangers involved is needed. Our open dissent is needed. And our objections must be sent to the president, our congressmen, and our local officials.

Again, we are reminded of Edmund Burke's forceful statement: "All that is necessary for the triumph of evil is for good men to do nothing."

Shall we allow the Equal Rights Amendment to become law by default — by our apathy? Or shall we stand up and be counted?

N.B. Among the fine groups opposing ERA are the *Eagle Forum,* whose president is Mrs. Phyllis Schlafly; a national organization of women and men who believe in God, home and country, and are determined to defend the values that have made America the greatest nation in the world; address: Box 618, Alton, Illinois 62002.

Women for Constitutional Government, now organized in 15 states; 117 Pleasant Street, Newton Center, Mass. 02159.

EXAMINATION OF CONSCIENCE

We spend so much time in checking things. We check our health and physical needs. We check our car and its needs. We check our studies and work. We check to see if the children are playing safely. We check to see if the dinner is cooked, etc.

And yet, we often fail to check the most important thing in our lives: *our souls and our standing with God.* Somehow, we let the matter of the examination of our conscience slip by us — sometimes from the time of one Confession until the next.

This is quite a failing, especially if we are really trying to live as God wants us to live. The saints and our spiritual advisors tell us that it is a good practice to examine our conscience, daily, particularly at bedtime when we pray our *Act of Contrition.*

If we do this, our contrition will have greater meaning; our resolutions will be more sincere.

A quick check for daily examination is the following:

Was God a conscious part of my day?

Did I, this morning, remember to offer Him my day?

Did I turn to Him in times of temptation?

Did I pray for my own needs and for the needs of others?

Were there opportunities wherein I could have "stood up" for God, Our Blessed Mother, the Pope, or the Church but did not do so?

Was I superstitious? Did I consult a fortune teller or an astrologer or did I attend a seance?

Was I guilty of presumption or despair?

Do I hate anyone? Was I unkind or intolerant of anyone? Was I prejudiced in my dealings with a person of a different religion, color or race? Did I spread such bias?

Did I give scandal?

* * * *

Did I use God's name without reverence or in anger?

Did I blaspheme or curse?

Was I faithful to my vows?

* * * *

Today (Sunday) did I get to Mass on time? Did I participate with love and devotion or did I go because I have-to or because my friends go? Did I attentively offer the renewal of Calvary, along with the priest: to adore God, to offer reparation, to thank Him, to ask His help for self and others?

Did I spend the day in unnecessary physical work? Unnecessary buying or selling?

Did I (a youth) disobey my parents? ridicule them? sass them?

Did I refuse to help a sick or needy parent?

Did I (a parent) give good example to my children? care for them properly? listen to their questions and problems?

Did I correct — and if necessary — discipline them? Was I too easy-going or too harsh with them?

* * * *

Did I do anything harmful to my health? eat or drink too much? ignore the diet necessary for my well-being? take drugs not prescribed for me? Did I work beyond my strength?

Did I (an alcoholic or drug addict) begin to drink or take drugs again?

Did I give in to anger? quarrel? fight?

Was I revengeful?

Did I give scandal?

* * * *

Have I been impure today: in thought, word or deed?

Did I dress immodestly? allow my children to dress immodestly?

Did I speak immodestly?

Did I read a salacious book, see such a movie, play or program? Did I permit my children to do so?

* * * *

Did I steal anything? Did I help someone else steal?

Did I cheat in school? Did I take credit for work for something which someone else did?

Was I unjust in my dealings with others?

Did I waste my employer's time or goods?

Did I give false weights or measurements? Did I charge exhorbitant fees?

Did I damage someone's property? or the school's? or the city's?

Did I accept a bribe? give a bribe?

Did I borrow something with the mental intention of not returning it?

* * * *

Was I a hypocrite?

Did I lie?

Did I hurt someone by backbiting, detraction or calumny?

Did I make a rash judgment about someone?

Did I start or spread gossip?

Did I betray a secret?

Did I center my thoughts on impure things?

Did I foster desires contrary to chastity?

Did I cultivate "interest" in another's husband or wife?

* * * *

Did I intensely wish for things that belong to someone else?

Did I rejoice at another's misfortune, hoping to acquire his job, property or goods?

Was I envious of my neighbor's prestige, wealth or success?

Did I wish evil upon anyone?

Checking our relation with God, our spiritual directors tell us, should be one of our most important daily checks. A good time to start this practice is now — today.

FALLEN-AWAYS

Time was when the problem of fallen-aways did not affect us personally. Now and then we may have heard about someone leaving the Church but not anyone close to us.

What a difference today!

Which of us does not have a son or daughter, fallen-away — "married" to a divorced person? A cousin, niece or nephew, fallen-away — shattered by loss of faith resulting from a university's false teachings about God, truth and morality? A brother or sister, fallen-away — having forsaken wife or husband for someone more alluring or more dashing? An uncle or an aunt, fallen-away — preferring to be a "gay blade" unhampered by the teachings of God and His Church? A friend in the priesthood or religious life, fallen-away — surrendering the precious privilege of serving God for the tarnishing tinsel of a "free life in the world"?

When news of such defections reaches us we are stunned and deeply grieved — at first. But as the days lengthen into months and years, what then?

Are we still concerned? Do we still offer daily prayers and sacrifices for these, our fallen-aways? Or have we become so blase' that it no longer seems so disastrous that these, our beloved lapsed ones, are in danger of eternal damnation?

Why?

Is it because we are so involved with personal ambitions and worldly cares that the thought of eternity is pushed into the background and hell seems unreal, even non-existent?

Is it because we dread the thought of our dear ones — or ourselves — being banished to hell and so we console ourselves thinking: surely, the loving, merciful God will never damn anyone to hell.

Right. God does not damn anyone. *People damn themselves.* God does not turn away from anyone. People turn away from Him — by wilfully, obstinately, persistently following their own wills rather than His Will.

Is it because we rarely hear sermons about death, judgment, heaven, hell, or the devil?

Is it because we are so ultra modern that we have lost our perspective, our sense of values? Have we thus forgotten Christ's pleading reminder: *"What does it profit a man if he gains the whole world but suffers the loss of his soul?"*[1]

Is it because we no longer appreciate the necessity for, and the power of, prayer, sacrifice and suffering?

Whatever the reason, the fact is that hell does exist. A hell of terrible suffering. A hell that is forever.

But, we may wonder, how do we know for sure? Who says so?

Our Lord, Himself. He warned us about hell, not once, but over and over again. To quote just one instance, speaking of the final judgment and punishment of the wicked, Christ said: *"Depart from me, you cursed, into everlasting fire. . ."*[2]

Unfortunately, ignoring the existence of hell and the plight of fallen-always, or taking the matter lightly, does not erase the devastating danger in which they live — *and in which they may die.*

The fact remains that if they are to come back to God, it will only be through His great mercy and goodness. Chances are that fallen-aways are doing little or nothing to obtain this tremendous favor and so, someone else must help them.

Who?

Isn't the "someone else" you and I and anyone who cares?

Our Masses, Holy Hours, Rosaries, Stations and other prayers will gain the necessary graces for our fallen-aways.

So will sacrifices — our time, effort and money expended in works of charity and apostolic endeavors.

So will suffering — patiently endured and lovingly offered.

So will little, daily acts of penance and mortification.

And so will reparation offered through such practices as the *Adopt-A-Soul Program, All-Night Vigils of Reparation,* the *Program of Reparation* and *Apology to God,* and *Night Adoration in the Home,* as well as the *First Friday*[3] and *First Saturday*[3] Devotions.

The *Adopt-A-Soul* program is an apostolate started in April, 1967 at St. John's Cathedral in Milwaukee. It conducts a Holy Hour expressly offered for the return of lapsed Catholics, every Thursday from 7 to 8 P.M. Further information, helpful instructions and its special reparation prayer booklet (35¢) are obtainable from the apostolate at 1518 East Capitol Drive, Milwaukee, Wisconsin 53211.

All-Night Vigils of Reparation are generally held between First Fridays and First Saturdays, on the eves of special feast days as that of Christ, the King and the Immaculate Heart of Mary, and at such times as New Year's Eve and Shrove Tuesday. These nights of prayer begin with the Holy Sacrifice of the Mass followed by Exposition of the Blessed Sacrament. The Holy Hours, interspersed with Scriptural Services, homilies and prayers prayed in common, end with an early morning Mass. Various groups sponsor such vigils, including the *Men of the Sacred Heart,* the *Ambassadors of Mary* and the *Blue Army of Our Lady of Fatima.* Further information is available from the Sacred Heart Center at 110 West Madison Street, Chicago, Illinois, 60602.

The *Program of Reparation and Apology to God* was first introduced in 1971 in twenty-five parishes in Southern California, by the Rev. Francis Larkin, SS.CC., national director of the *Enthronement of the Sacred Heart.* It consists of a meditated Rosary for world peace; a half-hour of reparation and apology, before the Blessed Sacrament exposed; Benediction of the Blessed Sacrament; followed by the Holy Sacrifice of the

Mass, in which the parishioners are invited to receive Holy Communion in *reparation for the sins that so offend the Sacred Heart today.* Copies of this program may be obtained by contacting the Sacred Heart Center, 6026 West Harwood Avenue, Orlando, Florida 32811; single copies are 25¢; discounts are available on quantity orders.

Night Adoration in the Home, inaugurated by the late, revered apostle of the Sacred Heart, Father Mateo Crawley-Boevey, SS.CC., consists of one hour of prayer offered in union with the Masses being celebrated during that hour throughout the world. It may be prayed by anyone or any family or group, at least once each month, between 9 P.M. and 6 A.M., before an image of the Sacred Heart.[4] Various adoration pamphlets, suitable for the individual, the family, students, nurses, religious and others, are obtainable at 25¢ each from the Sacred Heart Center, 6026 West Harwood Ave., Orlando, Florida 32811.

These and other prayers and sacrifices offered for our fallen-aways are the greatest love of neighbor. Most assuredly, our prayers, sufferings and sacrifices bring abundunt blessings from the loving, merciful Heart of Christ, for He gave His life for us all — especially for His "lost sheep".

[1]Matthew 16:26
[2]Matthew 25:41
[3]See Index
[4]Any picture or statue of the Sacred Heart may be used. A beautiful home shrine which is a replica of the National Shrine of the Enthronement is available, at $5.50, from the above address. Various pictures of the Sacred Heart are also available at nominal prices.

FAMILY LITURGICAL BLESSINGS AND CUSTOMS

Many of our ancestors lived in the great Catholic countries of Europe. To them, the Church was all-important and their Catholicity extended to the family circle.

The reception of Baptism, First Holy Communion and Confirmation were festive occasions. The evening Rosary and litany were "musts". Holy Water and the Sign of the Cross were devoutly used. Stories of the patron saints were told and retold and their feast days were joyfully celebrated.

Our ancestors sought the Church's blessings upon their engagements and marriages; their homes and children; their labors and endeavors; and their aged and suffering ones. They sought and received other blessings, too: upon their stables and animals; mills and grains; bees and meadows; orchards and vineyards; food and herbs.

Theirs was a Faith that lived the years close to God, along with the cycles in the liturgy of the Church: Advent, Christmas, Epiphany, etc. These seasons were reverently accepted and loved and their spirit was carried into home life.

But when the world grew lax and indifferent, when riches, power, worldly pleasures and speed took over, many of the ancient, beautiful customs of Catholic tradition in family life were ignored.

Recently, however, there has been an awakening interest in family liturgical blessings and customs. Many Catholics are bringing these family customs — both general and seasonal — back into their homes. They are, for example, making of Advent a time of real preparation for the coming of Christ. Family Advent prayers are said — some of the same Psalms that Jesus, Mary and Joseph prayed when They lived on earth. The Advent Wreath is used and the beautiful songs of Advent are sung.

A spirit of penance and sacrifice is fostered, and the children are encouraged to offer some of their small earnings and allowances for such charities as the ransoming of pagan babies as a special birthday gift for the Infant Savior.[1] A home nativity crib is an essential part of the home decorations and Christmas day and week are celebrated in the spirit of honoring Our Lord's birthday.

With a little thought and preparation, with prayer and effort, liturgical customs not only for Advent but also for the other Church cycles could easily become a part of our Catholic home life.

To help us do so, many informative and attractive items are available. Among these are such pamphlets as *Family Advent Customs; Christmas to Candlemas; The Twelve Days of Christmas Book; The Twelve Days of Christmas Kit; Holy Lent-Home Easter Renewal; Easter to Pentecost; Christ Lives In Our House; Family Life in Christ; and My Nameday-Come for Dessert.*

Also available are Advent wreath kits; Christmas silhouette scenes for windows and mirrors; nativity scene door posters, indoor and outdoor; a 15-piece set of colored nativity scene patterns for mounting on plywood; the distinctive Christmas records, *Star Over Bethlehem* and *There in a Stable* (in sheet music also); the record albums, *Sing We Now of Christmas* and *St. Francis and the Christmas Manger;* Christ candles, Madonna and Child candles and Easter candles; family meal prayer cards (Advent, Christmas, Lent, Easter, Pentecost); and Christmas and Easter cards, personal notes and correspondence seals.

A brochure describing these and many other attractive items is available from the *Christ in Christmas Apostolate,* 1518 East Capitol Drive, Milwaukee, Wisconsin 53211.

Our days on earth pass swiftly, gliding silently into eternity. We can bring added grace, beauty and joy into our days and years by living them prayerfully — as our ancestors did — along with the Church.

[1]See explanation on page 51

THE FATIMA MESSAGE

A recent Gallup poll disclosed that only 1½% of all Catholics in the United States really know the Fatima message. What a staggering and sad disclosure this is!

Why so, we may ask?

Because 98½ percent of American Catholics are ignoring — or are not aware of — God's plan for a just and lasting peace, a plan which He entrusted to Our Blessed Mother to reveal to mankind. A plan so important that God granted *a public miracle at a predicted time and place* "so that everyone would believe". A plan which Our Lady promised would save us from "the annihilation of nations".

The time was October 13, 1917. The place was Fatima, Portugal. And the now famous "miracle of the sun" was witnessed by over 70,000 people. An event so outstanding that it was reported in many secular newspapers of the times, including the influential *O Dia* and *O Seculo* publications.

At that time and in four previous apparitions to the three favored children, Lucia dos Santos (9) Francisco Marto (8) and Jacinta Marto (6), Our Blessed Mother warned us that wars are a punishment due to sin and that man must stop offending God "already too much offended." *And to offset sin, Our Lady asked for the amendment of our lives, for the daily Rosary, for consecration to Her Immaculate Heart, for the First Saturday devotion and for penance and reparation.*

Our Blessed Lady also gave a precise warning to mankind: *"If my requests are granted, Russia will be converted and there will be peace. If not, she will scatter her errors throughout the world, provoking wars and persecutions of the Church; the good will be martyred; the Holy Father will suffer much; and various nations will be destroyed."*

Evidently too many of us have *not* listened to Our Blessed Mother and have not answered her requests, for we have been the unhappy recipients of World War II, the Korean War, the Viet Nam War, conflicts in the Middle East and various other regional uprisings. And Communism has become a world power, sweeping nations before it and threatening a devastating nuclear World War III.

But, we may wonder, what about all the confusing statements and rumors relating to Fatima?

1) Is it true that the revelations of Fatima are private revelations and so we do not "have to" believe in them?

True. Private revelations are not dogmas which Catholics must believe. However, isn't it rather imprudent to lightly brush them aside as inconsequential or unnecessary?

In fact, theologians point out that there is a very definite distinction between personal revelations in which the message is *directed entirely toward the recipient* and other revelations whose message is *declared to be for mankind in general.* The former can be ignored but the latter must be taken seriously when they are officially approved by the Church.

The Fatima revelations certainly belong in the latter classification. Their message is important, it is directed to all mankind, and it is for the good of all. Not only has it been repeatedly approved by such distinguished popes as Pius XII, John XXIII and Paul VI, but each of them has earnestly recommended our belief in, and our adherence to, the message of Fatima. Added to this, is the obvious approval of God as indicated by the authenticated miracles that take place at the Fatima shrine, many of which occur at the time when the sick are blessed by Our Lord in His Eucharistic Presence.

2) Didn't the biblical-apostolic revelations of God end with the death of the last apostle?

Yes. But this does not mean that God may not communicate with man at any time — if He so wishes. And what better emissary could He use than Christ's own beloved mother, and ours?

3) Is there any doctrinal importance to the apparitions and the messages of Fatima?

Yes. A penetrating look at the apparitions and messages reveals the importance, as well as the confirmation, of several Catholic doctrines. For example:

(a) The *Real Presence of Christ in the Holy Eucharist:* when the Angel appeared to the seers in adoration of the Host and Chalice suspended in the air, the drops of Blood falling from the Host into the Chalice confirmed the Church's constant teaching that Christ is present, whole and entire, in both species.

(b) *Original Sin:* this doctrine is confirmed in the references to the Immaculate Heart of Mary, clearly implying the Immaculate Conception. Since Mary is immaculate, then the rest of mankind is, indeed, conceived in sin — as the Church has always taught.

(c) *Sin*: Our Blessed Mother explicitly confirmed the malice of sin, stating that men must stop offending God, already too much offended; that wars are caused by sin; and that devastating chaos is to follow unless mankind turns from sin.

(d) *Hell* Our Lady specifically mentioned hell and she taught the children a prayer to be said between the decades of the Rosary — a prayer which implores God "to save us from the fires of hell". The children were also given a terrifying vision of hell, thus confirming its existence.

(e) *Reparation:* Mary emphasized the Church's age-old doctrine of reparation by repeatedly asking for prayers and sacrifices, not only for themselves and the conversion of Russia but also in behalf of sinners. "Many souls," she sadly said, "go to hell because there are none to pray and to sacrifice for them."

Thus, the apparitions and messages of Fatima bring to the attention of our modern world confirmation of authentic Catholic doctrine.

(4) Is the message of Fatima pertinent to our post-Conciliar world? Shouldn't we be concerned with practicing love of neighbor, especially for the suffering, the oppressed and the down-trodden, rather than being concerned with the requests of Our Lady of Fatima?

Our Blessed Mother's foremost request was — and is — that *"man must stop offending God, already too much offended."* And the Vatican Council's first and true aim was designated as *interior renewal.* Therefore, the two purposes coincide.

In fact, those who listen to Mary's requests and to the directives of the Council — and follow through — will effectively be concerned with true love of neighbor because their adherence naturally promotes the interests of God and the welfare of neighbor. Such adherence necessarily excludes cruelty to one's neighbor — injustice, intolerance, bigotry, lying, cheating, stealing, slandering, envy, quarreling, murder and other evils.

(5) But, we ask, since the Church now stresses the liturgy whereas the Fatima formula calls for the daily Rosary, First Saturday Devotions, and consecration to the Immaculate Heart of Mary, doesn't this present a conflict of devotion?

No. Actually, the liturgy and Marian devotion are compatible, for true devotion to Mary leads to greater love of God and more frequent, more devout participation in the Mass and the Sacraments.

Although the Sacrifice of the Mass is the most perfect, the most desired form of prayer, still, Catholic worship does not exclude other approved devotions, such as the Rosary, etc. Ideally, Mass and Holy Communion should be a part of one's daily life but everyone cannot always get to daily Mass. In fact, this is often an impossibility, especially for the sick, the aged, mothers with little ones to care for, workers whose hours of employment disallow the time for Mass, and others in the army, etc.

But the Rosary can easily be prayed by anyone — Catholic or non-Catholic — at any time and as often as one may wish. The Rosary, devoutly prayed, can be a very efficacious means of growing in sanctity. It increases faith, hope and charity, and the lessons contained in the mediations inspire confidence in God, humility and obedience, patience in adversity, courage in afflictions, sorrow for sin, gratitude for blessings, etc.

Is it any wonder, then, that Our Blessed Mother asked for the daily Rosary not once, but over and over again?

As to the practice of the First Saturday devotion, this is extraordinarily timely today since offenses and blasphemies against the Immaculate Heart of Mary are so flagrantly being committed.

By participating at Holy Mass and Holy Communion on five consecutive First Saturdays in a spirit of reparation; by praying the Rosary and "keeping Our Blessed Mother company" for at least fifteen minutes, while meditating on the mysteries of the Rosary, we offer reparation for our own sins, for those of others, and particularly for those who have the misfortune to offend the Immaculate Heart of Mary.

Thus, the First Saturday Devotion is both a relevant and efficacious devotion — a devotion for which Our Lady of Fatima promised "to assist at the hour of death with all the graces necessary for salvation" those who respond to her plea for this reparation.

Regarding consecration to the Immaculate Heart of Mary, its importance was emphasized during the third session of the Vatican Council when on November 21, 1964 (the feast of the Presentation of Mary) Pope Paul VI, together with the assembled cardinals and bishops of the world, united in consecrating Russia to the Immaculate Heart of Mary.

In personally assuming consecration to the Immaculate Heart of Mary, we, too, choose Mary to be our mother, our perpetual help in life and in death. To her, we relinquish our prayers, sufferings and good works, that she may perfect them and present them to God, making use of them for God's greater glory, the welfare of others and our own good. And in wearing the Brown Scapular,[1] as a sign of our personal Marian consecration, we are reminded to imitate Mary's virtues so that striving to follow her example, and imploring her gracious help, we may be formed into the likeness of Christ.

The Church, after prayerful, lengthy and serious deliberation, approved the revelations of Fatima and declared them worthy of our belief. Our recent pontiffs, Pius XII, John XXIII and Paul VI all openly and repeatedly encouraged mankind to follow the directives revealed by God through His Beloved Emissary, Our Lady of Fatima. And on May 13, 1967, the golden anniversary of Mary's first appearance at Fatima, Pope Paul VI climaxed official approval by a public pilgrimage to the shrine — a unique event televised around the world.

Shall we, therefore, follow the inspiring lead of Christ's vicars on earth and accept the message of Fatima, using it as a means of personal sanctification, and as an effective instrument towards a just and lasting peace?[2] Or, do we prefer to remain among the unconcerned and the unbelievers?

[1]See the chapter, Brown Scapular

[2]For information regarding apostolates and books which promote the message of Fatima, see pp. 32

Among the Fatima cassettes are the following: *To Teach As Mary Did at Fatima*, a series of three one-hour recrodings in which Father Robert J. Fox transports listeners to the scens of the apparitions, instilling zeal and love of the Faith which Mary taught to the three Fatima seers; provides sound catechetical instruction within the context of the Fatima message; especially geared to the 8-13 age-group but interesting and valuable for anyone of any age; available at $10.50 from POPE Productions, P.O. Box 6161, San Rafael, California 94903.

The Youth Needs Fatima Cassette Library which narrates the Fatima apparitions with an easy to understand doctrinal message for the world today, attractively packaged in a lifetime album; available at $14.95 from the Franciscan Friars, 8000 — 39th Avenue, Kenosha, Wisconsin 53141.

Fatima apostolates for children and teens include the *Blue Army Cadets* c/o Ave Maria Institute, Washington, New Jersey 07882 and the *International Youth and Children's Day Honoring Our Lady of Fatima,* 725 West Colorado Blvd., Dallas, Texas 75208.

For high school graduates and young adults, there is a *Blue Army School of Apostolic Formation,* c/o Ave Maria Institute, Washington, New Yersey 07882; and *Youth for the Immaculata,* 8000 — 39th Avenue, Kenosha, Wisconsin 53141. Anyone who is interested in becoming a Marian lay apostle may contact these centers for full particulars.

"GIVING UP"

Quite often these days we hear the remark — sometimes given in a jeering manner — that such little sacrifices as giving up candy, cokes, movies, etc. during Lent or at any time is old-fashioned, unnecessary and even stupid. We are told, instead, to visit the sick, the old and the imprisoned. To do something rather than to give up anything.

What about this advice? Is it actually 100% proof or are there glaring holes in it?

To visit the sick, the aged or the imprisoned is indeed a most commendable practice if it is done *not because we are supposed to* but through love of God and through compassionate love for the afflicted.

To give up candy, cokes or anything else *not because we are supposed to* but because we love God and wish to offer Him small but loving sacrifices in union with His infinite sacrifices — this, too, is a commendable practice.

By encouraging *doing* exclusively and discouraging *giving up* entirely, aren't we treading rather dangerous ground?

To whom shall we look for the correct advice?

Our Divine Master gave us the formula when He said: "If any man will come after Me, let him deny himself, take up his cross daily, and follow Me." (Luke 9:23)

Deny himself: if we now teach our children not to deny themselves, not to bother giving up anything during Lent, Advent or other times, how are they going to develop strength of character to cope with daily situations which require greater self-denial?

Though it is certainly true that God gives everyone the graces necessary to combat temptations and endure trials and sorrows, still we know that there must also be cooperation on our part. Habits of giving-up are an effective means of building self-discipline. Without such training, meeting day-to-day problems can become quite rugged.

How, for example, when children want a toy or something which is not theirs, are they going to resist stealing it? Or when they are older, when they want to go along with their pals to see a sexy movie, how are they going to be able to resist going? Or when they are young adults, how are they going to resist those extra drinks which lead to intoxication? In these and in countless other situations, self-discipline is needed.

Take up his cross: if moderate, loving self-denial is not encouraged, how, when sickness, troubles and sorrows come their way, are they going to be able to take it? Never having learned to give up anything *voluntarily,* even for the short period of Lent, how much harder it will be for them to endure possible weeks, months or years of frustration, sorrow, pain, immobility.

Follow Me: Christ — for love of us — gave up food and drink for forty days prior to beginning His public ministry. He often gave up time needed for refreshing sleep in favor of spending the night in prayer. He continually gave up strength in exhaustive travelling, teaching and preaching. And finally, He gave up His very life — the ultimate act of love: "Greater love than this, no man has, that a man lay down his life for his friends." (John 15:13)

The point involved therefore reduces itself to: if loving self-denial is not made an important part of Christian living from childhood upwards, how are we ever going to develop the strength of character necessary to deny self-will, self-comfort and self-pleasure in favor of the sacrifices — sometimes great and agonizing — required to obey God's Commandments, to be faithful to marriage vows or religious vows, to love our neighbors as ourselves?

Aren't prayer, doing and giving up *all* very necessary ingredients for true love of God, spouse, family and neighbor?

Wanted: a better balance.

HOLY COMMUNION

One of the most poignant scenes in the life of Our Blessed Lord is the time when He spoke to the people about His forthcoming Presence in the Holy Eucharist — when He said: "I am the living bread which comes down from heaven. The bread that I will give is My flesh for the life of the world. If any man eat of this bread, he shall live forever."[1]

The Gospel of St. John (Chapter 6) tells us that when the people heard these words many of them murmured, unbelievingly, and turned away. And Christ, looking sadly after them turned to His apostles, saying: "Will you also go away?"[2]

Christ's deep sorrow on this occasion must have been heart-breaking but still, He let the people go. He did not call them back. He could not call them back, for His words spoke truth. His promise was clear and definite. Those present had heard His words. They either believed Him or they did not believe Him. There was no in-between.

Now, as then, the truth of Christ is the same. We either believe that Our Lord is present in the Holy Eucharist — Body, Blood, Soul and Divinity — or we do not believe. There is no in-between.

If we do believe, why is our faith and our love of the Holy Eucharist — generally speaking — so frail and so lukewarm? Why do we not receive this Living Bread frequently, even daily?

Is it because we may think that we are not worthy of receiving often? Of course, we are not worthy! We never will be worthy. But if we wait until we think that we are worthy, we will wait forever because we are human — we are sinners; and God is Divine — God is Perfection. So we can never be truly worthy. Not ever.

Does receiving Holy Communion just once a month, or once a year, make us any the more worthy to receive than those who communicate daily? Hardly. Those who receive Holy Communion often do so not because they are perfect, or because they think that they are perfect, but because they know that they are weak and imperfect. They know that they need the graces which God so generously gives in Holy Communion.

The Church teaches us that we may receive Holy Communion as often as possible, even daily, as long as we are in the state of grace (free from mortal sin); and if we are fasting from food and drink, according to the Church's regulations.

And, of course, we must approach the Holy Eucharist with a good intention: to please God, to be more closely united to Him, and to seek His Divine assistance. And we should prepare ourselves for Our Lord's coming by thoughts and prayers of faith, contrition, humility, love and adoration.

Our thanksgiving after Holy Communion should also be pleasing to God. Do we offer such a thanksgiving?

Although the closing words of the Holy Sacrifice tell us to "go in peace", this does not mean that there must be a rushing exodus from the church. Why must we hurry out and speak to priests and people when, actually, we should be in the Church, conversing with Christ — loving Him, thanking Him, begging pardon for our sins and those of others, asking for His blessings?

The Church has always recommended adequate thanksgiving after Holy Communion. The new Liturgy Regulations (May 4, 1967) have not changed this. In fact, they corroborate this idea, clearly stating:

". . . Union with Christ is not to be limited to the duration of the celebration of the Eucharist (the Mass) . . . Those who have been nourished by Holy Communion should be encouraged to remain for awhile in prayer . . ."

The graces received from frequent Holy Communion are invaluable: an abundance of the supernatural life; an increase in virtue; strength against temptation; fervor in the service of God; and a relish for the things of God. Holy Communion remits venial sins; preserves us from mortal sin; weakens the passions; and often imparts health and strength to the body. Holy Communion is the Viaticum for the dying, a pledge of everlasting life and a preparation for a glorious resurrection.

But, we may sometimes think, since Holy Communion is the reception of Our Lord, why doesn't God do something to make the unbeliever and the indifferent understand this — something miraculous to make His actual Presence known to everyone.

He has. And He still does.

From earliest Christian times, there have been numerous Eucharistic miracles authentically recorded in Vatican documents. Some of these miracles are also reported in various other publications. And in our own time, there is the miraculous phenomenon relating to Theresa Neumann of Konnersreuth, Bavaria, who died on September 18, 1962. It is a recorded fact, proven by both ecclesiastical and medical examinations, that this renowned stigmatist lived for thirty-five years with only the daily reception of Holy Communion — with no other food or drink.[3]

Besides this wonderous manifestation, there are the officially documented miracles which take place at such famous shrines as Paray-le-Monial, Guadalupe, Lourdes and Fatima. A great many of these miracles occur publicly at the very moment when Our Lord in the monstrance is raised in benediction over the sick.

Before leaving the world, at the Last Supper, Christ left us His infinite love — *Himself in the Holy Eucharist.* Today, and every day, we are privileged to receive Him in Holy Communion. Shall we do so, humbly and reverently, at every possible opportunity? Or shall we, too, be among those who turn away from Him?

Communion Prayer

O my Jesus, give me grace nevermore in any way to offend You, and grant that I, being refreshed by Your Eucharistic Presence here on earth, may be found worthy to come to the enjoyment, with Mary, of Your eternal and ever-blessed Presence in heaven. Amen.

[1]St. John 6:51
[2]St. John 6:68
[3]*The Mystery of Konnersreuth* by Rev. Thomas Matin, C.M.F., Ph.D. (Angelicum Press, Box 3214 Term. Annex, Los Angeles, Cal., $2; 10th edition, p. 75)

IDOLATRY

Adoring golden calves, jade goddesses or jeweled serpents seems far remote to us of the twentieth century. Such idolatry, we think, belongs to the dim past or to uncivilized people who may be living in some far-off, hidden corner of the world.

Of course, of course. But are we sure that in our proud modernism the golden calves, the jade goddesses and the jeweled serpents have not been superseded by other gods? How careful are we to listen to and obey the Voice of God in the First Commandment: *I am the Lord, thy God, thou shalt not have strange gods before me.*

Strange gods — they assume so many forms these days:

Riches — are we so intent upon living in comfort and luxury, in having only the best, that we will do anything to make money? Are we so involved in amassing wealth that lying, cheating, stealing, unfair practices, etc. are an accepted part of our business deals? Do we try so hard to please executives or clients that we think nothing of going off on Sunday fishing trips, thereby missing Mass? Or do we drink or gamble far too much, so as to be a "good Joe", the life of the party? Are we so busy that we push beyond our strength, ruining nerves and health. Is our climb to riches and power so absorbing that we ignore and abandon our duties toward God, Church and family?

Sex — has sex become such a consuming part of our lives that we defy the sixth and ninth commandments with hardly any qualms? Are we going steady with someone who is already married or with someone whom we know will not consent to marriage in the Catholic Church or to married life pleasing to God? Do our marriage vows, made in the presence of God, mean so little to us that we are seriously contemplating a divorce or have already obtained it? Do we presume to know better than God in the matter of another "marriage" after divorce, artifical birth control, sterilization or abortion?

Fame — is getting to the top in movies, TV, the stage, the arts, the sciences or the professions so all-absorbing that we are willing to crush anyone or anything in order to achieve our aims? Are we so intent upon acquiring fame and prestige that we flagrantly ignore God's commands about morality, justice and charity? And having won worldly glory and position, do we become little tin gods, believing that we are more brilliant, more talented, more important and better than others?

Our modern, pagan, materialistic, sensual world lifts the golden calf of riches, the jade goddess of sex and the jeweled serpent of fame and pride upon a towering pedestal. Do we, by our actions, bow down before them or do we stand up and fight against these strange gods?

PRAYER

O Lord, Jesus Christ, deliver us from all our iniquities and from all evils. Grant that we may always keep your commandments, and never permit us to be separated from You.

INTOLERANCE

A young Negro lady stops at our section of the hosiery department and we are about to serve her when a White woman stops by. So we leave the Negro woman standing there and wait on the White customer instead.

A Jewish family runs the corner delicatessen and we are often pleasantly and kindly served by them but, even so, we give our children strict orders not to play with their children.

Several Mexican families, workers at the _______ Ranch, have been coming to our Church for some time now but we make no effort to speak to them or to invite them to the coming parish supper.

When we were in Miami last week at a movie, we deliberately and very rudely pushed our way ahead of a Cuban family.

We were about to send our daughter to St. Mary's (a private high school) when we learned that the nuns had accepted four girls from the Indian Reservation so we sent our daughter to another school.

Well, why not? One has to be careful. Association with only the best, that is so important. So we say.

Is it? And who is the best? Did God make the souls of the Colored less important or any different from the White? Did He exclude Puerto Ricans, Cubans, Mexicans, Indians or Chinese from the human race? Did He deny Jews, Mohammedans, Arabs — or anyone — the inalienable rights we enjoy?

In effect, therefore, any unkindness or discrimination — word or deed — is an affront not only to the persons involved but also to God.

Though today's intolerance problem has many facets yet, on a personal level, it concerns our individual attitudes, words and actions — whether or not we are obeying God's command to love our neighbors as ourselves.

Are we doing to others as we would have them do to us?

Do we have the time and the energy to help apostolates and/or community endeavors which assist minority groups in solving their problems or alleviate the suffering of the poor, the sick, the orphaned or the aged?

Actually, such involvement is not something new. In fact, Our Lord commanded us to love our neighbors as ourselves — to wish them well; to treat them kindly and justly; to be concerned about their needs; to assist them in their troubles and sorrows, whenever possible. The Church, too, has always encouraged us to practice brotherly love through the spiritual and corporal works of mercy. Chief among these are:

Spiritual works: to admonish the sinner; to instruct the ignorant; to counsel the doubtful; to comfort the sorrowful; to bear wrongs patiently; to forgive all injuries; and to pray for the living and the dead;

Corporal works: to feed the hungry; to give drink to the thirsty; to clothe the naked; to ransom the captive; to shelter the homeless; to visit the sick and the imprisoned; and to bury the dead.

The need and the obligation for involvement is, therefore, nothing new. Rather, the current emphasis on such assistance merely pinpoints our failures resulting from selfishness, greed and indifference.

If we care enough to help others, if we are in a position to do so, we are reminded to accompany our action with prayers and efforts toward personal sanctification, for without the blessing of God, nothing worthwhile is ever accomplished.

Recent pontiffs, as well as the Fathers of Vatican II, have repeatedly stressed the importance of combining prayer and the practice of virtue along with apostolic efforts, lest our charitable endeavors descend to humanistic social service. We are therefore expected to place things in their proper perspective, not to subordinate the divine to the human, the eternal to the temporary, the spiritual to the material. And we are further reminded that if we accompany our just and merciful words and deeds with humble, persevering prayers and sacrifices, then the services given are rendered not only to our brothers in need but also to Our Lord Himself, for Christ identified Himself with the poor, the downtrodden and the suffering.

MY DAILY PRAYER[1]

Keep us, O God, from pettiness.
Let us be large in thought, in
word, in deed. Let us be done
with fault-finding and leave off
self-seeking. May we put away
all pretense and meet each other
face to face without self-self-pity
and prejudice. May we never be
hasty in judgment and may
we always be generous.

Let us take time for all things;
make us grow calm, serene, gentle.
Teach us to put into action our
better impulses, straightforward
and unafraid. Make us realize
that it is the little things that
create differences; that in the
big things of life we are as one.

May we strive to know the great,
common, human heart of us all; and,
O Lord God, let us not forget to
be kind.

Recommended Reading:
Discrimination and Christian Conscience (Statement of the Bishops of the United States, published in booklet form by Our Sunday Visitor Press, Huntington, Indiana 46750; 10¢ each.)

Meet Saint Martin. (Patron of social and interracial justice); by Rev. Norbert Georges, O.P.; available from the St. Martin de Porres Guild Press, 141 East 65th Street, New York, New York 10021; 25¢ each; 5 for $1.00.

Among the apostolates specifically promoting racial harmony and justice are:

The Catholic Interracial Council — 55 Liberty St., New York, N.Y. 10005. *St. Martin De Porres Guild* — 141 East 65th St., New York, N.Y. 10021

Among the apostolates promoting harmony in Judaeo-Christian relations are:

The Edith Stein Guild — 48-27 211th St., Bayside Hills, New York 11364

Notre Dame de Sion — 3823 Locust St., Kansas City, Mo. 64109.

[1]Copies of this prayer are available from the Benedictine Convent of Perpetual Adoration, Clyde, Missouri 64432; 1¢ each; $1 per hundred, plus postage.

(Author: Mother Janet E. Stuart, R.S.C.J. Reprinted by permission.)

KNIGHTS OF THE IMMACULATA

An important apostolate specifically encouraging involvement in apostolic endeavors through total dedication to the Immaculate Heart of Mary is the *Knights of the Immaculata.* This apostolate stems from the work of a very saintly, very heroic priest, Father Maxmilian Kolbe, O.F.M., Conv. He died a hero, offering his life for another man's, in a concentration camp at Auschwitz on August 14, 1941, the eve of the feast of Mary's Assumption.

Realizing the needs of the world and the importance of Mary's role in all our lives, Father Kolbe had organized, in 1917, a small group — himself and five seminarians — whose purpose was to convert and sanctify souls through the mediation of Mary Immaculate.

Father Kolbe firmly believed that Mary is indeed the *Mediatrix of All Graces* and that with her help we can accomplish successful action for God's glory and the good of mankind. And Our Lady confirmed his faith and confidence, for not only was he able to overcome monumental obstacles and produce outstanding spiritual and corporal works of mercy, but he also developed the *Militia of Mary Immaculate* — now known as *Knights of the Immaculata* — into a worldwide apostolate. In fact, today there are over two million members from among the clergy, religious and the laity from all walks in life. International headquarters are at Rome. The American center is at Marytown, 8000—39th Avenue, Kenosha, Wisconsin 53141.

Father Kolbe, who was beatified by Pope Paul VI in an impressive ceremony at Rome on October 17, 1971, called his program a militia because its members are to be *Knights of the Immaculata,* offering themselves to her service, giving her their prayers, works and sufferings that she may "make use" of them for the sanctification of souls and for the conversion of sinners, unbelievers, heretics, schismatics and the avowed enemies of God and His Church.

Membership, through enrollment, is personal and does not require meetings or dues. The qualifications for becoming one of Mary's Knights are:

First of all, *total consecration of self to the Blessed Virgin Mary.* Since anyone who wishes to bring about the sanctification of others, must first start with himself, and since the surest and best way to go to God is through Mary, then it follows that total consecration is essential; a complete surrender of self, all that we are, all that we have, all that we hope to be; an entire offering of our daily life, with its prayers, works, joys and sorrows, so that in Mary, with Mary, for Mary and through Mary, we may love and serve God more perfectly.

Secondly, *we must endeavor to become fit instruments in Mary's service* by surrendering ourselves unreservedly to her as her exclusive property. This means the daily living of our consecration by the avoidance of all deliberate sin, by frequent participation at Mass, by the frequent reception of the Sacraments, and by fidelity to the duties of our particular state in life. Thus, through good example, through prayer, through work and through patience under trials, graces are won for souls.

Thirdly, *we must do the will of the Immaculate:* we must let ourselves be totally guided by her; and in this perfect obedience, Mary will reveal her will and make use of us as her instruments. To each one in particular, Our Lady will indicate what he or she is to do, and when the proper time comes, each will understand her desires. Mary's wishes will be known in various ways: through very special circumstances; through obedience to lawful superiors; through spiritual reading; through sermons, missions or retreats; or through the advice of another.

The Immaculate will obtain for each of her *Knights* the graces needed to enlighten and strengthen them to act in God's service at the proper time. Therefore, *it is left to the discretion and zeal of each individual to carry out the aim of this apostolate according to one's state in life and the circumstances surrounding him.*

Fourthly, *it is necessary to be enrolled in the Knights of the Immaculata* since its aim is best accomplished in spiritual union with others, rather than "on one's own".

Finally, *members are to wear the Miraculous Medal*[1] as a reminder of their consecration to Mary and to gain the special graces promised by Our Blessed Mother to its wearers.

The *Knights of the Immaculata* movement is ecumenical in purpose, spirit and action. As its founder repeatedly stated: "*The Knight of the Immaculata* does not confine his heart to himself, nor to his family, relatives, neighbors, friends or countrymen but embraces the whole world, each and every soul, because, without exception, they have all been redeemed by the Blood of Jesus. They are all our brothers. He desires true happiness for everyone, enlightenment in faith, cleansing from sin, inflaming of their hearts with love towards God and a love towards neighbor, without restriction. The happiness of all mankind is in God and through the Immaculata. Behold, this is the dream of the *Knights of the Immaculata.*"

Blessed Kolbe's "dream" has extended to *Youth Mission for the Immaculata (YMI)* inaugurated in 1975 at the Marytown Center in Kenosha. This program of apostolic formation and involvement is for youth 16 to 24. Aware of the great potential among youth to make sacrifices for the extension of the Kingdom of God when properly motivated and guided, the Friars are asking youth to spend some of their time in apostolic endeavors for Christ and His Church. The program exposes them to a deeper understanding of their faith and the spiritual life, as well as giving them opportunities to get actively involved in apostolic activity so that they will become saintly Catholic leaders in whatever state in life they eventually choose. The main thrust of YMI is to further in a systematic way the *Knights of the Immaculata Movement.*

This training program consists of conferences on the history of the Church, the decrees of Vatican II, the liturgy, sacred scripture, theology, the role of Our Blessed Mother in personal life and in the life of the Church, the mysteries of the Rosary, and lay spirituality. Classes include studies in salesmanship, public speaking, positive approach techniques for home visitations, photography, printing, management techniques and other subjects which develop leadership qualities. Practical experience in making home visitations combine theory with practice. Above all, the training period fosters a solid foundation in the spiritual life with ample opportunity for community and private prayer.

Two five-week sessions for young men are held in the summer and one five-week session is given for young women. Further information may be obtained by writing to the Director of YMI, Marytown, 8000—39th Avenue, Kenosha, Wisconsin 53141.

Throughout his priestly life, Blessed Kolbe continually stressed the importance of Mary's role in God's plan of salvation. "Modern times," he said, "are dominated by Satan and will be more so in the future. The conflict with hell cannot be engaged by man, even the most clever. *The Immaculata alone has from God the promise of victory over Satan.* However, assumed into heaven, the Mother of God now requires our cooperation. She seeks souls who will consecrate themselves entirely to her, who will become in her hands forceful instruments for the defeat of Satan and the spread of God's kingdom."

The *Knights of the Immaculata* is an inspiring legacy for the clergy and the laity alike. Wherever people hear or read about this saintly priest's life, they are deeply inspired, for, from the natural standpoint, how this sickly man with only one lung could accomplish so much is beyond understanding. It can only be explained by his tremendous confidence in God and his complete dependence upon Mary. In his own words: *"I can do all things in Him who strengthens me, through the Immaculate Virgin!"*

And so, we are invited to become *Knights of the Immaculata* — to leave the ranks of the apathetic and join the ranks of the apostolic: for God, for His Church and for all mankind.

CONSECRATION TO MARY IMMACULATE

O Immaculate, Queen of heaven and earth, Refuge of sinners and our most merciful Mother: Thou, to Whom God entrusted the entire order of mercy: I, N., unworthy sinner, humbly beseech Thee to accept my whole and entire self as Thy possession and property, and to dispose of me, of all my faculties of soul and body, of my whole life, death and eternity, as it pleases Thee.

Make use of me, if such be Thy will, entirely without reserve to bring about that which was said of Thee: "She will crush thy head," and again, "Thou alone hast destroyed all the heresies in the whole world", so that in Your Immaculate and Merciful hands, I might become a useful instrument towards implanting and developing Thy glory in a most eminent degree in the many strayed and indifferent souls, and thus become instrumental in spreading the Kingdom of the Most Sacred Heart of Jesus, for wherever Thou dost enter, there Thou obtainest the grace of conversion and sanctification — since through Thy hands flow all the graces from the Heart of Jesus.

V. Vouchsafe that I may praise Thee, O Sacred Virgin.
R. Give me strength against Thine enemies.

Recommended Reading:

The Death Camp Proved Him Real: this recent paperback of the original book, *Our Lady's Fool,* authored by Maria Winowski, is written in an interesting, live style which captures the spirit of Blessed Kolbe and his apostolate; 95¢ per copy.

The Militia of Mary Immaculate: a beautiful, inspiring special edition of *Immaculata* magazine; relates the life of Blessed Kolbe and the start and development of this apostolate; 50¢ per copy.

The Beatification of Maximilian Kolbe: a very impressive issue describing Father Kolbe's life, priesthood, apostolate; death and beatification; highlighted by numerous photographs, including colored pictures of the beatification ceremony held at the Vatican on Oct. 17, 1971, in the presence of Pope Paul VI, many cardinals and the 300 bishops attending the Second Synod of Bishops; 50¢ per copy. (These publications are available from the Franciscan Marytown Press, 8000—39th Avenue, Kenosha, Wisconsin 53141).

[1]See index

THE LAY APOSTOLATE

So often these days we hear the expression, the Lay Apostolate. Too often, the words are just words. They do not reach us. They should.

Since we, Catholics, know what a favor it is to be sustained by the graces of the Mass and the Sacraments — in joy and sorrow, in sickness and health, in life and in death — how is it that we are not more active in work for God, His Church and our neighbor? Is it because we think that such efforts are the duty of priests and religious?

True. But such work is not for them, exclusively. Rather, it is the privilege of the laity, also. We are all — clergy and laity — members of the Mystical Body of Christ. As such, we have the right, the duty and the privilege to bring Christ and His Church to those who do not know Him and to the poor, the suffering and the oppressed.

There is so much that we, the laity, can do. There are so many efforts open to us, especially in circumstances where the clergy and the religious cannot possibly be.

Take convert-making, for example. Most of our priests, brothers and nuns have few opportunities for meeting non-Catholics. So what about our in-laws, our neighbors, the mechanic in our garage, the lady in the delicatessen, the classmate in the lab, etc.? Who is going to tell them about the truth, the peace, the beauty, the joy to be found in Christ's Church — the Catholic Church?

How do we do this? Should we continually be pushing the subject of religion? No, of course not. On the other hand, neither must we stop anyone's interest in anything Catholic by answering his questions with a blunt, "Oh, I never discuss politics or religion!"

Such a reply may be quite a disappointment and a failure. Perhaps the questioning non-Catholic may really want to know the Catholic belief or position on this or that point;[1] he might like to read some of our Catholic books and magazines; he might like to be invited to go with us to a Mass, Bible service, novena, retreat or mission; and when he comes with us to a neighborhood wedding or funeral, he might wish that we would explain the ceremony.

These and similar contacts are simply thoughtful kindness extended to others. With prayer and good example, such contacts may become the opening door to Catholicism. Contacts are important. In fact, how many a convert, happy in his Catholicity, has often asked: "Why didn't someone tell me about the Catholic faith before?"

Of course, convert-making is only one phase of the lay apostolate. There are so many other endeavors. If we like, we may join the choir, assist with catechetical classes, help care for the altars and altar linens etc. We could also become members of such apostolates as the *Men of the Sacred Heart,* 6026 Harwood Ave., Orlando, Florida 32811; the *Blue Army of Our Lady of Fatima,* c/o Ave Marie Institute, Washington, New

Jersey 07882; the *Catholics United for the Faith,* 222 North Avenue, New Rochelle, New York 10801; the *Archconfraternity of Christian Mothers,* 220 — 37th Street, Pittsburgh, Pa. 15201; the *Legion of Mary,* c/o Montfort Fathers, 40 South Saxon Avenue, Bay Shore, New York 11706; the *Society of St. Vincent de Paul,* c/o Railway Exchange Bldg., St. Louis, Missouri 63101 or other approved apostolates. Perhaps we could help start a parish adoration program or perhaps we could activate a "dead" parish guild by injecting a specific project aiding the poor, the sick, the handicapped, the aged, the missions, the orphans, the lepers, the prisoners. Perhaps we might even like to serve with one of the lay-missionary apostolates.[2]

Sounds good, we say, but we just don't have the time for apostolic endeavors. Really? Just as we have the time — or we take the time — for bowling, golf, bridge, etc., so, too, we have — or could take — the time to do something for Christ, also.

All of us? Even the aged, shut-ins or the handicapped?

Yes, indeed. There are a number of apostolates specifically designed for this purpose. Among these are the *Apostolate of Suffering* and the *Catholic Union of the Sick in America.*[3]

The sick and the well — irrespective of whether they belong to any apostolate — may also engage in such efforts as sewing scapulars,[4] making rosaries[4] or collecting used stamps or old gold jewelry or trade stamps for the missions and the poor.

We could also assist the endeavors of various apostolates by enclosing the organizations' promotional leaflets in our correspondence, as, for example, the *Markham Prayer-Card Apostolate* (60 Compton Road, Cincinnati, Ohio 45215) which distributes a prayer-card specifically designed to assist the dying of any religious denomination; the *Apostleship of Prayer: League of the Sacred Heart* (515 East Fordham Road, New York, New York 10458) which spreads *Morning Offering* leaflets; the *Calix Society* (7601 Wayzata Blvd., Minneapolis, Minn. 55416); whose leaflets encourage alcoholics to break away from drinking, and also enlist prayers from everyone for God's assistance in helping alcoholics to overcome their problems; and the *St. Martin de Porres Guild* (141 East 65th Street, New York, New York 10021) which promotes devotion to this great Negro saint and interracial brotherly love.

We may also spread interest in various apostolic radio programs by mentioning the programs to others whenever the opportunity may arise. Among such programs are the *Ave Maria Hour* emanating from Graymoor, Garrison, New York 10524; the *Christopher Radio Program* from New York, New York 10017; the *Sacred Heart Program* from St. Louis, Missouri 63108; the *Family Rosary Crusade Program* from Albany, New York 12208; and the *Marian Hour* from Powers Lake, North Dakota, 58773; P.O.P.E. Presents the *Catholic School of the Air* from San Rafael, California; and other Catholic radio and TV programs.

And, of course, anyone — priests, religious and the laity — may become a co-missionary. Co-missionaries are adults and children who spiritually adopt a specific missionary by pledging themselves to offer their prayers, works, duties, joys and sufferings of one or more days per week for this missionary and for the souls entrusted to his care. The pledge does not involve any meetings, correspondence, dues or financial obligations. Membership is obtained by writing to the *Co-Missionary Apostolate,* St. Mary's Seminary, Techny, Illinois 60082. A certificate of membership, a picture of the "adopted" missionary and an explanatory leaflet is sent to each co-missionary.

Christ needs our co-operation. He needs not only the help of His dedicated ones — His priests, brothers and sisters — but He also needs the help of His laity. Each of us has a part to play in the apostolate of the world. Each of us is necessary for the common good. And although no one can do everything, yet, if each does his part, then definite progress for the glory of God and the good of mankind will result.

Perhaps we may be thinking about getting into some phase of the lay-apostolate but feel hesitant and inadequate. Perhaps, too, we may be looking for a model, for someone to help us.

Mary, Christ's Mother and ours, is the perfect model. She was the first of all lay apostles. She brought Our Lord into the world and then she served Him faithfully through prayer, sacrifice, suffering and effort.

In fact, the Church in its Vatican II Document, the *Decree on the Laity,* Chapter I reminds us: "The perfect example of the spiritual and apostolic life is the most Blessed Virgin Mary. All should devoutly venerate her and commend their lives and their apostolate to her motherly care."

Among the apostolates specifically encouraging participation in the lay apostolate through total dedication to the Immaculate Heart of Mary is *Knights of the Immaculate,* reported in another section of this book.

If we ask her, Mary will teach us and help us. She will ask God for the graces indispensable for anyone who wishes to love and serve God and neighbor. She will obtain for us the zeal and the willingness to sacrifice self, time and energy; the humility, the patience and the charity to withstand the obstacles, rebuffs and misunderstandings; the courage and the strength to perserve.

With Mary's help, we can stand firmly on the side of Christ, courageously doing the best that we can, serving God — as she did — in prayer, sacrifice, suffering and apostolic action.

"All that is necessary for the triumph of evil is for good men to do nothing."

Edmund Burke

"God has created me to do Him some definite service; He has committed some work to me which He has not committed to another. I have my mission — I never may know it in this life, but I shall be told in the next . . . I have a part in a great work. I will trust Him, whatever, wherever, I am . . ."

John Henry Cardinal Newman

"I shall pass through this world but once.
Any good, therefore, that I can do or any kindness that I can show to any human being, let me do it now.
Let me not defer or neglect it, for I shall not pass this way again."

Etienne de Grellet

Most Holy Spirit, through the Sorrowful and Immaculate Heart of Mary, make me your instrument in spreading the reign of Jesus on earth.

[1]Among the helpful publications for this purpose are: *100 Common Questions About the Catholic Faith* (Our Sunday Visitor Press, Huntington, Indiana, 46750; $2.00) and *The Faith Explained* (Lumen Christi Press, P.O. Box 13176, Houston, Texas, 77019; $2.95).

[2]See Index

[3]See Index

[4]Materials for sewing scapulars may be obtained from the Scapular Apostolate, 329 East 28th Street, New York City, N.Y. 10016; materials for rosary-making are available from Our Lady of Fatima Rosary Making Club, 4611 Poplar Level Road, Louisville, Kentucky 40213.

MARY, OUR MOTHER

From the cross, our dying Lord gave His beloved Mother to St. John — and to us — to be our spiritual Mother.

With what piercing anguish must He have realized that there would be many who would reject Mary, blaspheme and belittle her.

No Catholic worthy of the name would ever reject, blaspheme or ridicule Our Blessed Mother but, sad to say, there are some misguided ones who belittle Mary's role in Catholicism and disdain approved devotion to her.

Does hearing or reading such remarks and opinions make us question Marian devotion? Are we concerned about rumors that the Second Vatican Council downgraded Mary? Are we wondering if the practice of devotion to the Mother of God is now out-dated?

On the contrary. Such remarks, opinions and rumors are decidedly false. Anyone who reads the Council's documents — particularly Chapter Eight of *Lumen Gentium* (Dogmatic Constitution on the Church) can see for himself that the Council Fathers give great honor to Mary and emphatically encourage us to love her, honor her, and seek her efficacious intercession with God.

Vatican II defines and honors Mary as the Mother of Christ, Mother of the Church, Mother of us all. It recognizes the fact that true devotion to Mary leads us to God, to a greater love and participation in the Mass and the Sacraments, and to a more perfect love of neighbor.

Nowhere do the Council's documents state that we are to ignore Mary. Rather, its *Decree on the Apostolate of the Laity,* Chapter I, No. 4 clearly states: *"The perfect example of the spiritual and apostolic life is the most Blessed Virgin Mary. All should devoutly venerate her and commend their lives and their apostolate to her motherly care."*

Neither does Vatican II forbid approved Marian devotions. Rather, its Document on the *Dogmatic Constitution on the Church,* Article 67, encourages devotion to Mary, stating: *"Let the faithful hold in high esteem the practices and the devotions to the Blessed Virgin approved by the teaching authority of the Church in the course of the centuries."*

And the Council's *Dogmatic Constitution on the Church,* in its Chapter Eight, No. 69, also specifically encourages us to turn to Mary in our personal and universal needs, stating: *"Let the entire body of the faithful pour forth persevering prayer to the Mother of God and the Mother of men. Let them implore that she who aided the beginnings of the Church by her prayers may now, exalted as she is in heaven above all the saints and angels, intercede with her Son in the fellowship of the saints . . ."*

Added to these specific directives are those contained in the American Bishops' Pastoral Letter, *Behold Your Mother: Woman of Faith,* issued in November, 1973 and in the Apostolic Exhoration, *Marialis Cultus,* dated February 2, 1974, issued by Pope Paul VI, encouraging devotion to the

Blessed Virgin Mary and "the restoration, in a dynamic and more informed manner, of the recitation of the Rosary."[1]

It is therefore clearly evident that such approved devotions as the Rosary, the Angelus, the Memorare, and the Litany are still very relevant. And such approved practices as Total Consecration to the Mother of God, the Scapular Devotion, the First Saturday Devotion, pilgrimages to Marian shrines, and the Pilgrim Virgin Statue Movement[3] are to be promoted, rather than downgraded.

Perhaps the reason why Marian movements are sometimes belittled is because their purpose and methods are misunderstood. The Pilgrim Virgin Statue Movement, for example, stems from a pilgrimage authorized by the hierarchy of Portugal in 1946. At that time, in celebration of the 300th anniversary of the patronage of the Immaculate Conception of Our Lady over Portugal, the bishops arranged for the image of Our Lady of Fatima to be carried in solemn procession from the Cova da Iria — where our Blessed Mother appeared in 1917 — to Lisbon.

This first pilgrimage was accompanied by so many miraculous events, both spiritual and temporal, that the news spread quickly throughout the world. Most amazing of these phenomena was the "miracle of the doves" witnessed by thousands of people from all walks in life. It lasted from November 29 to December 25, 1946. Without food or drink or sleep, these doves acted as a "guard of honor" for the first Pilgrim Virgin Statue for nearly thirty days.

The following year at the International Congress of Catholic Girls held at Fatima, one of the girls proposed that a copy of the Fatima statue be blessed and sent on a pilgrimage throughout the world so that Mary would be honored and so that knowledge of her request for prayer, sacrifice, consecration to her Immaculate Heart, and personal amendment would reach people of all nations. This idea was soon approved and in the United States the Pilgrim Virgin statue visited at many cities through the co-operating assistance of such dedicated Marian apostles as Monsignor William McGrath, S.F.M., and Vern Stacks, Monsignor Harold Colgan, the Rev. James Keane, O.S.M., and John Haffert.

The Pilgrim Virgin Statue Movement has an efficient program. The care of each Pilgrim Virgin statue is the responsibility of a lay custodian assisted by a group of men called the Guard of Honor. The custodian contacts pastors, inviting them to host the Pilgrim Virgin statue and asks permission for home visitation within the parish. The statue is usually enshrined in the church for a week during which time special services honoring Our Lady are held. Parishioners who wish to "welcome the Pilgrim Virgin" into their homes then indicate their preferred date.

No special preparations are necessary other than provision for a table covered with a white cloth. The Guard of Honor brings candles and flowers. They also bring various pamphlets such as *Our Lady of Fatima's*

Peace Plan from Heaven (which narrates the Fatima apparitions) and *Fatima or Moscow?* (which relates the message of Fatima to self). In this way the family's knowledge and appreciation of Mary's visitations at Fatima are increased.

Families are encouraged to invite their relations, friends and neighbors to come to their home on the welcoming evening and also to stop-by throughout the week for evening prayers consisting of the Rosary, the Litany of Loretto, and Consecration to the Immaculate Heart of Mary. Some families arrange to have the prayers in the afternoon as well as in the evening, for the convenience of elderly people. Teaching sisters often bring their students to the home during the day, also.

The purpose of the Pilgrim Virgin Statue Movement[3] is to honor our Blessed Mother, to offer reparation, to pray for world peace, and to pray for the needs and intentions of the family and the parish. And our Blessed Mother, through these prayers and sacrifices, obtains from her Beloved Son graces and blessings for the people taking part in the program, for the men who conduct it, and for the parish: conversions, the return of lapsed Catholics to the Sacraments, the sanctification of family life, and great personal favors.

In recent years a new dimension has been added to the movement: the combination of the Enthronement of the Sacred Heart[4] in the home with the Pilgrim Virgin visit. On the occasion of the arrival of the Pilgrim Virgin Statue to a home, the family is told about the option of having the Sacred Heart of Jesus enthroned the following Saturday night. An explanatory booklet is then left at the home. Countless families have responded and continue to respond.

Thus, for a week our Lady "prepares" for the coming of her Son as a permanent "Guest" of the family. For seven days the Rosary, the Litany and the consecration to the Immaculate Heart of Mary are offered. And then, at the end of the week, when the men return for the closing ritual, an image of the Sacred Heart is enthroned and the family is consecrated to the Sacred Heart of Jesus.[4]

In this way Christ is invited to become King of the home. And in this way, Jesus — through Mary — conquers homes for His kingdom.

Devotion to the Mother of God is a definite and necessary part of our "modern" Catholic life. In fact, Mary's role in the life of the Church is both ancient and modern. Our Blessed Savior loved and honored His beloved Mother. So did the apostles. So did saints and popes. And so have millions of people — priests, religious and laymen — throughout the centuries. Wisely, they have accepted Mary as their spiritual Mother, loved her, praised her, and implored her assistance "now and at the hour of death."

In the memorable words of St. Bernard, for example, we find the moving entreaty: "In dangers, in sufferings, in doubt, think of Mary and invoke her aid. Let Mary be always in your heart and often upon your lips. To obtain her help in death, follow her example in life. In following her, you will not go astray; by praying to her, you will not despair; if you cling to her, you will not go wrong. With her support, you will not fall; under her protection you have no fear; under her guidance you do not grow weary; and by her gracious help, you will reach heaven."

Recommended Reading:

The Glories of Mary: this Marian classic, written by St. Alphonsus Liguori, is still regarded as a "must" for all people of all times; available in two volumes, $3.95 each, from the Ave Maria Institute, Washington, New Jersey 07882.

The Heart of Mary by Heinrich Keller, S.J., is a popular paperback which summarizes Catholic love of Mary and depicts her Immaculate Heart as a symbol of her personal love for us, just as the Sacred Heart of Jesus is the symbol of Christ's love for us; especially timely since at the close of the third session of Vatican II, Pope Paul, in the presence of the Bishops of the Church, solemnly renewed consecration of the human race to the Immaculate Heart of Mary; $1 per copy; available from the Reparation Society, 100 East 20th Street, Baltimore, Maryland, 21218.

The Sorrowful and Immaculate Heart of Mary, an interesting paperback concerning this devotion; 70¢ per copy; available from the Franciscans at 8000—39th Avenue, Kenosha, Wisconsin 53141.

The Marian Catechism, authored by the Rev. Robert J. Fox; covers briefly and accurately Marian doctrines and devotions; answers related questions; suitable for all ages; available from Our Sunday Visitor Press, Huntington, Indiana 46750; $1.95 per copy.

[1] Both documents are available from Our Sunday Visitor at nominal prices.

[2] See the Index for reports on each of these practices.

[3] Detailed information about the movement's procedures for conducting local programs may be obtained by contacting the Immaculate Heart of Mary Center, 5851 West Madison Street, Chicago, Illinois, 60644.

[4] See chapter on the Enthronement of the Sacred Heart.

THE MASS

On Calvary, over nineteen hundred years ago, Our Lord gave up His life for our salvation. Perhaps we have sometimes regretted that we could not have been present, standing at the foot of the Cross, with our Blessed Mother and St. John. Although we did not have this great favor, still we are privileged to be present at Mass — at Calvary renewed.

The Holy Sacrifice is Christ offered to God for His glory, for our sanctification. The Mass is the time when angels, saints and sinners unite to offer God a perfect sacrifice of praise, adoration, reparation, petition and thanksgiving. It is a special time in which God looks upon us in loving benediction. The Mass therefore is — or should be — the center of our life.

Sometimes, sad to say, we fail to realize this. Too often we are "Sunday Catholics", only. Too often we go to Mass because we "have to", not because we want to.

An exaggeration? Not really. How long is it since we attended Mass on a week day or a second Mass on Sunday? Why? Is it because we are spiritually lazy and because things are too easy for us?

Quite possibly. Maybe we would be less apathetic, more appreciative, if, now and then, we would give a thought to Catholics who live in places where freedom of worship is prohibited. How difficult it is for them to be deprived of the Mass. In fact, from various escapees, we know of the great sacrifices which many have made — often at the risk of their lives — to attend Mass, secretly offered. And they report that, like the martyrs in early times of persecution, many of their relatives and friends lost their lives in the attempt.

This is a far cry from us who are free to attend Mass as often as we wish. We have so many opportunities not only in the morning but often at noon and at evening, too.

On the other hand, maybe we are not apathetic. Perhaps our failure to appreciate the Mass, to participate in the Holy Sacrifice, is rather because we do not understand it or its importance. A little reading, a little study, could do so much to deepen our appreciation and love of the Mass.

Perhaps we do not attend daily Mass simply because, for one reason or another, we never got started. Some day, we tell ourselves, we will start going to daily Mass but somehow that "some day" never comes.

This is a distinct loss to ourselves, to others and to the Souls in Purgatory. Yesterday is gone; tomorrow may never come; the only way to start going to daily Mass is to go *today*. The first few times may take real effort and determination but the sacrifice involved cannot be compared to the infinite value of the Mass.

Of course, there are many times when we may wish that we could get to daily Mass but poor health, the inconvenient time of work, the care of little ones, the sick or the aged, really prevent our attendance. Still, there are times when, with a little re-arranging of schedules, a little sacrifice of sleep or time, we actually could get to daily Mass.

But if we honestly can't participate every day, could we, at least, attend one weekly Mass? Could our entire family attend at least one weekly Mass together? Could the members of our family take turns at daily Mass, so that our family is always represented?

But, we may say, we would love to have someone from the family in attendance at daily Mass but we parents can't always get there and our pre-teens and our teens just aren't interested.

Why not? What can we do to help them become interested? Multiply the folk and the rock Masses? Add more sentimental, emotional, fun-music and songs?

Is that *really,* the answer?

Many pastors, Parents and teachers emphatically state that this does *not* bring about true and lasting appreciation of the Mass. And they pose the penetrating question: what happens when teens become young adults and the so-called teen Masses no longer appeal to them? What then?

Not only do objections to folk-rock Masses come from the "over 30" crowd but also from the teens, themselves. In fact, all teens are decidedly *not* attracted to, nor in favor of Masses "just for them". Many say: "I don't particularly care for such Masses; I go to them because others do and it seems that I'm expected to like them. Actually, I don't like them and neither do my close friends. Why should the Mass be made 'entertaining' for us? We can get enough entertainment outside of church. Aren't we supposed to go to Mass to offer God our prayers and our love and to receive His love?"

We are, indeed, supposed to go to Mass to offer God our love, adoration, thanksgiving, reparation, and our petitions — and — to receive Him, His love, and His blessings for ourselves and for others.

Therefore, isn't the answer to drawing pre-teens and teens towards greater appreciation of the Mass to be found in giving them the example of our own appreciation and love of the Mass; in teaching them what the Mass really and essentially is, and what it can mean — *must mean* — to each of us, not only for today but for every day of their, and our, lives?

There are many fine books designed to help us understand and love the Mass. Among these is the impressive classic, *The Hidden Treasure* written by St. Leonard of Port Maurice; now available as a paperback, $1.00 per copy, from the Apostolate of Christian Action, P.O. Box 24, Fresno, California 93707; and among the recent popular paperbacks is *The World's Greatest Secret* written by John Haffert; 95¢, available from Ave Maria Institute, Washington, New Jersey 07882. Reading such a book within the family circle can be an effective means of learning to appreciate the Holy Sacrifice of the Mass. And if we like recordings, among the popular Mass tapes is the *Talking Catechism* entitled *The Glorious and Holy Sacrifice of the Mass* by the Rev. Robert J. Fox. This inspiring tape reminds us that the Mass is the highest form of worship; places us on Calvary in time; and relates its fruits, reaching beyond time into eternity. The cassette ($5.50) and the reel ($6.50) are available from Pope Publications, Box 6161 San Rafael, California 94903.

And if our parish were to have Mass celebrated in Latin — but according to the New Ordo — perhaps at one Sunday Mass each week, this would do much towards giving youth an opportunity to cultivate an appreciation of the beauty and glory of the traditional liturgy which otherwise might be lost to them. Helpful for this purpose is a new booklet, *Approved Presentation of the New Order of Mass in Latin and English,* bearing the imprimatur of the Most Rev. John F. Whealon, archbishop of Hartford. The use of this arrangement was inaugurated at the Cathedral of St. Joseph on October 20, 1972 at the Mass celebrated by the archbishop during the Northeast Regional Forum of *Catholics United for the Faith.* It met with appreciative, enthusiastic response from the nearly four hundred Catholics in attendance.

The text, chiefly compiled by Francis J. Haggerty, is aimed at combining the beauty and solemnity of the Latin with the familiarity of the vernacular. It preserves the traditional Roman Canon while the parallel English is according to the translation of the International Committee on English in the Liturgy. The booklet is available from the apostolate's national headquarters at 222 North Avenue, New Rochelle, New York 10801; single copies are priced at $1.00 with generous discounts on quantity orders.

But, we may question, isn't the use of the Latin in these post-Vatican II times, now forbidden?

Definitely not!

Although the Church has granted permission for the celebration of Holy Mass in the vernacular, still, Pope John XXIII, Pope Paul VI, the Fathers of Vatican II (Constitution on the Sacred Liturgy, Nos. 36, 54) and Post Conciliar Commissions have emphatically stated that the liturgical Latin should also be retained and made available to the faithful. The use of Latin in the New Ordo is also authorized by the Liturgical Instructions Document issued in June, 1971.

The Church also acknowledges the value of Gregorian Chant and recommends its continued use. (Constitution on the Sacred Liturgy, Nos. 112, 118). It is noteworthy that since a great many persons asked for the use of Latin and Gregorian Chant, Pope Paul VI graciously responded to this request. In April, 1974 he sent a booklet, *Jubilate Deo (Rejoice in the Lord)* as his personal gift to every Roman Rite Catholic Bishop and to major Religious Superiors throughout the world. It contains a minimal repertoire of Gregorian Chant which the Pontiff wishes to be used in the Roman Rite Eucharistic Liturgy.

The booklet was accompanied by a document of the Vatican Congregation for Divine Worship, signed by its prefect James Cardinal

Knox. It states that Pope Paul "desires the faithful in every country to know at least some Gregorian Chant in Latin, as for example, the *Gloria,* the *Credo,* the *Sanctus,* the *Pater Noster,* and the *Agnus Dei,* so that they can be helped to associate themselves in spirit with all their brothers in the faith and with the living traditions of past centuries."

The Vatican document noted that unity in faith and charity among the faithful is highlighted in a special manner by the use of Latin and Gregorian chants "which for so many centuries accompanied sacred celebrations in the Roman Rite, nourished faith and piety, reached such artistic perfection as to be justly considered one of the Church's patrimonies of inestimable value, and were recognized by Vatican II as the singing 'proper to the Roman Liturgy'".

In response to the Holy Father's wishes the Benedictines at St. John's Abbey have issued a Gregorian Chant Booklet presenting a collection of the desired chants which may be sung in unison by the faithful. The booklet may be obtained from the Liturgical Press, Collegeville, Minnesota 56321; $1.50 per copy.

Perhaps we could also interest our parish organizations in promoting attendance at daily Mass by establishing a unit of the *Daily Mass League.* Cooperating assistance may be obtained from the league, 10 Pleasant Street, Rochester, New York 14604, which supplies leaflets, application blanks and posters.

Christ's gift of the Mass to us, our gift of the Mass to God, is a perfect sacrifice from which great graces flow. In failing to attend daily Mass, we are losing a great deal.

Why do we miss daily Mass?

> "IF MEN ONLY KNEW how the Eternal Father regards this Sacrifice, they would risk their lives to be present at a single Mass."
>
> Padre Pio,
> (The saintly stigmatist whose cause for beatification is now in process)

Recommended Reading:

Mystery of Faith (Mysterium Fidei) — Pope Paul VI's encyclical on the Holy Eucharist; (Daughters of St. Paul Press, 50 St. Paul Ave., Boston, Mass. 02130; 25¢ per copy).

MENTAL PRAYER

The saints, as well as our spiritual advisors, tell us that the habit of Mental Prayer is a very wise habit because through it we learn to live in the presence of God, even in difficulties and sorrows. But sometimes we shy away from Mental Prayer, mistakenly thinking that it is something too difficult.

Mental Prayer is simply the process of thinking about the things of God; in the presence of God; and then, applying the thoughts to self.

In making a Mental Prayer we place ourselves in the presence of God. Of course, we are always in God's Presence since He is everywhere, but God also dwells within the souls of those who are in the state of sanctifying grace. Remembering this, we can then more easily become aware of God's Presence within us.

Next, we are to think about God or something pertaining to the spiritual life. To think about the things of God is easy. Every day we do a lot of thinking about ourselves and about other persons, places or things. We think about our families and friends; our school or work; our interests and plans. In the same way we can think about God and the things of God — about the commandments, eternity, the life of Our Lord, Our Blessed Mother, heaven, hell, the souls in Purgatory, the saints, etc.

In the practice of Mental Prayer we are to apply these thoughts to ourselves. In thinking about the things of God, in the presence of God, we naturally begin to make such an application. We instinctively look into ourselves and see whether or not we are living in a manner pleasing to God. And we are then moved to make good resolutions.

Finally, we end our Mental Prayer with a colloquy — a little chat — with God. We tell Him in a simple manner how we feel about things: of our sorrow for sin; our desire to please Him; our thanks for His graces; our need for His continued guidance and blessing.

Making a Mental Prayer is really not difficult. A subject easily comes to mind by recalling a Rosary mystery or by reading a short passage from the Bible, or the *Following of Christ, or Jesus, King of Love,* or a few paragraphs from a book about Our Blessed Mother, the Saints or Angels. If, for example, we were to open the Bible at random and thereby glance at a few verses in the seventeenth chapter of St. Luke, we would note that only one of the ten lepers whom Our Lord cured returned to thank Him. A very short Mental Prayer stemming from this ingratitude might be as follows:

Subject Chosen: gratitude

Act of Recollection: Lord God, help me to spend this time of prayer with You.

Meditation: The ten lepers see Jesus coming along the road to Jerusalem . . . they hurry towards Him, hopeful and excited . . . they cry out: "Jesus, Master, have mercy on us!" . . . Jesus, seeing their misery, looks upon them with loving compassion and tells them to go and "show themselves to their priests" . . . the men rush away, filled with joy, anxious to return to their families and friends . . . one comes back to thank Our Lord for his miraculous cure . . . only one . . . Jesus asks: "Where are the other nine?"

Colloquy: Lord, I am sorry that all the cured lepers did not come back to thank you . . . And I'm sorry about the countless times when I, and so many others, fail to thank you . . . for all the wonderful graces, gifts, and even miracles which You so generously give us . . . We take so much for granted: the gift of life, the grace of Faith, the tremendous gift of Confession in which we receive Your loving forgiveness, the marvel of Your gracious presence in the Holy Eucharist . . . our family, friends and all the glories of nature, from the beauty of a rose to the majesty of the mountains . . . for these and all Your blessings and gifts, help me and others remember to thank You daily and often . . . Thank You, dear Lord, for everything!

The events of daily life also furnish many opportunities for meditation. For example, perhaps this morning we attended the funeral of a friend and so the thought of our own death naturally presents itself. From such a thought, we could make a short Mental Prayer, such as:

Subject Chosen: My Death

Act of Recollection: Lord God, help me to spend this time of prayer with You.

Meditation: Some day I am going to die . . . that is certain . . . nothing could be more certain . . . perhaps I may not suffer terrible tragedies . . . accidents . . . poverty . . . disgrace . . . but I cannot avoid death . . . some day I shall be placed in a coffin . . . brought to the church . . . laid in the grave . . . covered over with dirt . . . then left alone . . . when will that be? . . . I don't know . . . maybe today, maybe tomorrow, maybe years from now . . . but each moment brings me nearer to death . . . nearer than when I got up this morning . . . nearer than when I started this meditation . . . should this frighten me? . . . no . . . only one thing should make me fear death . . . mortal sin because then I could not come to You.

Colloquy: Lord God, I know that some day I must die . . . help me to remember that death means coming home to You . . . please keep me far from all mortal sin, because that would keep me away from You forever.

Of course, the foregoing Mental Prayers are very short meditations, simple examples which may be expanded as one chooses. There are a number of books designed to help us with Mental Prayer. Among these is the popular, excellent little book, *My Meditation on the Gospel,* by the Rev. James Sullivan; available from the Confraternity of the Precious Blood, 5300 Ft. Hamilton Parkway, Brooklyn, New York, 11219.

The Church encourages us to practice Mental Prayer daily — at least a few moments, preferrably fifteen minutes — because it helps us to conform our lives to God's Will. Mental Prayer perfects our spiritual life because if we meditate well, then we will be anxious to please God and we will try to improve ourselves.

Recommended Reading:

Progress in Mental Prayer by Rev. Edward Leen (Sheed & Ward) 64 University Place, New York, N.Y. 10003.

A Guide to Mental Prayer With Mary in Mind edited by Rev. Howard Rafferty, O. Carm. (Carmelite Press) Aylesford, Downers Grove, Illinois 60615.

MODESTY

A young mother, in a large eastern city, goes about her washing, ironing, cooking, cleaning in a continual daze. Her beloved little girl is dead. Suddenly, unnecessarily. The mother relates that her daughter was playing on the sidewalk when a car jumped the curb and crashed into a tree, knocking the child to her death; and that the tragedy occurred because the driver had turned to take a second look at a young lady immodestly dressed in fashionable attire. The look caused him to hit another car, careen over the sidewalk, and strike the child.

But, we may ask, "Isn't this an extraordinary event?"

Possibly. Let's hope so.

The point, however, is that the need for modesty and for awareness of responsibility is evident, for immodesty is so prevalent that it has even invaded the sacredness of the house of God. In fact, mini-skirts, shorts, etc. are often worn at Mass and at the reception of the Lord of Lords, the Holy of Holies.

But, comes the protest, what's the difference? Everyone wears such styles, and besides, God doesn't care about fashions, as long as we get to Mass.

Doesn't He?

Isn't that actually our own opinion, rather than His? Doesn't He expect us to follow His commands regarding purity and the virtue of modesty which guards purity? And didn't He voice very strong condemnation of scandal-givers?

Added to the irreverence and the immorality of immodesty, are the physical dangers involved. It is common knowledge that in these times girls and women feel that they cannot safely walk alone on city streets at night, even in the early evening. Statistics on sexual crimes continue to rise higher and higher. Ways and means of preventing such crimes are being investigated but one simple means which could be of tremendous help — *the promotion of modesty* — is being widely ignored.

What, we ask, can we do about promoting modesty?

There are so many things which could be done. Naturally, any corrective measures must start with self and within the family circle before such efforts can extend into the community and ultimately into "the world". First of all, you and I — men and women — must dress modestly at all times. Next, mothers and fathers must set a good example; must instill in their children an appreciation of the importance and the beauty of the virtue of modesty; and then, see to it that their children practice modesty and purity.

Of course, sometimes we may have to shop around quite a bit and we may have to settle for a different color or fabric from the kind which we wanted to buy. We may have to lengthen hems and/or make other alterations — a bother, of course — but it can be done, it should be done.

We could also sew, or have others sew, our clothes. These days there is such a marvelous array of materials, colors, designs and patterns that very lovely clothes can be made — and at worthwhile savings! We could also start a sewing circle, even with just a few friends.

Efforts toward modesty should next extend to the community: pastors, teachers and parents could cooperate in efforts to promote modesty, particularly in establishing modest dress codes.

Many teens and women are not happy about wearing current styles but they feel that they must "go along with the crowd". Over and over, teens say that they need and want norms to follow. Many women say: "how I wish that these styles would change!" And parents repeatedly say: "I wish that we could have some help in this area. And I wish that our priests would occasionally preach about modesty and purity. Silence on these subjects just adds to the misconception that 'it doesn't matter what we wear or do.' We need the help of our priests and religious to back-up our efforts toward modesty and purity."

Next, family and community efforts toward the promotion of modesty could reach "the world" if we care enough to be concerned about this problem. Instead of complaining to one another about "how terrible the styles are", *why don't we complain where it will bring results?* If we, and the members of our parish and school groups, would tell the clerks in our shops that we don't like short or tight-fitting clothes, strapless formals, abbreviated swim suits, etc., *at the same time refusing to buy them,* then the clerks would relay our protests to the managers. In time our complaints would reach designers and manufacturers, and a change to modest fashions could result because our refusal to buy and our positive complaints would touch the trade where it hurts — in the cash register.

Another effective means of combatting immodesty is the distribution of pertinent leaflets in parishes, schools, and in one's correspondence. Among the most popular of these items is the leaflet, *Fashions, Books and Movies,* available from the Sacred Heart Center, 6026 West Harwood Avenue, Orlando, Florida 32811; 20 copies for $1.00; and the pamphlet, *Modesty,* published by the Apostolate of Christian Action, P.O. Box 24, Fresno, California 93707; 25¢ each.

It is interesting to note that the late holy stigmatist, Padre Pio, whose cause for beatification is now underway, often deplored the prevalence of immodesty and repeatedly urged a return to modesty. In the book, *Roads to Padre Pio,* (Marytown Press, 8000 — 39th Avenue, Kenosha, Wisconsin 53141; $3.00), its authoress, Clarice Bruno, also states that "Padre Pio promised that a very special blessing will follow those who work towards bettering this condition."

And Sister Mary of the Immaculate Heart (Lucy) to whom Our Blessed Mother appeared at Fatima, recently stated: "When I think of the United States I think about this: one of the things which Our Lady especially asked for was modesty in dress. There does not seem to be much modesty in the life of the women of your country. But modesty would be a good sacrifice to offer Our Lady, and it would please her if the Catholics in your country would make a league for modesty in dress . . ."

Effort and cooperation, backed by prayer, patience and perseverance, could turn the trend away from immodest styles to modest fashions. After all, the present immodest designs did not occur all at once. Rather, they began slowly — first, with medium short skirts. Our silence and apathy emboldened paganistic ones to go forward with more and more immodest designs. Now we are flooded with them. It will naturally be difficult to stem the tide but with God's blessing, it can be done. It may be an uphill struggle but then the start towards modesty must be made. As the old saying goes; "the longest journey of a million miles begins with a single step."

Modesty in dress is not the only modesty to be promoted. There is also modesty — custody — of the tongue, the eyes and the minds.

Do we use our tongues to tell dirty jokes, thus encouraging the practice and enlarging the flow of impure thoughts? Our tongues are precious organs, the recipients of Our Lord in Holy Communion. Surely, we Catholics — especially — should not use our tongues for dirty jokes, vile language, or other evil speech.

As to custody of the eyes and mind, what do we do with pornographic cards or pictures which come in the mail or which our children bring home? Do we keep them and laughingly pass them around or do we report them to school and postal authorities?

Pornography should be reported. That is the effective way of fighting this demoralizing two billion dollar a year racket. The FBI and many government and church leaders warn us that this devastating evil is so successfully promoted because it is an undercover business and the average contact is too timid to report it. They urge us to be alert and to report pornography and to combat it in our community.[1]

Among the informative pamphlets on this subject are *Printed Poison and Fight Newsstand Filth,* 10 cents each, available from the *Citizens for Decent Literature,* 5670 Wilshire Blvd., Los Angeles, California 90036.

And what about trashy bestsellers? Are such books in our homes? Are they in our schools — even in some Catholic schools — as "required reading, under supervision"?

Required by whom? Certainly not by God.

But, some teachers and parents say, these books are necessary. Our young people should have knowledge of what is going on in the world. They must understand that there is a great deal of evil in the world, evil which they must encounter.

True. But in these days of such frankness in reporting and such public scandals, which of our teenagers and young adults does not know about existing evils? Besides, youths can be cautioned without unnecessary, unwise descriptions.

Why, then, is it necessary to encourage students, or anyone, to read about evil suggestively presented in detail?

But, we argue, isn't it better for our youngsters to read such books in school, under supervision, rather than on their own.

Better? For whom and for what? Truthfully, isn't it better that these books not be read at all — in school or out of school?

But, we object, if we disapprove and forbid suggestive, immoral reading, aren't we being extremists? After all, the Old Testament openly reports transgressions against the sixth and ninth commandments, and yet we encourage the reading of the Bible, don't we? What's the difference?

Yes, the Bible does report sin. Unfortunately, sin existed then, as it does now. But there is a vast difference between the Bible's reporting and the writing found in suggestive reading.

In the Bible the commission of sins is mentioned briefly, calmly, with no suggestive details. But in our modern objectionable books, vile and obscene and blasphemous language is used repeatedly, and sin is passionately and vividly described in minute detail and circumstances. In fact, sin is often promoted as no sin at all. Rather, it is written off as the normal and expected thing. How vastly different from the Bible!

Actually, we may rationalize the matter in any way that we wish but the truth is: God gave us the wonderful gifts of eyes and minds to use intelligently for His glory and for our own good and that of our neighbor — not to use sinfully.

What about sexy movies, plays and TV programs? Do we shrug off this immorality as just an "accepted" part of modern life? Do we excuse our viewing on the grounds that the photography is magnificent or the acting is superb or that people are flocking to see them?

Do we ever "bother" to protest offensive advertising, TV programs, movies or plays?[2] So often we think that our protests are insignificant. On the contrary. They are of great importance because they constitute public opinion — the yardstick of decisions made by many advertisers, writers, actors, directors and producers. For example, Dana Andrews, former president of the Screen Actors Guild, has stated that although the industry's code bars nudity, still an aroused public can do much to counteract the increasing pressure on movie actresses to pose in the nude. In a newspaper report, he stated; "If the American public puts up with it, if society tolerates nudity, then the situation will get worse and worse."

Regarding offensive TV movies and programs, it is not enough just to turn the dial. Rather, it is objections made to local channels, to the networks, to sponsors and to newspapers which run display ads on X-rated movies (and certain places of amusement) which form the public opinion to which executives listen.

Evaluating assistance can be obtained by the use of movie TV ratings available from the Division for Film and Broadcasting, United States Catholic Conference, 1011 1st Ave., New York, N.Y. 10022. These listings could be posted on parish bulletin boards and included in Sunday Bulletins.

It is encouraging to note that members of *Morality in Media*[2] and other groups are circulating a petition which reads:

> "We, the undersigned, are objecting to the nudity, obscenities and extreme violence that is being brought into our homes by way of television. Let us keep TV clean for our children and ourselves to enjoy. We hereby request the Federal Communication Commission to deny renewal of a license to any television station not honoring the above request."

Anyone or any group may circulate similar petitions. Completed petitions may be sent to *Morality in Media,* 487 Park Ave., New York, New York 10022.

An inspiring example of ecumenical cooperation in this matter is a group known as *Women of Faith* organized recently by the Rev. Francis J. Caffrey, M.M., assisted by Mrs. Edith Perry. Leaders in the group are Mrs. Joanne Walsh, a Catholic, and Mrs. Gloria Dameron, a non-Catholic. Its eighty members of various denominations are circulating the above petition and writing protesting letters to TV stations, advertisers and network officials. They are also writing to their congressmen asking support for the Bill which Senator Strom Thurmond introduced to amend the 1934 Communications Act which governs television programming. The group also distributes free copies of *Open Letter to Man* and *Open Letter to Woman.*

Anyone interested in starting a similar project may contact Father Caffrey, M.M., at P.O. Box 4278, Mountain View, California 94040.

Although in our modern, paganistic world, we are bombarded with the promotion of immodesty and impurity, although far too many "good" people are apathetic about such matters, yet it is encouraging to know that there are still priests who are courageous enough to preach modesty and purity; still nuns who do not tolerate students wearing immodest fashions; still parents who give good example and who teach their children the value of modesty and purity; and still teenagers who want norms and discipline and a change in current fashions, literature and entertainment. In fact, as one youth recently put it — bluntly and cogently: "Just because the trade pushes immodest styles on us; just because books, plays and movies are more and more disgusting; just because advertising is often in such poor taste, do we have to take all this stuff? Do we have to be such fools?"

Well . . . do we?

[1]See section on Pornography.

[2]Morality in Media is continuing its campaign to Federal Communications Commission Chairman Richard E. Wiley, urging public hearings on gratuitous sex-violence TV programming, so that the people can be heard. For petition sheets, write Morality in Media, 487 Park Avenue, New York, N.Y. 10022.

THE MORNING OFFERING

Long ago Our Blessed Lord told His apostles — and us — to "pray always."[1] How can we do this? Our spiritual advisors tell us that we may do this through a devout *Morning Offering,* for if we are free from mortal sin, then our every work, joy, suffering and sorrow of the day become a prayer.

The *Morning Offering* is a short prayer, taking just a moment or two of our time. But sometimes we forget to say it. Sometimes we pray it hurriedly and unthinkingly so it does not mean much. But it could mean a great deal. It could make a great difference in our lives, for through a devout, daily *Morning Offering* we give God ourselves and all of our days on earth.

There are several *Morning Offerings*. The one to the Sacred Heart of Jesus is perhaps the best known:

> O Jesus, through the Immaculate Heart of Mary, I offer You my prayers, works, joys and sufferings of this day for all the intentions of Your Sacred Heart, in union with the Holy Sacrifice of the Mass throughout the world, in reparation for my sins, for the intentions of all our associates, and in particular for the intentions of our Holy Father for this month.

This is a very powerful prayer since it unites our daily prayers, works, joys and sufferings with the tremendous value of the Mass — not only with the Holy Sacrifice offered in our parish church, or even in the churches of our own diocese, but with all the Masses celebrated each day throughout the world. A treasure beyond evaluation.

The *Morning Offering* also carries the added inestimable value of the presentation of our humble offerings to God through the Immaculate Heart of Mary, Christ's beloved Mother, the most perfect of all God's creatures.

And Mary, conveying our gifts, particularly offered for the intentions of the Sacred Heart and those of the Holy Father, His divinely appointed vicar on earth, obtains graces and blessings for us and for all mankind — favors beyond estimation; graces powerful enough to bring about the conversion of Russia and world peace.

In fact, we know that throughout her apparitions at Fatima, Our Blessed Mother asked that our daily prayers and sacrifices — especially those necessary for obedience to God's commandments and for the fulfillment of the duties of our particular state in life — be offered to her, in reparation to the Sacred Heart of Jesus, so that she might use their value for the salvation of the world.

Can we, therefore, afford to forget the *Morning Offering?* Wouldn't it be wise not only to offer this prayer, individually, but also as a daily *family* prayer? Many families do so. For this purpose, some are using an attractive, three-color prayer-card inscribed with the *Morning Offering* and with a prayer to Christ, the King.

This card was designed by the Catholic Youth Council of the diocese of Ogdensburg, New York and is available[2] from the Precious Blood Monastery at 135 Keyes Avenue, Watertown, New York, 13601. The card is made of durable, washable plastic and its adhesive backing makes it ideal for placement on mirrors, glass, medal or wood — in the home, on office or school desks, on our car's dashboard, etc. Thus it serves as a quick reminder to pray and live each day, in union with Mary, for Christ and for his Church.

The *Morning Offering* extended throughout our day by quick remembrances of it, especially in times of trials and temptation, becomes a powerful deterent to the enticements and snares presented by the devil and his agents for our downfall into evil.

In fact, united in prayer to the Sacred Heart of Jesus through the Immaculate Heart of Mary, we find the graces necessary to avoid sin, to frequent the Sacraments, to deepen the love of God within ourselves and to bring this love to those whom we meet daily in the little world around us.

Recommended Reading:

From A Morning Prayer by John Haffert (Ave Maria Institute, Washington, New Jersey 07882; 75¢ per copy)

[1]St. Luke, 18:1.

[2]The cards are priced at 5¢ each; in lots of 100, the cards are 3¢ each; and in lots of 1,000, the cards are 2¢ each.

PARENTS

Loud, angry voices break the still of a quiet, summer evening. Mr.__________ and his teenage son, Ted, are at it again. A few more minutes of bitter yelling, then Ted tears out of the house, slamming the door behind him.

Too bad, we think. They are both such nice persons. It is just too bad that they do not seem to get along.

Why not? Is it because they — and we — are ignoring the Fourth Commandment?

If children are allowed to stand against parents, dictating to them instead of obeying them; if parents do not explain reasons for difficult commands; if discipline is extreme — too lukewarm or too severe; if father is so engrossed in business or sport that he gives little or no time to his wife and children; if mother is so busy with clubs and community affairs that she neglects companionship and care of her family; if children are allowed so many outside activities that they are seldom at home or are permitted to go-steady during high school days, how can there be family love, peace and happiness? How can our homes resemble — as they should — that of the Holy Family?

God's law places the father and mother in command, imposing upon children the duty of respect and obedience: simple, prompt and constant.

Of course, along with parental authority, there comes the responsibility of providing a holy, happy home. A home where God is King, where His laws are honored and obeyed, where there is prayer and good example. A home where kindness is the rule; where children, young and old, know that they can depend upon their parents and can go to them for help and advice in all their difficulties — great or small.

In such homes children truly love and honor their parents. Situations and problems are discussed and ironed out. Arguments do not extend into bitter quarrels. There is no back talk, no rebellion.

Children from such homes do not have to be reminded of their obligations to parents. As adults, they remain loving and loyal. They would not think of turning away from sick or aged parents. Rather, they go out of their way, sacrificing self, time and money in order to help their parents. And whenever possible, they willingly and lovingly take their widowed mother or father into their own homes, instead of relegating them to nursing homes or homes for the aged.

Well, we think, such a home sounds great but how do we achieve it?

Our spiritual advisors give us the answer: *by accepting God's laws, by prayer and by effort.*

In accepting God's laws, parents must assume their God-given roles as the representatives of Christ — the father as head of the family, the mother as its heart.[1] Fathers and mothers must follow God's laws, themselves, and they must teach and command their children to do likewise. Parents must also see to it that their children study and understand their catchetical lessons so that they will truly grow in the knowledge and the love of God.

Among the practical pointers for assisting parents are the following recommendations — originally presented in a Liguorian Sunday Bulletin[2]:

"*Try to improve yourself* a little every day. Become more pious, more virtuous. Give your children a good example and let them see that you obey God and all lawful authority.

"*Demand punctual obedience* from your children. Teach them to obey for the love of God, because God wants it. Teach your children to deny themselves and to bear unpleasant situations patiently.

"*Be reasonable.* Do not expect too much from a young and inexperienced child. Remember that even a year or two can make a great difference. With the oldest child, especially, parents may prove too demanding. They must realize that a child of seven is still only seven, even if there are younger brothers and sisters.

"As children grow older, parents should begin to explain the reasons for their commands; but they should not give the impression that obedience is simply a debate in which the one who can marshal the better reasons will prevail.

"*Be patient.* A young child lacks foresight, doesn't hear when preoccupied, has a short attention span, forgets easily, and sometimes has an uncanny knack of irritating father or mother. All this puts a severe strain upon the patience of parents. Only continued effort and great love can bring some measure of success in this difficult virtue.

"*Be consistent.* If a child knows what to expect from parents in certain circumstances, he will gradually conform. However, if the same action calls for different responses, ranging from the violent disapproval to apathetic indifference, the boy or girl becomes confused. Parents should also be consistent in the treatment of all their children so that one is not favored over the others. Moreover, father and mother must present a united front to prevent the youngsters from cleverly playing off one parent against the other.

"*Praise for work well done.* It is not wise to bribe a child to do what is right but it is good to reward him at least occasionally. The approach should not be: 'If you wash the dishes I will buy you some ice cream,' but 'Since you did the dishes so well, we will get some ice cream.'

"Let good order govern your home and insist that everything be done at a regular hour. For instance, do not permit your children to eat, play or sleep at unsuitable times or when the humor strikes them.

"*Punish to help, not hurt.* Punishment should enter the picture only when the child has committed a deliberate moral fault. If he makes a mistake because he doesn't know what to do, because he forgets or becomes confused, parents should correct but *not* punish the child. At times a mere glance or a quiet word may be all that the occasion calls for.

"Punishment should fit the 'crime', as well as the personality of the child and the parent. Often, prohibiting a privilege that has been abused is the best method of punishment. Thus, the child who violates family rules about TV could well be restricted in his use of TV for a period of time.

"There is a great controversy about the use of corporal punishment. Some hold with the Scriptures that the rod is a necessary method of training; others contend that a child should never be spanked. The greater weight of opinion seems to be returning to the attitude that moderate corporal punishment does have its place in disciplining. Sometimes a slap or a spanking at the moment of misbehavior is the only language that a small child will understand. Usually, a delayed spanking is not much value. Too frequent and severe spankings are definitely harmful.

"Parents should be careful not to humiliate the child so that it feels worthless and rejected. Like all the rest of us, even a wee "criminal" must not be deprived of hope, and it must be made clear that his parents are punishing him because they love him and want him to be better.

"*Use supernatural means of discipline.* Instead of always harping upon the negative, parents should often hold before their children the example of Christ who, as a Child, was subject to His parents and obeyed them. The Cross can easily teach a child the meaning of sin, as well as the merciful goodness of God. Confession can be an efficacious means of rooting out small faults. Communion will bring the child closer to Christ and instill the motive of love as a stimulus for right conduct.

"Gather your family together for daily prayers. See that your children are on time for church and school. Accompany them in the frequent reception of the Sacraments. Encourage them to take an active part in the liturgy and church affairs.

"*Keep a watchful eye on your boys and girls,* both young and older, in the home and out of it, on their reading and entertainment, and on their companions. Recognize the value of having the children bring their friends home.

"Believe that you know more than your children do about life and do not lose your self-confidence when they tell you that you do not understand what is good for them.

"*Forbid any kind of dating in grade school.* Permit group activities for freshmen and sophomores but do not allow them to go to these affairs as dating couples. Place very restricted dating patterns on juniors and seniors and encourage group associations. Encourage them to go to college or to work before becoming serious about love and marriage.

"*Let your children see the depth of your faith in God and your love for each other. Keep a happy atmosphere in your home so that your children will appreciate a truly Christian way of life.*"

Many parents find that it is very helpful, both to them and their children, when a family code is set up and followed. The following is a popular code which was originally published in *The Scapular Magazine*:[3]

Obedience and Respect: To parents and others who take the place of parents, children are expected to give obedience and respect as to the representatives of Almighty God.

By the practices of Christian courtesy and etiquette, we will show our love and respect for each other.

By proper clothes and conduct for each occasion, we will show our respect for ourselves.

Home: Any problem can be solved if you will talk about it with us. Try to understand our viewpoint as we will try to understand yours.

Permission must always be obtained to use the property of another.

Phone calls must be limited.

All will remain at table until Grace has been prayed.

If you are involved in any difficulty outside our home, we expect to hear about it from you first.

Chores: We will each care for our personal belongings.

Home chores will be assigned by weekly schedule.

Your weekly allowance will be based on job performance.

TV: The evening programs for the whole week will be selected on Sunday, with due regard for the wishes of each member.

Study: Two hours of home study or reading (besides school study periods) will be expected in preparation for each school day.

Two failure grades bring the loss of all social privileges (dates, car, job, extra-curricular activities) until the next report card.

Social Life: Every Sunday is *family* day.

No evenings out when there is school the next day.

Drive-in theatres are not permitted for dates.

Steady dating is not permitted until after graduation.

Alcoholic beverages are permitted — if at all — only for members of our family and only when we are present.

Your friends are welcome in our home.

We expect to be told where you go and with whom.

All of us are expected to phone when we will be later than expected.

Curfew will be: freshmen, 10 P.M.; sophomores, 11 P.M.; juniors, 11:30 P.M.; seniors, 12 P.M. One hour later for very special occasions.

The importance of prayer in obtaining a peaceful, holy, happy home is beyond question and so habits of prayer[4] should be fostered — praying *Grace* at meals; the daily *Morning Offering* prayed, together, at breakfast; and the evening family *Rosary;* attending *Mass* and receiving the *Sacraments,* together, whenever possible. Some families also make it a practice to attend at least one daily Mass, together, each week. Other families who cannot get to week-day Mass, together, represent the family by taking turns at going daily or on a set day or days each week.

Prayer — liturgical, family, private — all are indispensable ingredients for happy, holy family life. The reading and discussing of spiritual books[4], as well as the practice of family liturgical customs[4], are also beneficial.

Speaking of reading, one of the disturbing problems in far too many families is a child's inability to read. From this there stems tantrums, misunderstandings, problems of discipline, and general frustrations and unhappiness. Sometimes this becomes a stepping-stone towards skipping school, getting into street gangs and petty thievery which often extends into serious crimes.

It is encouraging to note that there is now a very effective, highly recommended means of teaching children to read. It is the *Professor Phonics Kit* which was developed by Sister Monica Foltzer, O.S.U., for use in either homes or schools.

The kit contains an attractive, intensive phonics practice book and reader entitled *Professor Phonics Gives Sound Advice* — easy to follow, suited to all age levels including pre-school age; an instruction manual which provides simple, page by page, helps for parents and teachers; and thirty-eight vividly colored picture key word cards. Parents and teachers of primary students need the entire kit ($7.50) but only the book and manual ($4.50) are needed by parents with older children having difficulty with reading or spelling. All items are available from S.U.A. Phonics Department, 1339 McMillan Street, Cincinnati, Ohio 45206.

Other efforts conducive to family peace and joy are sharing family entertainment and participating in family sports; developing family hobbies or projects; encouraging children to bring their friends home; and allowing children to take part in preparing meals, family plans and activities — especially on Sunday, Christmas, Easter, holy days and holidays.

One of the most important things that parents can do for themselves and their children is to have the ceremony of the *Enthronement of the Sacred Heart of Jesus* (reported in another section of this book). Millions of families throughout the world have consecrated themselves to the Sacred Heart in this special way and their dedication has brought — and is bringing — them many family blessings and joys, as well as special graces of strength and courage during times of sufferings and trials.

Peace and joy in family living are ideals obtainable by those who face reality and who care enough to base their lives on the love of God and of neighbor. Their prayers, sacrifices, loyalty and trust in the loving, merciful Heart of Christ bring the abundant, magnificent rewards which He promised to families devoted to Him:

"I will establish peace in their families.

"I will re-unite divided families.

"I will bless every house in which the picture of My Heart shall be exposed and honored.

"I will give them all the graces necessary for their state in life.
"I will console them in all their difficulties.
"I will be their refuge during life and especially at the hour of their death."

A PARENT'S PRAYER[5]

My God, make my home a happy home, dedicated to You and founded on Your principle of unselfish love and sacrifice.

Grant me prudence in judgment, perseverence in effort, and humility and strength in the performance of all my duties.

Help me appreciate more fully the importance of "eternal values" and the joy in accepting "Thy will be done."

Direct me in teaching Your children and mine these sacred and essential truths and principles.

Assist me in guiding each of my children with love, understanding, wisdom and justice.

Give me courage to say "No" to them when I should, regardless of their pleading and temporary sadness.

Increase my patience in correcting misbehavior and settling quarrels calmly and fairly.

Thus, O God, let my children see in me some faint glimmer of Your virtue and goodness.

May my conduct and speech inspire and encourage them in their steps toward You.

And one day, in Your mercy and love, may all of my family be united in Your eternal home, to live with You in perfect happiness and peace. Amen.

ACT OF CONSECRATION TO THE HOLY FAMILY

O Jesus, behold our family. Once more we consecrate ourselves to You — our trials and joys — that our home, like Yours, may ever be the shrine of peace, purity, love and faith. Protect and bless all of us, absent and present, and be merciful to those departed.

O Mary, loving Mother of Jesus, and our Mother, pray to Jesus for our family, for all the families of the world, to guard the cradle of the newborn, the schools of the young and their vocations.

O Joseph, Holy Guardian of Jesus and Mary, assist us by your prayers in all our necessities. Watch over our home, at the pillow of the sick and the dying, so that we may all be united to Jesus with Mary and you for all eternity. Amen.

Recommended Reading:
Are We Short Changing Our Youth?, a popular paperback which alerts parents, pastors and teachers to the problems of youth and suggests positive means of assistance; highly recommended; available from the Sacred Heart Center, 6026 West Harwood Avenue, Orlando, Florida 32811; $1.25 postpaid.

[1]An apostolate especially designed to help mothers recognize their God-given role, to help them strengthen Catholic home life and to assist them in educating their children according to the principles of the Gospel is the *Archconfraternity of Christian Mothers.* Details for establishing local units are available from its headquarters at 220 — 37th St., Pittsburgh, Pa. 15201.

[2]Reprinted here by permission.

[3]Reprinted here by permission

[4]See index.

[5]This prayer was composed by Rev. Joseph E. Keller and originally appeared in *Our Sunday Visitor.*

Copies of this prayer are now available in card form in quantities of 10 for 50¢, 25 for $1.00, 100 for $3.00, and 500 for $10.00 from: Miller Printing Co., Box 1206, Springfield, Ohio 45501.

A five stanza abridgment of this prayer in an attractive 6x8 wall plaque is obtainable at local religious goods stores. (Manufacturer; The Gerffert Co., Inc., 54 — 60 Lafayette St., New York, N.Y. 10013).

Reprinted by permission.

THE POPE

Are we among those who find it quite fashionable to question the Holy Father's decisions and teachings, to belittle his encyclicals, to cast doubts upon his official judgments?

What about this?

We know that Christ, the King of Love, appointed St. Peter to be His first official representative — the supreme leader and teacher of His Church — His vicar on earth.

The early Christians understood Peter's divinely appointed role. They honored him, loved him, and obeyed him. But Peter's enemies hated and rejected him — to such an extent that they took his life. Since that time succeeding pontiffs have been loved and despised, accepted and rejected.

In our modern, materialistic, paganistic world the authority of the Holy Father has been challenged, openly defied, and even rejected. It has become quite fashionable to question the Pope's decisions and teachings, and to belittle his encyclicals on the grounds that these documents are not infallible and that everyone has the right to follow his own conscience.

What about this? What did Christ say? What does His Church teach?

Our Lord said; "Whatsoever you shall bind upon earth, shall be bound in heaven." (Matthew 16:19).

This is certainly a definite, positive statement. Its meaning is clear — beyond question.

As to encyclicals, these are official documents coming to all Catholic people from the Supreme Teacher of Christ's Church. No conscience is a right conscience, or even a well guided conscience, if it does not take this into account. In fact, Vatican II clearly and emphatically reminds us of this obligation. In the *Dogmatic Constitution on the Church (Lumen Gentium) No. 25,* the Council Fathers state:

"This religious submission of will and of mind must be shown in a special way to the authentic teaching authority of the Roman Pontiff, even when he is not speaking ex cathedra. That is, it must be shown in such a way that his supreme magisterium is acknowledged with reverence, the judgments made by him are sincerely adhered to, according to his manifest mind and will. His mind and will in the matter may be known chiefly either from the character of the documents, from his frequent repetition of the same doctrine, or from his manner of speaking."

We, therefore, have a serious and imperative obligation to form a correct conscience, according to the Holy Father's directives — not according to our own likes or our own wishes.

Although it is true that man must always follow his conscience if he would avoid sin, still it must be a correct conscience. This Pope Paul and many other authorities have repeatedly declared. Man's conscience can only be correct when it conforms to God's Will, and God's Will can only be known with absolute certainty through the Catholic Church of which the Pope is the authentic interpretor.

The Church's teaching is that if one errs through invincible ignorance, he is justified in following his erroneous conscience. However, he must correct it as soon as he discovers his error. No Catholic can honestly claim that he does not know — or cannot learn — what the Catholic Church teaches.

The Pope is not "just another theologian". He is the divinely appointed guardian and teacher of the Church. His vocation is to proclaim truth even though it may bring him virulent attacks, contempt rather than respect, and the loss of some Catholics and even some potential Catholics.

The responsibility of a pope to teach and guard truth, and of the faithful to acknowledge and obey, are clearly defined in many documents. Among such is the encyclical, *Humani Generis,* issued by Pope Pius XII, in which he states:

". . . If the Supreme Pontiffs in their official documents purposely pass judgment on a matter up to that time under dispute, it is obvious that the matter, according to the mind and will of the same Pontiffs, cannot be any longer considered a question open to discussion among theologians.

". . . God has given to His Church a living Teaching Authority to elucidate and explain what is contained in the deposit of faith only obscurely and implicitly. This deposit of faith our Divine Redeemer has given for authentic interpretation not to each of the faithful, not even to theologians, but only to the Teaching Authority of the Church."

Obedience and loyalty to the Holy Father are therefore hallmarks of true Catholics. We certainly do not need to be ashamed of "standing" along with the Pope. We need not be concerned about being labelled old-fashioned or of not being "with it". Rather, we should feel honored, for our allegiance to the Holy Father — candidly faced — is actually to be "with it": with Christ, with His Vicar, with His Church.

We have a forthright, encouraging reminder of this from a very great, very holy pontiff, the pope of the Eucharist, St. Pius X, who said:

"When people love the pope, they do not discuss his orders; they do not question the extent of their obedience, nor in what matters they are to obey. When people love the pope, they do not pretend that he has not spoken clearly enough, as if he were obliged to whisper in each one's ear that which he has often expressed so clearly in words and encyclicals. They cannot cast doubt upon his order under the pretext so commonly adduced by those who are unwilling to obey, that it is not the pope who commands but those who surround him; they cannot limit the ground on which he may and ought to exercise his authority; in matters of authority, they cannot give preference to persons whose ideas clash with those of the pope, however learned these may be, for though they be learned, they are not saints."[1]

This is "telling it as it is". This is emphasizing the truth that disobedience and insults against Christ's Vicar are in reality disobedience and insults against the loving Heart of Christ.

The important question is, therefore, where do we stand? With Christ's Vicar or against him?

> Lord Jesus, shelter our Holy Father, the Pope, under the protection of Your Sacred Heart. Be his light, His strength and his consolation.
>
> V. Let us pray for our Pontiff
>
> R. The Lord preserve and give him life, and make him to be blessed upon the earth, and deliver him not up to the will of his enemies.

> "In order that the Episcopate itself might be one and undivided, Christ placed Blessed Peter over the other apostles, and instituted in him a permanent and visible source and foundation of unity of faith and fellowship. All this teaching about the institution, the perpetuity, the force and reason for the Sacred Primacy of the Roman Pontiff and of his infallible teaching authority, this Sacred Synod again proposes to be firmly believed by all the faithful."
>
> (Dogmatic Constituion on the Church,
> Chap. 3, Sec. 18)

[1]*Jesus, King of Love* by Rev. Mateo Crawley-Boevey, SS.CC. chapter 18, P. 194.

PORNOGRAPHY

The atmosphere at the meeting of the Duluth City Council on October 29, 1973 was extremely tense. The people present — proponents and oponents ofordinances establishing anti-pornography laws — "held their breaths" as the votes of the commissioners were being recorded.

Ordinance No. 8019 prohibited the sale and distribution of obscene materials and ordinance No. 8020 prohibited the use of sexual material, nudity and obscene words in public advertising displays. Legal definitions of obscenity terms were included in the ordinances and exemptions for the use of such materials by physicians and other qualified persons were stipulated.

The result of the tabulation indicated decisions in favor of both ordinances.

Particularly jubilant over this decision were Robin Tellor, a Catholic, and John McAllister, a Lutheran. They had become friends through meetings at previous sessions of the City Council. At that time both men had courageously spoken against pornography.

Their joy was short-lived, however, because the Council's resolutions were soon challenged by the *Minnesota Civil Liberties Union.* In fact, that organization immediately began to circulate a petition to repeal the ordinances on the grounds that they were unconstitutional because they allegedly violated freedom of speech and of the press. As soon as the required number of signatures was obtained, the *Minnesota Civil Liberties Union* presented the petition to the City Council. The City Attorney and a Judge subsequently ruled that the petition was invalid because both ordinances had been placed on the same petition.

Not satisfied, the *Minnesota Civil Liberties Union* appealed the ruling to the Minnesota State Supreme Court. On May 2, 1975 Judge Lawrence Yetka handed the matter back to Duluth officials with the order that the Council either remove the ordinances from the city's books altogether or present them as referendums for the citizens' approval or disapproval. The City Council then decided to submit the referendums at the same time as the election of city officers to be held on November 4, 1975.

This led Tellor and McAllister to contact their friends and associates who formed a local unit of *Citizens for Decency Through Law.* (National headquarters are at 5670 Wilshire Blvd., Suite 1680, Los Angeles, California 90036 from which information on how to ban pornography may be obtained). A series of meetings were then held at various church clubrooms and community centers.

At these meetings, it was emphasized that, contrary to wide-spread misconceptions, the United States Supreme Court and the Constitution do *not* protect pornography; in fact, that in June 1973 and again in June, 1974 the Supreme Court handed down decisions on pornography which gave individual communities the *right to clean up pornography*. The justices also bluntly stated that local law enforcement officials should get on with it.

Members further learned that the ordinances were drawn up in consultation with the city attorney and that similar ordinances had been tested and could be enforced.

Members were reminded that although legislation by and of itself cannot create moral persons, still governments have the duty to promote moral decency and goodness; also, that as citizens, everyone has a right to protest against evil; and that society has a right to set standards and the states have a right to legislate to protect those standards.

Members also heard various national reports stating that many psychiatrists, judges and policemen attribute a definite connection between pornography and the increase in sex crimes; and that numerous case histories from across the nation indicate that the criminals themselves admit that their sex crimes were directly linked to obscene materials and X-rated movies.

During these meetings arguments of the opposition were also discussed so that members would be familiar with these aspects and be able to answer possible objections intelligently.

Being thus informed *Citizens for Decency Through Law* were ready to carry on a concerted campaign to alert Duluthians to the need of making their voices heard and of voting for anti-pornography laws.

Their efforts included the following:

1. Personal contacts were made to relatives, friends and neighbors, explaining the issues involved.

2. Numerous telephone calls were made. (Many senior citizens, even some in nursing homes, joined in making these calls.)

3. Officers and key members appeared on radio talk shows and spoke to church, school and civic groups, as well as at church breakfasts and similar gatherings.

4. The bishop was contacted with the request that pastors be advised to alert parishioners to the need for voting for decency laws; and notes were sent to pastors of all churches, Catholic and non-Catholic, suggesting that anti-pornography information be placed in church bulletins and mentioned from the pulpit.

5. Pertinent literature, including a special edition of *News for Good Neighbors* (available from the Christian Family Renewal, P.O. Box 73, Clovis, California 93612) were distributed.

6. Candidates up for election were invited to their meetings.

7. Support of the president and other officials of the local university and college was solicited.

8. Contributions to cover the cost of mail and of ads were sought. (One such ad covered a full page and listed the names of 1,500 people who favored anti-pornography laws.)

9. Attractive postcards explaining the ordinances were mailed to peo-

ple in each district.

10. Weekly meetings were continued at which time progress was reported, ideas exchanged, and momentum accelerated.

11. Ads were placed in the city's newspapers.

12. Open letters were sent to the editors.

Some of these open letters were short and to-the-point, simply stating that a person or a group favored the passage of decency laws. Other letters, as the following one, provided important information:

Dear Editor:

Duluth voters will be going to the polls to elect a mayor, city councilmen and school board members. In addition, some special propositions will be on the general ballot. Proposition 1. deals with the sale and distribution of obscene materials. Proposition 2. prohibits public displays of obscene materials. Both are against hard-core pornography.

As the Supreme Court has ruled to place the responsibility on the local community, it is up to us to decide what is best for the good of our community in this regard.

As to the legality of the ordinances, it should be noted that these were carefully drawn up with legal counsel, the ordinances being essentially similar to those adopted by a number of cities in the U.S. Their enforcability has been tested in the following cases: Marvin Miller vs. State of California; Paris Adult Theatre vs. Lewis R. Slaton, District Attorney, Atlanta Judicial District and many more, including Albuquerque, New Mexico and Rapid City, South Dakota.

To vote intelligently is to exercise one of our prized freedoms. To vote responsibly is an opportunity of improving our world. May we do both.

(Signed)

As a result of these and other efforts, on November 4th the voters expressed their overwhelming desire for anti-pornography laws by a 3 to 1 majority.

And so, concerned Duluthians won their battle against pornography. Of course, it was not an easy fight but similar measures can also be effective in other localities, large or small. All that it takes is prayer, enthusiastic dedication, organized effort, patience and perseverance.

Although the cooperation of many persons is ideal, still successful strategy can be accomplished by lesser numbers. In Duluth (population about 100,000) the movement was spearheaded by the two originators, plus a nucleus of fifty very dedicated men and women, plus the cooperation of many occasional helpers including senior citizens.

It is noteworthy that many personal prayers beseeching God's guidance and blessings were offered. And all of the *Citizens for Decency*

Through Law meetings were opened and closed with a prayer. Thus, by prayer and action, this was indeed a true ecumenical endeavor since the members belonged to various denominations.

They all realized the truth of the old adage that "all that is necessary for the triumph of evil is for good men to do nothing" and so they were determined not to be apathetic. Rather, they decided "to do something" to defeat evil.

And they did!

N.B. Besides Citizens for Decency Through Law, another group promoting decency is Morality in Media, 487 Park Ave., New York City 10022. Among other endeavors, it is continuing its campaign to Federal Communications Commission Chairman Richard E. Wiley, urging public hearings on gratuitous sex-violence TV programming, so that the people can be heard. For petition sheets, write to the above address.

PRAYER

We know that prayer — humble, sincere, reverent prayer — is speaking with God: to adore Him, to offer Him reparation, to thank Him and to seek His blessings.

Prayer is, therefore, a four-point program. But what about this program? How many of these points do we make a living part of our daily prayers?

Do we pray when we need or want something — health, a job, etc.? We know that praying to ask such favors is necessary and good, for God is our Father Who loves us; Who is interested in our problems and needs; and Who answers our pleas in the best way possible. But do we pray *only* when we are in need or when we want something?

And what about our prayers of gratitude? Do we remember to thank God frequently — not only for His many special favors but for the gifts which we take so lightly and so for granted: our life, our Faith and our freedom?

Prayers of gratitude are simple courtesy. They are prayers which God expects of us. When Christ cured the ten lepers and only one returned to thank Him, Our Lord's remark was a sorrowful rebuke, not only to the lepers but to us all: "Were not ten cleansed? Where are the other nine?"[1]

And how about our prayers of love and adortion? How often do we tell God that we are happy to be His creatures; that we acknowledge His Kingship; and that we want to live as He wishes? How often do we ask His blessing and guidance so that we may learn to be more holy and more pleasing to Him? Often? Once in awhile? Never?

And what about our prayers of reparation? How often do we tell God that we are sorry about our own sins and the sins of others — that we are sorry about all the sufferings which these sins have caused Him?

Do we remember to pray for the needs, the intentions and the endeavors of our Holy Father, our bishops, pastors, missionaries, priests, religious and lay apostles?

Our priests and religious deeply appreciate our prayers and surely our defected ones are much in need of compassionate prayers. Among the new, short prayers for priests, living and dead, is the prayer offered for them to the Sacred Heart of Jesus through the sorrows of the Immaculate Heart of Mary. A free copy is available upon request, accompanied by a stamped, self-addressed envelope, from the Sacred Heart Center, 6026 West Harwood Ave., Orlando, Florida 32811. Among the recent booklets is the *Holy Hour For Priests,* published by the Carmelite Apostolate For Priests, available at 25¢ per copy from the Aylesford Carmelite Center, Box 65, Westmont, Illinois, 60559.

And if we wish, we may become members of the *Lay Associates of the Priesthood,* open to men and women who wish to say the apostolate's daily prayer for priests plus the offering of *one* of the following practices which may be changed from time to time according to member's preference or circumstances: five decades of the Rosary prayed daily; a weekly or monthly Holy Hour or two half-hours (which could include the Mass and Rosary); a nocturnal hour of prayer spent in the church or at home between 8 P.M. and 6 A.M., weekly or monthly. Members who are ill may offer an hour of suffering, daily.

A special division, open to nuns, is the *Confraternity of Mary, Mother of Priests* whose members offer prayers and sacrifices for a particular bishop or priest, for the sanctification of all priests, and for priests who may have "lost their way".

Anyone who might be interested in either of these apostolates and/or in learning about a vocation with the Handmaids of the Precious Blood may write to Mother Bernadette, H.P.B., at Jemez Springs, New Mexico 87025.

Do we also pray for an increase in religious vocations? Do we pray for the gift of Faith for unbelievers and for the conversion of sinners? And what about the suffering, the dying, the imprisoned, the oppressed and down-trodden, people in captive countries, the poor, the aged, the lonely, the confused and troubled? How often do we pray for them?

Each day brings many and varied opportunities for prayer: the Morning offering, the Mass, Holy Communion, Visits, Holy Hours, the Rosary, the Stations, the Angelus, Spiritual Communions, and numerous "little" prayers.

Speaking of Spiritual Communions, we may use any formula that we choose. A popular example is the following composed by St. Alphonsus Liguori:

> My Jesus, I believe that You are present in the Blessed Sacrament. I love You above all things and I desire to receive You into my soul. Since I cannot now receive You sacramentally, come at least spiritually into my heart. As though You were already there, I welcome You and unite myself wholly to You. Never permit me to be separated from You.

Spiritual Communions, such as this one, may be made frequently, not only in Church but also at home, school, work, etc.

As to the "little" prayers, these require so small an effort but they are so fruitful. For example, in his book, *You Can Change The World,* Father James Keller points out a "little" method of praying in reparation for sins and for the needs of others. He says: "When you go into a bus or streetcar, into a theatre, or to a football or basefall game, or down to the beach, say a passing prayer for everyone there."

There are so many daily occasions for such "little" prayers. For instance, couldn't we say

A prayer when we hear an ambulance or fire siren, for whoever may be in difficulty;

A prayer when we read the obituary column, for those newly dead and for those who are to die this day or night;

A prayer when passing or visiting a hospital, for God's blessing upon the patients, the doctors and nurses;

A prayer of reparation when someone uses the name of God in vain in our presence: *Praised be the name of Jesus!*

These and other short prayers, such as *Lord Jesus Christ, have mercy on me;*[2] *Sorrowful and Immaculate Heart of Mary, pray for us; and Jesus, Mary, Joseph, I love you, save souls;*[3] are obviously important and they extend our *Morning Offering* into constant prayer. Daily prayers, both great and little, make us conscious that we live in the presence of God and they bring His blessings upon us and upon others.

But, we may ask, is daily prayer really so important? I don't pray very much any more. Frankly, I wonder whether God actually hears our prayers. I wanted something so much and I prayed so hard for it, but I didn't get it. God didn't answer my prayers.

Didn't He?

Rather, wasn't His answer, "no"?

God answers every sincere prayer, though not always as we may wish the answer to be. As the God of Love, the God of Divine Providence, sometimes His answer must be a "no" because our request, though it seems very pleasing to us, is actually not good for us to receive. Even though we may not see it that way, the "no" is truly for our own good — just as any loving father will say "no" to something which is harmful or not in the best interest of his child.

And when God does refuse a specific request, still our humble, sincere prayers are meritorious for us and for others — sometimes indicated in very apparent and wonderful ways; sometimes hidden from us until eternity. And so, our petitions should be expressed with their disposition to be left to God's Will, and with complete confidence that God will always take care of us and our needs in the best way, according to His infinite wisdom and goodness.

At times God's answer may be "not now, later on". In such cases God may be testing our faith or teaching us patience and perseverance, thereby allowing us to grow in grace. But since God is never outdone in generosity, the blessings and favors He then grants are often far beyond expectation — as in the case of St. Monica who prayed for years for the conversion of her son, and finally received not only a converted son, but a saint.

At other times when God's answer is "yes", not only do we receive countless daily graces and gifts but often extraordinary personal favors and even public miracles, as those manifested at Paray-le-Monial, Lourdes, LaSalette, Fatima, Beauraing, Guadalupe and other shrines.

Whether God's answer to our prayer is "yes, no, or later", the fact remains that prayer is indispensable.

But, we may wonder, why should we spend so much time in going to daily Mass, in praying the Rosary, in making visits and holy hours, in praying the Stations, etc.? Shouldn't we use our time and energy in works of mercy rather than in personal prayer or in furthering apostolates directly related to prayer, to God or to Our Blessed Mother?

Looking at Our Blessed Lord for the answer, we see that He spent His apostolate in both prayer and involvement. Although He expended Himself in preaching, teaching and in compassionate assistance to the poor, the suffering, the discouraged, the discriminated, still He found the time — took the time — to pray.

Christ prayed and fasted for forty days before beginning His public ministry. He prayed both at the temple and "apart alone". He taught us how to pray the *Our Father.* He told us "to ask and you shall receive." He warned us to "watch and pray lest you enter into temptation." He prayed at the Last Supper and in the garden of Gethsemane. And on the cross, His dying words were prayers of love, forgiveness and surrender to the Will of His Father.

On the human level, looking at just three of the world's greatest heroes of loving, compassionate involvement, from three different times and circumstances in life, we see:

St. Francis of Assisi whose name is synonymous throughout the world with loving kindness and compassionate concern for the poor and the suffering; St. Frances Cabrini who left her beloved Italy to come to the slums of New York, Chicago and other cities, expending her frail health in merciful works for the poor, the orphans and for the sick; and St. Martin, the humble mulatto of Peru, who ministered to the suffering and the downtrodden, whether White, Negro, Indian or Spanish; whether Catholic, non-Catholic or atheist.

These great ones probably never consciously thought of the words, commitment and involvement. They just loved God *first,* with all their hearts and souls, with all their strength. And their outstanding love of God, nourished by daily prayer, by the Mass and the Sacraments, and by a deep and constant devotion to the Blessed Sacrament and to Our Blessed Mother, poured forth into the fulfillment of the second commandement: love of neighbor as of self — into commitment and involvement.

Though our own commitment and involvement in works of love and mercy may never reach the heights of a Francis, a Cabrini or a Martin, still, if it is to be persevering and effective, it must be accompanied by prayer and sacrifice, for without the blessing of God involvement becomes ineffective and sporadic and falls flat into failure.

We know that Christ valued prayer. So did our Blessed Mother. At Fatima, for example, she asked Lucia, Jacinta and Francisco to "pray, pray very much and make sacrifices for sinners, for many souls go to hell because there is no one to make sacrifices for them." And she begged the seers, over and over again, to "tell the people to pray the Rosary."

Therefore, can we, who are just falteringg humans, afford to ignore daily prayer or belittle the importance of prayer?

Recommended Reading:
Pray Without Ceasing by Rev. Brice Inglesby, C.P.; explains how the constant, quiet miracle of grace takes place hourly in hearts of those who have discovered that prayer supplies them with a steady flow of sustaining power in daily life; available from the Marian Fathers Press, Stockbridge, Mass. 01262; 95¢ per copy.

[1]St. Luke, 17:17
[2]This prayer, known as the Jesus Prayer, deepens awareness and appreication of the merciful love of Our Lord for all mankind. An inspiring explanation of this prayer, its purpose, and its powerful effects is contained in the interesting paperback, *Pray Without Ceasing,* authored by the Rev. Brice Ingelsby, C.P.; available from the Marian Fathers Press, Stockbridge, Massachusetts 02162; 95¢ per copy.
[3]The importance and the efficiency of this prayer are portrayed in the book, *Jesus Appeals to the World;* cloth, $3, paperback, $2; available from the Divine Love Press. P.O. Box 24; Fresno, California 93707.

THE PRAYER IN SCHOOLS AMENDMENT

From the days of the little red school house, prayer or the reading of the Bible were always offered at the beginning of each school day. But in recent years along came objections to this practice — at first, not very noticeable, then more and more often, louder and louder. And so a movement to ban prayer from the nation's public schools developed.

Madalyn Murray, generally "credited" with spearheading the continued disension, together with friends and associates, lobbyed so persistently and so effectively that on June 17, 1963 the United States Supreme Court handed down a decision in the *Schempp* and *Murray* cases which banned prayer from the public schools in the United States.

And so, to the utter dismay of millions of people of many denominations, prayer went out of the classrooms. This disappointment still exists, as is evidenced by the fact that a Gallup Poll, conducted in the fall of 1974, indicated that 77% of the people queried want the adoption of an amendment restoring the practice of prayer to the schools.

A return to prayer in the schools is an important matter for obvious reasons. Noteworthy is the fact that parents of many children are no longer affiliated members of any particular church and therefore all too often the recognition of God and the practice of prayer are missing elements in their children's upbringing. It is also noteworthy that statistics show a sharp rise in crime among students of school age after 1963. There has also been a noticeable decline in the former atmosphere of respect for teachers and fellow students. These statistics, combined with the steady drop in scholastic aptitude tests after 1963, confirm the fact that the attitudes and behavior of school children have been markedly affected by the Supreme Court's ban of school prayer on June 17, 1963.

Some time ago Congressman G. William Whitehurst introduced a Bill which would return prayer to the schools. It is sitting in the Subcommittee on Courts, Civil Liberties and the Administration of Justice on the House Judiciary Committee and it could very well die there. So on July 17, 1975 Representative Whitehurst filed a discharge petition to bring the school prayer amendment to the House floor for a vote. To accomplish this, the signatures of at least 218 Representatives are needed.

We can help in getting these signatures by writing to our own Representatives, c/o House of Representatives, Washington, D.C. 20515 and by encouraging others to write to their respective Congressman, also.

Our letters need not be long or elaborate. Rather, just a few lines are required, simply stating that we are in favor of the passage of an amendment which would return prayer to public schools; and asking the Representative to sign the Whitehurst Prayer Amendment Discharge Petition.

Perhaps some of our representatives may send replies stating that they do not believe in signing discharge petitions or that there should be hearings on the prayer amendment first, or other declining reasons. And so a second or even third letter, perhaps mentioning the findings of the Gallup Poll, to the Congressmen may be necessary. Unfortunately, persistence seems to be the name of the game in scoring with many of today's politicians.

If enough persons could get their Representatives to sign the discharge petition, this would be a major step forward. Then when the Bill is in debate, follow-up letters to the Representatives, as well as to the Senators and President could bring victory in this issue.

Our letters, plus our prayers seeking God's assistance, require a little time and a little effort but thereby we "do something" for God's glory and the welfare of the children of our nation.

PURITY

Mary, the Immaculate One, showed the children of Fatima a glimpse of hell and told them that more souls are in hell because of sins of the flesh than for any other reason.

A devastating remark. A terrible warning for us all. So terrible that the devil has done, and is doing, a masterful job of hiding this fact from us.

With the aid of the unscrupulous, he presents immodesty and impurity as the accepted norm, the essence of popularity, the height of a so-called good time. And the world co-operates with him, presenting advertisements, literature, fashions and entertainment designed to entice the senses and destroy the soul. Satan even uses misguided teachers, psychiatrists and other professionals to promote the theory that illicit sexual indulgence — pre-marital or extra-marital — is simply the fulfillment of personality, a modern necessity.

With such a daily bombardment promoting immodesty and impurity, shouldn't we be alert to realize that the highly advocated *new morality* — no matter how it may be expounded — *is actually no morality?* Shouldn't we be very careful that we are not drawn into erroneous thinking and judgments? And shouldn't we check ourselves in matters of modesty and purity: in what we think, what we read, what we say, what we do, what movies, plays and TV we see, what places of entertainment we frequent, and how we act on dates?

There are other pertinent points to be considered. For example, if we are going steady, or are engaged, are we involved in heavy kissing, parking and petting — justifying our actions because "everyone is doing it"?

Everyone? Not really. There are many couples who respect themselves and each other too much for that. And more to the point, they want to please God — rather than offend Him — so they do not engage in sinful embracing.

Perhaps we are going steady and we know that we are too young. Perhaps we may even wish that we were not going steady but it is the custom. Everyone, but everyone, goes steady in high school.

Maybe so. But why does this have to be? Just because the custom started is no reason why we should let it continue, especially since teenage going steady is a certain sign of social immaturity. Why? Because going steady normally leads to courtship, and courtship to marriage. The problem is as basic as that. Teen-agers are not ready for marriage. Therefore, they are not ready for going steady. Social maturity is basic for the married state.

Ever thought of meeting with parents, teachers and student council members about stopping teen-age courtships at your school? It can't be done? On the contrary. Something can be done. In fact, in some localities, in both parochial and public schools, parents, teachers and students have organized especially for this purpose. Through their meetings and discussions principles have been set for social patterns. These patterns end boy-and-girl parties for children below high school age; reduce social activities; and re-establish the senior prom as the top social affair, at the same time, abolishing all-night prom parties. With co-operation, unwise and unsound social acceleration in our schools actually can be corrected. In many communities high school boys and girls are turning, more and more to group activities, without formal dating. Students report: "It's more fun that way"; "We like it a lot better this say"; "It eliminates the pressures arising from dating."

And then there is the very serious problem of unwed fathers and mothers. Sudden weddings and unwed fathers and mothers are no longer the exception but, rather, the quite ordinary, the matter of fact. Statistics show an appalling increase in these heart-breaking disasters. Unfortunately, statistics are not just cold numbers. The figures listed represent human beings, many just youngsters. The numbers on the charts show impersonal figures. What they do not show, what they cannot show, are the attendant misery, heartbreak and despair. The searing scars never completely healed. Never completely forgotten.

The alarming crescendo in such statistics covers a terrible and distinct failure. Who is to blame? What is the reason? What can be done to change the picture?

Doesn't the blame lie upon clergymen, parents and teachers? — for our failure to advocate modesty and purity, our lack of interest, our apathetic attitudes, our failure to acknowledge responsibility and our lack of courage "to do something about it"?

Many pastors, psychiatrists and educators attest to this judgment. In fact, the need for corrective action and for personal and public amendment re modesty and purity is so apparent and so urgent that many concerned people — even those in the secular field — are publicly calling attention to this matter. For example, an editorial in the *San Francisco Examiner,* entitled *The Appalling Erosions of Moral Standards,*[1] states, in part:

". . . Since the end of World War II we have seen our national standards of morality lowered again and again. We have seen a steady erosion of past principles of decency and good taste. And — we have harvested a whirlwind. As our standards have lowered, our crime levels and social problems have increased.

"Today, we have a higher percentage of our youth in jail, in reformatories, on probation, and in trouble than ever before. The statistics on illegitimate births, on broken marriages, on juvenile crimes, on school drop-outs, on sex deviation, on dope addiction, and on crimes of passion are higher than ever. And going higher.

"Many clergymen, parents, police authorities, educators and thoughtful citizens in all walks of life are deeply disturbed. *They should be. For they are responsible. We of the older generation are responsible.* We encouraged permissiveness. We indulged youth. We granted maximum freedoms, and we asked for a minimum in respect and in responsibility.

"Rules and regulations that prevailed for generations as sane and sensible guides for personal conduct were reduced or removed. Or ignored. Prayer was banned from the schoolroom and the traditional school books that taught moral precepts as well as reading were replaced with the inane banalities of 'Dick and Jane.'

". . . As prayer went out of the classroom so, too, did patriotism. No longer are our children encouraged to take pride in our nation's great and glorious past. Heroes are down-graded.

"We believe that this is wrong. We are convinced that a majority of our citizens would welcome an increase in patriotism and prayer and a decrease in the peddling of sex, sensationalism, materialism and sordidness.

". . .If the general public is as deeply disturbed as we are by the decline in national morals and in national pride, let it speak out. *Together, we can put down the sex peddlers. And, with God's help, we can put prayer and patriotism back in our classrooms. And in our hearts and homes, as well."*

Among the psychiatrists who have publicly cautioned people about parental responsibility is Dr. Paul M. Kersten whose report, *Are We Stealing Childhood from Our Children?,* was originally published in the Iowa State Medical Society Journal and later reprinted in pamphlet form. The response brought a great many concurring comments from medical personnel, religious leaders, parents and teachers. The following are excerpts from his report:[2]

". . . I believe that my question, 'Are we stealing childhood from our children?' must be answered unequivocally in the affirmative. I believe we American parents *are* robbing our youngsters of their childhood. I believe that we are doing this by default, rather than directly. I believe that the mechanism is a lack of application, or a mis-application, of the parental prerogative. From my own vantage point, the medical, social and psychiatric implications of this mistake are alarming.

". . . One can't do much about preventing illegitimate pregnancy or promiscuity in teenagers when such evils already are established facts. The work of preventing such behavior must start early in the children's lives, and parents must instill the requisite attitudes largely by serving themselves, as models of proper values, goals and aspirations for their sons and daughters.

". . . What are some of the activities in which we are negligently permitting our children to engage before they are old enough? We allow boy-girl activities at too early an age. We permit or actually encourage social dancing for children. We permit unsupervised boy-girl activities and we countenance chronic "going steady." These are just a few of them. I think that the all-too-prevalent lack of chaperones for early-youth activities also puts excessive pressure on children. I seriously question the appropriateness of providing automobiles to most youths.

"There is a general lack of supervision of the things children read and the programs they see at the movies and on television. From all sides, children are being bombarded by distortions of the way life really is, and we adults seem to approve this faulty orientation to life when we fail to object. It seems that there is a general lack of concern, among parents, about the type of friends their children choose and about the effect those friends can have on particular children. All of these instances of parental neglect, many of them subtle, thrust the child into excessively stimulating situations before he or she is capable of dealing with them satisfactorily.

"It has been my observation that in our contemporary culture, parents are afraid of their children. Generally speaking, parents have the mistaken idea that to love one's children means to give in to them — acceding to the demands of the individual child, or to group demands and expectations. Often the parent does this even though he realizes that it is unwise. Children perceive this giving-in on the part of parents, and they look upon it as a sign of weakness. Their recognition of parental weakness produces anxiety in the child, a feeling of dis-ease which is often expressed as restlessness, actual physical symptoms or unacceptable behavior. Oftentimes, to love is to say, "No." Children want this love, this expression of authority, this structure and guidance.

". . . By fearing the disapproval of children — their own youngsters or the youth of the entire community — parents place themselves in an untenable position. Parents cannot delegate this responsibility but all too often, I think, they expect the school, the church, the Y, the scouts or the police to do their task for them. Those agencies have their places but they can't adequately replace parents.

"It is time for us to reappraise our role as parents, to reappraise our rights, our duties, our responsibilities and our prerogatives, ethically, legally and practically. The standard for this evaluation must not be what the individual child or the group of children may want, but instead it must be what, in our mature judgment as parents, seems truly best for the child — what is within the capacity of the child to adjust to, and what is proper for his age . . ."

It is significant that many of our youth decry the fact that adults have failed them by permitting — through apathy or moral weakness — a climate in which immodesty, impurity, pornography, illicit sex, contraception and abortion are advocated as a modern necessity.

Teens and young adults not only complain about this among themselves but they also appeal for help. To quote just one such incident: Louise Bailey, in her article, *Our Young People Speak,* published in the Canadian Layman, said: ". . . The world today is in the throes of strife over civil rights and human equality yet current pornographic plays, literature, movies and TV programs are intent on human debasement denying the interior spirituality of man and his creation in the image of God, and conveying him as a missionless animal controlled by lust and passion. We, the growing youth, must assume the leadership and responsibility of our country one day, yet how can we do this if we ourselves have no respect for our minds and bodies and for those of others?

". . . We, the young, seek a decent world to live in, and we ask you, we beg you, to give us a chance to survive. Give us moral standards to cling to, to live by, to be solid citizens. Do not claim to worry about pollution of our country and yet not worry about the pollution of us, the future citizens!"

And so the challenging question arises: *what are we doing to stem the ever-widening cesspool of moral pollution?*

Facing truth, we can impress upon ourselves and our families the eternal fact that we are creatures having not only a body, but also, a soul created by God. That, because *we have this soul, we are children of God* as well as children of our parents. That we, therefore, owe God, ourselves and others, reverence and respect. And that virginity among the unmarried and fidelity among the married are of the greatest responsibility.

We can acknowledge and accept the fact that God has given each of us the commands of His Divine Law, the Ten Commandments. And that of these, His commandment, *Thou shalt not commit adultery,* excludes not only adultery but *all* impurity and immodesty.

So acknowledging and so accepting God's commands, we can do our best to live by His wishes and to teach our children to do so, also. We can counteract modern false teachings about sex[3] with positive truthful teaching: that sex is a sacred gift from God enabling married couples to become co-creators, with God, of new life; that the gift is to be used in lawful, valid marriage, *only*; and that God demands that the gift never be abused.

And we could impress upon them the fact that no matter how emphatically people, organizations, government agencies, or the news media may advocate contraception, abortion, and sterilization for the direct purpose of preventing procreation, the truth of the matter is that *these are intrinsically evil, abhorrent to God, and absolutely forbidden!*

So taught and so understood, our youth will see the necessity of reverence and respect towards God, self and others. Thus, if they are told by some misguided teachers and school counsellors — and this is often being done — that "pre-marital sex is the accepted, modern practice, and that the answer to unwanted pregnancy is to use contraceptives and, if necessary, to have an abortion", they will recognize the evil of such teaching, will report the matter to parents, and will then not be taken in by such immoral advice.

Helpful in recognizing and counteracting widespread errors concerning premarital sex, homosexual acts, and masturbation is the document entitled *Declaration on Certain Questions Concerning Sexual Ethics* which was published on January 15, 1976 with the approval of Pope Paul VI and signed by Cardinal Franjo Seper, prefect of the Doctrinal Congregation, and by Archbishop Jerome Hamer, its secretary.

It reaffirms traditional teachings on sex and stresses "esteem for the virtue of chastity, its beauty and its power of attraction." This virtue, it states, "increases the human person's dignity and enables him to love truly, disinterestedly, unselfishly and with respect for others."

The document declares that it is the responsibility of bishops to "instruct the faithful in the moral teaching concerning sexual morality, however great may be the difficulties in carrying out this work in the face of ideas and practices generally prevailing today" and to see to it that "sound doctrine is taught in schools of theology and in seminaries."

The *Declaration* also states that "it rests with bishops, priests and their collaborators to alert the faithful against the erroneous opinions often expressed in books, reviews and public meetings." And it cautions "artists, writers and all those who use the means of social communication to exercise their profession in accordance with their Christian faith and with a clear awareness of the enormous influence which they can have."

The document further states that "each individual, in his or her domain, must show tact, discretion, moderation and a true sense of values. In this way, far from adding to the growing permissiveness of behavior, each individual will contribute towards controlling it and even towards making the moral climate of society more wholesome."

Copies of the *Declaration on Certain Questions Concerning Sexual Ethics* are available from the Wanderer Press, 128 East 10th Street, St. Paul, Minnesota 55101, 35¢ per copy; discounts on quantity orders.

We could also be more alert about checking where our youth go and with whom — at the same time welcoming their friends into our homes. We could encourage them to join organizations[4] which truly uphold God's principles and provide friendships with others of similar ideals. We could be more vigilant in supervising our children's reading, TV, movie and other entertainments. We could explain the evils resulting from excessive drinking and from the abuse of drugs and encourage them to refrain therefrom. And we could join with other parents in establishing codes which prohibit all-night prom parties and discourage high school going-steady.

We could also join in the activities of national organizations promoting modesty and purity. Among these are the *Apostolate of Christian Action,* P.O. Box 24, Fresno, California 93707; the *Christian Family Renewal,* P.O. Box 73, Clovis, California 93612; *Citizens for Decent Literature,* 5670 Wilshire Blvd., Los Angeles, California 90036; and *Morality in Media,* 487 Park Avenue, New York, New York 10022.

We could also cooperate in the endeavors of such entertainment-communications apostolates as *Mary Productions,* 58 Lenison Avenue,

Belford, New Jersey 07718. Its scripts — religious, historical, patriotic and comic — are suitable for use in schools, retreat houses, monasteries, convents, diocesan and religious societies; and its puppetry kits are popular with the young and the not-so-young. Mary-Eunice Spagnola, co-founder with her husband, Joseph, also presents her excellent monologue sketches, in costume, at various gatherings and at special events, such as those held at shrines.

Modesty and chastity are definitely not the "impossible to attain" virtues falsely stated by today's promoters of permissiveness. Throughout the centuries our saints, pontiffs and other spiritual leaders have repeatedly taught that these virtues can be — *must be* — achieved and maintained and that daily prayer and the frequent reception of the sacraments are vital for this purpose.

The reward for the practice of these virtues is inestimable. Our Lord Himself promised: *"Blessed are the clean of heart, for they shall see God."*[5]

DAILY PRAYER FOR PURITY

Hail Mary (three times) By your Immaculate Conception, O Mary, make my body pure and my spirit holy.

Recommended Reading:
Charity, Morality, Sex and Young People, authored by the Rev. Robert J. Fox. In this important paperback, Father Fox insists that young people, properly guided, are capable of great sacrifices to do right. By presenting the doctrine of the right use of sex and the sanctity of marriage, he appeals to their best instincts. It is an excellent treatment of sex, explaining the "whys" of the Church's teachings. The book is available at $1.95 from Our Sunday Visitor Press, Huntington, Indiana, 46750

Let's Take the Hard Road: this book prepares boys to develop their moral and physical health and encourages the practice of the virtues to enable them to live, and to stand-up for, their Faith; acclaimed not only by pastors, parents and teachers but also by youth themselves; available from the Franciscan Marytown Press, 8000 — 39th Avenue, Kenosha, Wisconsin 53141; $3.95 per copy.

Sex and the Mysteries; this recent book is an antidote to the modern promotion of impurity; it emphasizes the fact that sex is a gift of God to be used in valid marriage, only; and that purity is not an impossible ideal but a positive reality which brings joy of heart in this life and God's promise of heaven; the book offers a method of help for children, the single, and the married in attaining and keeping a "clean heart" through application of the mysteries of the Rosary to daily living. (Ave Maria Institute, Washington, New Jersey 07882; 95¢ per copy.)

[1]Reprinted by permission; copies are available from the *San Francisco Examiner*

[2]Reprinted by permission.

[3]See chapter re Sex Education.

[4]Among these national groups for youngsters are the *St. Dominic Savio Clubs,* 148 Main Street, New Rochelle, New York 10802 and the *Tarcisians,* 3 Adams Street, Fairhaven, Mass. 02719; for teens, college students and young adults, the *Chi Rho Society,* 19767 Yorba Linda Blvd., Yorba Linda, Calif. 92686; the *Student Alliance for Christian Renewal in America,* 8 Struble ave., Butler, New Jersey 07405 and the *Blue Army Apostolic Formation,* 8901 West Vernon Street, Detroit, Michigan 48209.

[5]Matthew 5:8

REPARATION

Our daily newspapers are filled with reports of adult and teenage crimes — murder, arson, armed robbery and other major evils. They are crimes which defy God and which demand reparation. For all of these terrible deeds and for the blasphemies, the sacrileges, the broken vows, the murderous abortions, the immoralities, the disobedience, injustices, hatreds and cruelties — and — for our own misdeeds, reparation must be made.

Unfortunately, we seem to go along our way, quite unconcerned about the necessity for reparation. We do not seem to realize that mortal sin is a deliberate, willful rejection of divine authority, a heinous insult to God, a flagrant outrage deserving eternal punishment. Mortal sin cost our Blessed Lord His very life — a sacrifice that He made willingly and lovingly. Knowing this, how is it that we, offenders in serious or lesser matters, fail to make reparation an important part of our lives?

The need for reparation is so great that it caused the Sacred Heart to complain to St. Margaret Mary about our indifference and ingratitude. He even found it necessary to ask for the First Friday devotion, for holy hours of reparation and for the establishment of the feast of the Sacred Heart of Jesus.

In loving appreciation of our response, the Sacred Heart of Jesus promised a very great reward. "I promise you," He told St. Margaret Mary (and us) "in the excessive mercy of My Heart, that its all-powerful love will grant to all those who communicate on nine consecutive First Fridays of the month the grace of final repentence. They shall not die in My disfavor nor without receiving the Sacraments, and My Divine Heart will be their assured refuge at the last moment."

Of course, the promise demands co-operation on our part. It goes without saying that we must have the *right intention.* Otherwise, the effort is meaningless and without merit. In fact, no one can expect the reward of God's promise if he has the erroneous attitude: "I will make the First Fridays and afterwards I will do as I please about God's laws because I am going to be saved anyway" — for such an approach is certainly not sincere. Neither is it faith and love but, rather, it is hypocrisy and presumption.

The First Friday promise, as well as all the promises made by the Sacred Heart, was carefully examined by the Church and found to be worthy of credence. In fact, the promises have been referred to in several public papal documents and they were also incorporated in the Apostolic Bull of the Canonization of St. Margaret Mary on May 13, 1920.

Succeeding pontiffs — including Pope John XXIII who opened the Second Vatican Council and Pope Paul VI, its reigning pope — have all approved and promoted devotion to the Sacred Heart. In fact, in 1965, the 200th anniversary of the institution of the liturgical feast of the

Sacred Heart, Pope Paul issued an Apostolic Letter, *The Unfathomable Riches of Christ,* to all the hierarchy of the world. In this document the Holy Father clearly stated:

"This seems to us to be the most suitable ideal: that devotion to the Sacred Heart — which, we are grieved to say, has suffered somewhat in the estimation of some persons — now reflourish daily more and more. Let it be esteemed by all as an excellent and acceptable form of true piety, which in our times, especially because of the norms laid down in the Second Vatican Council, must be rendered to Christ Jesus, the King and center of all hearts . . ."

Besides the First Friday devotion special reparation may be offered through several other approved practices: in the home, through *Night Adoration in the Home;* by children through the *Tarcisian Movement;* and in public by the *Program of Reparation and Apology.*

Night Adoration in the Home began through the efforts of the late, saintly Father Mateo Crawley-Boevey, SS.CC. who established the apostolate of the Enthronement of the Sacred Heart[1] at the approval and command of Saint (Pope Pius X). It consists of one hour of prayer offered in union with the Masses being celebrated during that hour throughout the world, by anyone or any family or group, at least once each month, between 9 P.M. and 6 A.M., in the home, before an image of the Sacred Heart. Various pamphlets for this purpose are available from the Sacred Heart Center 6026 West Harwood Avenue, Orlando, Florida 32811, at 25¢ each. Among these are *Family Holy Hours; Holy Hour for the Home; My Hour With Jesus; Holy Hour for Students; Night Adoration for Nurses; Night Adoration for College Students; and Holy Hour for Religious.*

The *Tarcisian Movement,* also started by Father Mateo, is a speical reparative apostolate for children. It encourages members to offer the Sacred Heart love and reparation through daily prayers, little sacrifices, and devout participation at Mass and Holy Communion. Experience has proved that this program is capable of bringing out the best qualities in a child — obedience, honesty, generosity, concern for others, etc. Interested pastors, parents or teacher may obtain detailed information for establishing local *Tarcisian* units by contacting the Sacred Heart Center, 6026 West Harwood Avenue, Orlando, Florida 32811.

The *Program of Reparation and Apology to God* was first introduced in 1971 in twenty-five parishes in Southern California by the Rev. Francis Larkin, SS.CC., national director of the *Enthronement of the Sacred Heart.* It consists of a meditated Rosary for world peace; a half-hour of reparation and apology before the Blessed Sacrament exposed; Benediction of the Blessed Sacrament; and the Holy Sacrifice of the Mass in which the parishioners are invited to receive Holy Communion in *reparation for the sins that so offend the Sacred Heart today.*

Thus, the program renders public atonement and apology to God; offers special prayers for God's guidance upon spiritual and world leaders so that families and nations will come back to Christ and *His* way of truth and love; and serves as an effective means of emphasizing individual, family and parish awareness of the necessity and importance of reparation.

Further information, including a printed copy of the program, may be obtained by contacting the Sacred Heart Center, 6026 West Harwood Avenue, Orlando, Florida 32811.

Other approved reparation practices include the *First Saturday Devotion, All-Night Vigils of Adoration*[2] and the *Adopt-A-Soul Program.*[2]

Regarding the *First Saturday Devotion* — a devotion requested by Our Lady on Dec. 10, 1925 — this practice consists of going to Confession and participating at Holy Mass and Holy Communion on five consecutive First Saturdays in a spirit of reparation; praying the Rosary and "keeping Our Blessed Mother company" for at least fifteen minutes while meditating on the mysteries of the Rosary. Through this devotion, we offer God reparation for our own sins, for those of others, and particularly for those who have the misfortune to offend the Immaculate Heart of Mary.

Thus, the First Saturday devotion, for which Our Blessed Mother promised "to assist at the hour of death with all the graces necessary for salvation" those who respond to her plea, augments the practice of First Fridays.

Most certainly, the Masses, Holy Hours, prayers and sacrifices which we offer in reparation are pleasing to God. These, together with the daily acceptance of the monotony and hardships of our work, sufferings, struggles, disappointments and heartaches, bring great favors and blessings from the merciful Heart of Christ, for God is never outdone in love or generosity.

Recommended Reading:

Enthronement of the Sacred Heart $3.00; *Jesus, King of Love* $3.00;

Honestly, Have You Tried Everything $1.25; *The Nun: St. Margaret Mary* 50¢; *The Firebrand: Father Mateo* $4.00; *Blessed Claude* 50¢; all from the Sacred Heart Center, 6026 West Harwood Ave., Orlando, Florida 32811.

"I Will Reign Despite Satan," a special reparation issue of *Divine Love;* 50¢ per copy, discounts on quantity orders; available from the Apostolate of Christian Action, P.O. Box 24, Fresno, California 93707.

Night of Love; an interesting book about All-Night Vigils $2.50; *Why Five First Saturdays?;* Leaflet, 10¢; both items available from the Ave Maria Institute, Washington, New Jersey 07882.

The Five First Saturdays and Reparation to the Immaculate Heart of Mary: this booklet written by Lawrence F. Harvey tells how each of us can help to avoid the grave disasters that threaten humanity and how to save sinners from hell; 25¢ each; available from the Marian Fathers, Stockbridge, Massachusetts, 01262.

Among the Apostolates specifically designed to answer Our Lady of Fatima's pleas for reparation are the *Blue Army of Our Lady of Fatima,* Ave Maria Institute, Washington, New Jersey 07882 and the *Reparation Society of the Immaculate Heart of Mary,* 100 East 20th Street, Baltimore, Maryland 21218. Pertinent publications regarding the First Saturday devotion, as well as the entire Fatima message, are available from both apostolates.

[1]See the index
[2]See index for explanation of these programs.

ACT OF REPARATION

Eternal Father, we offer You the Body and Blood, Soul and Divinity of Your Most Beloved Son, Our Lord and Savior, Jesus Christ, in atonement for our sins and the sins of the world.

For our irreverences in Your holy temple:
 we ask pardon and make reparation;

For the wanderings of our minds and hearts during the Holy Sacrifice of the Mass:
 we ask pardon and make reparation;

For our lack of preparation in receiving the Sacrament of Your love:
 we ask pardon and make reparation;

For our lukewarm thanksgiving:
 we ask pardon and make reparation;

For the blasphemies of the impious against You, Your Immaculate Mother, and Your Vicar on earth:
 we ask pardon and make reparation;

For the outrages committed against You by those who should love and honor Your Sacred Heart and the Immaculate Heart of Mary:
 we ask pardon and make reparation;

For our failure to sanctify Sundays:
we ask pardon and make reparation;

For broken vows:
we ask pardon and make reparation;

For sins of pride:
we ask pardon and make reparation;

For sins of disobedience:
we ask pardon and make reparation;

For abortions and all other murders:
we ask pardon and make reparation;

For all crimes of violence:
we ask pardon and make reparation;

For hatred, injustice and dishonesty:
we ask pardon and make reparation;

For sins of impurity and immodesty:
we ask pardon and make reparation;

For the abuse of drugs and intemperance in food and drink:
we ask pardon and make reparation;

For the sins of which we have been the cause:
we ask pardon and make reparation;

For the bad example which we have given:
we ask pardon and make reparation;

For all the sins of our past life:
we ask pardon and make reparation;

For the sins of all mankind:
we ask pardon and make reparation.

Eternal Father, we offer You the Most Precious Blood of Jesus Christ in atonement for our sins and those of all mankind.

RETREATS

Have we ever made a retreat? No? Is the thought of making a retreat a little awesome or a little puzzling? It need not be. A retreat is a time of tranquillity and beauty. It is a time of being sheltered from the restlessness and the distractions of a busy world. A time for learning to know God and self.

The days of a retreat are spent close to God, beginning with the Mass and closing with Benediction of the Blessed Sacrament. During the day there are quiet talks in the chapel. The retreat master does not preach. Rather, he directs and stimulates reflection. Then there is time to meditate on the thoughts presented and to apply them to one's own life. And if anyone has questions or personal problems, a retreat master is available to help through private conferences.

Wondering what it is like to make a retreat? Let's "go" to a typical week-end retreat:

It is Friday — late afternoon — and you and I and others arrive at the retreat house. A courteous nun receives our registration and introduces us to the other retreatants. We are given a program of events and then shown to attractive rooms.

Later a bell rings announcing the dinner hour and we gather in the dining room to enjoy a delicious meal and a pleasant period of conversation and get-acquainted-ness.

At eight a bell summons us to the chapel where we meet the retreat master and listen to his first direction of meditation. This is followed by Benediction of the Blessed Sacrament, after which there is silence until the close of the retreat. From now on, although in the company of others, we are alone in spirit — alone with God and self.

On Saturday morning the awakening bell rings at 7:30. Private meditation is at 8:00; Holy Mass at 8:15; then breakfast. The first conference, or meditation, is in the chapel at 10:00; the examination of conscience at 12:00; the second conference at 12:15; and lunch at 1:00.

In the afternnon Benediction is at 4:00; the third conference is at 4:15; and then, a period of opportunity for going to Confession. Dinner is at 6:00; and the last meditation of the day is at 8:00, followed by another opportunity for Confession.

The program for Sunday follows that of Saturday until 4:00 when we take part in a beautiful procession and a public act of Consecration to Mary, the Mother of God. Then we listen to the retreat master's final meditation and advice. And then we receive his priestly blessing, the Papal blessing and the Blessing of God in the last Benediction.

The week-end has gone but it has brought us nearer to God and to a deep realization that we are brothers and sisters of Christ, sons and daughters of God, the Father. It has brought us to the stirring knowledge that God is with us in the life of our souls and in the life of the Church.

And it has brought gifts of grace, good resolutions and added strength to face the trials, hardships and temptations of a busy life.

The opportunities for making a retreat are many and varied. In many cities there are year-round week-end retreats; retreats offered during the summer months by many of our Catholic colleges; special retreats for married couples, teen-agers and other groups; and family retreats.

Family retreats are very popular. Housing is provided; matrons baby-sit with infants; and the nuns take pre-school tots on a "vacation" around the grounds, showing them the wonders of nature and telling them about God, their Creator. The rest of the family attends the retreat sessions, together.

A family retreat is something special since it is also a means of solving marriage problems. The husband and wife can be counselled together; and the presence of the children on the premises helps the mothers find a peace of mind which they would not have if the children were miles away.

The retreat movement is becoming more and more popular. Retreats are now being attended by Catholics and non-Catholics, by the young and the old, by the lowly and the great. There was a time when a retreat promotor found it difficult to interest others but now there does not seem to be enough retreat houses nor enough retreat week-ends to satisfy the growing demand. In most cases reservations must be made well in advance of the time set.

The days of a retreat are days of peace, grace and inspiration. They are days spent close to God, a rest for the soul and the body. This year — and every year — we are invited to treat ourselves to a retreat.

Note:
Some retreats now combine several discussion periods with the customary "silence, alone with God".

THE ROSARY

Back in 1208 Our Blessed Mother promised St. Dominic that the Rosary would be the means of converting sinners and that it would obtain many favors for the just.

Of course, we can't measure the countless times that this promise has been fulfilled privately but we do have definite knowledge of the public fulfillment of this great promise: the tremendous victories at Muret in 1231, at Lepanto in 1571, at La Rochelle in 1627 and at Temesvar in 1716. Some of the early accounts of these battles state that it was not generals nor battalions nor arms that brought victory but, rather, Our Lady of the Rosary.

Closer to our own times and in our own country, we have public knowledge of another great Rosary favor. It happened on January 8, 1815 in New Orleans. At that time, in our war against the British, we were caught in a threatening catastrophe: 6,000 Americans in battle against 15,000 British. General Andrew Jackson was in command. Realizing that we were hopelessly cornered, the general, the troops and the citizens turned to God in prayer for deliverance.

Over in the Ursuline convent the good Sisters gathered in their chapel before the Shrine of Our Lady of Prompt Help. And the terror-stricken wives, mothers, daughters and sisters of the soldiers joined them. Together they spent the night of January 7 in a vigil of prayer. Over and over again they prayed the Rosary, beseeching Our Blessed Mother's help.

Mary received their prayers and offered them to God, and victory came — suddenly and decisively.

With the dawn of January 8 the battle began. At about the same time the Very Rev. William Dubourg, Vicar General, offered Holy Mass at the main altar above which Mary's statue had been placed. And "at the moment of Holy Communion, a courier rushed into the Chapel, announcing the glad tidings of the enemy's defeat!"[1]

The victory was a spectacular one. It came within 25 minutes of battle and with an American loss of only 37 men!

No one could reasonably doubt Our Lady's miraculous intervention. And Jackson, himself, did not hesitate to admit Divine assistance, for he and his staff went to the convent to thank the nuns and women for their prayers. The general ordered a day of public thanksgiving. Ever since that time the people of New Orleans have commemorated this great victory.

The years go by and we sometimes forget these great Rosary favors. And we forget that Our Blessed Mother has often asked that we pray the Rosary. At Fatima, for instance, Mary told Lucia, Jacinta and Francisco — and us: "*You must say the Rosary every day and say it properly. Pray; pray much. Make sacrifices for sinners. Many souls go to hell because there are none to make sacrifices and to pray for them."*

Our Blessed Mother also asked that the prayer, *"O my Jesus, forgive us our sins, save us from the fires of hell, bring all souls to heaven, especially those in most need of Thy mercy",* be added to each decade, following the Glory.[2]

But, we may wonder, isn't the Rosary passe' these days?

On the contrary.

Speaking of devotions, the Second Vatican Council, in its *Dogmatic Constitution on the Church* (Article 67) points out: *"Let the faithful hold in high esteem the practices and devotions to the Blessed Virgin approved by the teaching authority of the Church in the course of the centuries."*

Most certainly, the Rosary is among the popular, approved devotions. In fact, the Rosary devotion has been recommended in at least thirty-five encyclicals from the time of Pope Leo XIII to the present. The most recent of these is the inspiring encyclical, *Christi Matri Rosarii* (Rosaries to the Mother of Christ) issued by Pope Paul VI on September 15, 1966. And his Apostolic Exhortation, *Marialis Cultus,* (February 2, 1974) also recommends the Rosary: "the compendium of the entire gospel."

It is also noteworthy that the revised *Raccolta* — an official compendium of indulgenced prayers and good works — gives significant mention of the Rosary, with special emphasis placed on the communal nature of this prayer and the granting of a *daily* plenary indulgence upon its *common* recitation, in church, the family, a religious institute, at apostolic gatherings, funeral wakes, etc.

Couldn't we, therefore, include the Rosary in our daily prayers? It takes such a little time — about fifteen minutes. Surely, in a twenty-four hour day even the busiest of the busy could find the time to pray at least one Rosary. So little a thing to do; so great the rewards promised.

We may pray the Rosary at any time and it need not be said entirely at one time. An ideal time for saying the Rosary is together with the family. The family praying together is then together with Christ, for He told us that "where two or three are gathered together in my Name, I am in their midst." (St. Matthew, 18:20)

But, we may protest, we just can't get our family together for the daily Rosary.

Really?

How hard have we tried? Isn't it a fact that we generally take the time — make the time — to do whatever we really want to do?

Many families have found that if they set a definite time — usually just before or after the evening meal — the family Rosary becomes a feasible and beloved family practice, followed even when some members are not present. An added interest is given to the family Rosary when members take turns in suggesting a special intention. Offering the Rosary for the needs of others, besides personal intentions, heightens awareness of the problems of others and brings a compassionate desire "to do something" to help the less fortunate and to serve the Church.

Many parents also find it wise to hold the children's attention by using Rosary picture-booklets, picture albums, slides and recordings, available from the Family Rosary Crusade, 773 Madison Ave., Albany, N.Y. 12208 and from many Catholic book stores. Among these items is *The Rosary For Children* by the Rev. P. J. Gearon, available from the Apostolate of Christian Action, P.O. Box 24, Fresno, California 93707; $2 per copy.

But, we may object, the Rosary is no longer relevant or meaningful these days.

Isn't it?

Properly understood and properly prayed, it is actually both relevant and meaningful. Praying the *Creed,* which is basic to our religion, reaffirms and strengthens our faith in God. The *Our Father* is biblical in origin, taught by Christ Himself to the apostles. The *Hail Mary* stems from the prayer offered by the Angel Gabriel at the time of the Incarnation, the beginning of Christianity. And the *Glory* is a short form of the ancient prayer glorifying the Blessed Trinity.

The meditations on the joyful, sorrowful and glorious events in the lives of Jesus, Mary and Joseph are also biblical in origin, as well as pertinent to Christianity. Through these mediations we learn to live in the presence of Jesus and Mary. For example: adoring the Infant Jesus with Mary and Joseph at Bethlehem; standing with Mary at the foot of the cross; rejoicing with Our Lord and Our Blessed Mother at the glory of His Resurrection. Thus, they help us to know and love the Holy Family, to imitate Their virtues, and to turn to Them for assistance in all of our needs.

Therefore, can anyone truthfully say that these prayers are not important or that they are without meaning?

There are a number of books, recordings, cassettes and slide albums designed to help us with Rosary meditations. Among these are St. Louis de Montfort's renowned classic, *The Secret of the Rosary,* now available as a paperback, 50¢, from Montfort Publications, 40 South Saxon Avenue, Bay Shore, New York 11706; *The Mysteries of the Rosary,* unique meditations through inspiring poetry written by Edith Myers, augmented by beautiful silhouettes cut by Sister Mary Jean Darcy, O.P.; available from the Lumen Christie Press, Box 13176, Houston, Texas 77019; $3.00 per copy; *The Rosary* a special issue of *Immaculata,* magazine; of interest to both Catholics and non-Catholics; contains instructions on how to pray the Rosary; the Rosary mysteries; 45 illustrated pages on such topics as the Liturgy and the Rosary; the Radio Rosary; the Rosary and the Blessed Sacrament; the Rosary and Conversions; Famous Rosary Shrines; and Chains of Unity for all Christians;

available from the Franciscan Marytown Press, 8000 — 39th Avenue, Kenosha, Wisconsin 53141; single copies, 50¢; discounts granted on quantity orders; *The Living Rosary,* a recording beautifully presented by two priests; one reading the Scriptural passage pertaining to the mystery and the other explaining its meaning; mono-aural, LP 33-1/3 RPM; $3.98; available from the Blue Army of Our Lady of Fatima, Ave Maria Institute, Washington, New Jersey 07882; *The Rosary Cassette* by Rev. Robert J. Fox who uses scripture, tradition, and Vatican II quotations to describe the Virgin's powerful role in assisting mankind; relates inspiring meditations on the Rosary mysteries; $5.50 from P.O.P.E. Publications, Box 6161, San Rafael, California 94903; and *The Rosary In Art:* 225 color slides prepared by the Rev. Canon Joseph Strugnel who visited many of the great museums of the world and gathered the finest quality slides of art works depicting scenes from the mysteries of the Rosary as portrayed by renowned art masters. Along with the slides is a book giving a corresponding scripture text or special reading relating to the pictures. The set is recommended not only as an excellent addition to any parish, school, retreat house or groups who promote the Rosary but also as an interesting and valuable presentation for art and history classes; available at $145 per set, postpaid, from the Maryfaithful Center, Powers Lake, North Dakota 58773.

If we love the Rosary enough to be interested in helping others — including "the public" — to know and love this prayer, a very effective means for doing so are the books, films, radio and TV programs available from the Family Rosary Crusade, 773 Madison Avenue, Albany, New York 12208.

And among the most popular of the Rosary programs produced independently is the *Marian Rosary Hour.* This program is broadcast direct and live each Sunday from the National Shrine of Our Lady of the Prairies located in Powers Lake, North Dakota. The program is a devout recitation of the Family Rosary with a musical background, ending with a short talk, and the blessing of a priest. It draws a tremendous amount of appreciative mail and the unusual aspect about this is that almost half of the letters is from people of many denominations who wish to join Catholics in praying for the lasting peace which guns cannot obtain. Anyone — or any group — interested in getting the *Marian Rosary Hour* on local stations may obtain helpful information for this purpose by contacting the program at Powers Lake, North Dakota 58773.

And if we would like to arrange a local Rosary Rally, this can be done without too much effort. Briefly stated: choose a centrally located church; consult the pastor; decide on a suitable date; plan a program (usually consisting of a procession with a statue of Our Lady; recitation of the Rosary; a homily; and Benediction); send announcements to each parish, encouraging pastors to speak about the forthcoming rally and to include the information in weekly Sunday bulletins for at least four weeks before the date; send notices to diocesan and local newspapers; invite the bishop, clergy, religious, local organizations and school groups to participate; distribute leaflets explaining the Rosary; provide posters for church vestibules, schools and club rooms; arrange for choir, organist, flowers, and hymn sheets; and have extra rosaries on hand.

Thus, with prayer and cooperation, a very inspiring and effective Rosary Rally can be accomplished in any community.

But, we may object, the Rosary was intended for past times when people were illiterate. In our modern times, other forms of Marian prayer are better, aren't they?

Yes, the Rosary did originate in early times when the ordinary person did not know how to read or write. But in 1917 when Our Blessed Mother begged the children of Fatima, over and over again, to *"tell the people to pray the Rosary"*, schools, newspapers and books were widely in existence and people did know how to read and write.

Surely, Our Blessed Mother must have been aware of the needs of this century and the changes still to come. Still, she did not stipulate a time limit for praying the Rosary. She did not say: pray the Rosary this year, or until next year, or until fifty years from now. She simply said: *"Tell the people to pray the Rosary."*

Could it be that Mary requested the Rosary because the Rosary is a prayer which can be said easily and quickly at anytime by anyone? At anytime: in a visit at church, at home, while traveling, while walking, etc. By anyone: from a small child to a harried housewife to a busy worker to a distinguished scientist to a saintly pontiff.

But, we may question, in these ecumenical times, shouldn't other forms of Marian devotion be investigated and used?

Marian devotion is indeed being studied by church officials and perhaps in time new forms of Marian prayer may be developed. However, this does not mean that the Rosary is to be ignored or downgraded. Surely, there is room for both the Rosary and new Marian approaches to God. Surely, in acquiring and using the new, it is not necessary or prudent to trample upon the traditional which is good.

Also, isn't it conceivable that the Rosary — if more generally encouraged — could actually become an efficacious connecting link between Catholicism and other religions?

A very effective means for this purpose could be the use of the recently issued *Rosary Card for Wakes*. This beautiful folder is especially designed for the use of non-Catholics attending Catholic wakes. Its cover presents a courteous invitation to join in the prayers of the Rosary offered for the deceased. Its inside pages give an explanation of the Rosary, the Rosary prayers, and short Rosary meditations indicating their biblical origin. Use of the *Rosary Card for Wakes* could indeed be a unifying step towards helping non-Catholics realize that in praying to Mary, there is absolutely no adoration. It would help them see that in our devotion to

Our Blessed Mother there is only love and confidence that she will graciously intercede for us with her Divine Son now and at the hour of our death.

The use of the *Rosary Card for Wakes* could be very acceptable to non-Catholics since there already are many non-Catholics who *do* appreciate the Rosary and pray it often. This is evidenced by correspondence received from those who tune in on Rosary radio and TV programs; by the attendance of non-Catholics at Rosary-Prayer rallies; and by non-Catholic fathers or mothers who join their families in praying the daily Rosary. It is also noteworthy that a Methodist minister and theologian, the Rev. J. Neville Ward, recently authored a popular book about the Rosary entitled *Five For Sorrow; Ten for Joy*. It has an obvious ecumenical dimension but it is also an unintended rebuke and spur to Catholics who have neglected the rich treasury of prayer and meditation that is the Rosary.

So wouldn't you like to see this *Rosary Card for Wakes* made available in your local mortuaries?

It may be obtained from the Sacred Heart Center, 6026 West Harwood Avenue, Orlando, Florida 32811.

But, we may ask, what about our young people and the Rosary? Teens seem to object to the repititious element contained in praying the Rosary.

Possibly some do. But doesn't the fault lie, not in praying the Rosary but, rather, in the failure to teach children and youth how to meditate — how to think about the joyful, sorrowful and glorious events in the lives of Jesus, Mary and Joseph?

Isn't it a fact that when we meditate while we pray the Rosary, we are not specifically conscious of the words of the prayers or of the number of prayers being said? Isn't it also a fact that while meditating, the repitition of prayers does not even bother us?

The Rosary is renowned as one of our spiritual treasures. Our Blessed Mother and her Divine Son's Vicars on earth have asked us, over and over again to pray it often, not only for ourselves but for the conversion of sinners and ultimately for peace in the world.

Have we prayed the Rosary today?

[1] *Manual of the Pilgrim to the Shrine of Our Lady of Prompt Help*, published by Ursuline Convent, New Orleans, p. 11.

[2] The S.A. Penitentiary, Feb. 4, 1956, authorized the recitation of this special Fatima prayer after each decade of the Rosary in private and public devotions. (Office of Indulgences, 878:56)

THE SACRAMENTALS

A lovely painting of an autumn woodland scene graces the sitting section of our living room. The book-ends on the mahogany table are wood carvings of Abraham Lincoln. A small bust of Beethoven sits on our piano. Three Hummels are perched on the mirrored shelving over the dining alcove. And six graduated floral etchings line the wall along the staircase.

This is a Catholic home? A visitor would hardly recognize it as such. There is no picture or statue of the Sacred Heart[1] — even though we know that Christ promised St. Margaret Mary, and us, that He would bless every place in which a picture of His Sacred Heart is exposed and honored — nor a picture or Our Blessed Mother, nor a crucifix, nor anything Catholic.

Well, we do have a small medallion of Our Lady on one of the bedroom walls.

On the bedroom wall? Why not in the living room? Have we forgotten that a blessed holy picture, a crucifix, a statue, a medallion are among the sacramentals?

Sacramentals — too often we do not make use of them at all or we use them without thought or devotion.

Take the Sign of the Cross, for example. This is a very powerful sacramental, one which was loved and used extensively by the early Christians. They used it on rising and retiring, before any undertaking, in times of dangers, sickness and temptations, and in frequently blessing their children.[2]

Down through the centuries the Sign of the Cross has been regarded as an effective weapon against the devil. It has been the means of obtaining great favors, even miracles. St. Benedict, for example, made the Sign of the Cross over a poisoned cup of wine intended to kill him, and the goblet was immediately shattered to pieces. St. Louis Bertrand, confronted by a would-be assassin, made the Sign of the Cross and the gun pointed at him was instantly changed into a crucifix. St. Vincent Ferrer, St. Dominic and many other saints worked numerous miracles through this Sign.

Knowing this, how is it that we use the Sign of the Cross so rarely and often so mechanically and haphazardly?

Many times this is also true of our use of holy water, another most powerful sacramental, one which the devil hates because of its power over him. Although holy water is used at liturgical services, it is also intended to be reverently used in our homes. In fact, the rubric in the *Roman Ritual* states: "The faithful may receive holy water in their own containers and take it home to sprinkle it on their sick ones, their houses, fields, vineyards and other objects; also they may keep it in their homes to sprinkle themselves with it every day, and even often during the day."

Among the petitions which the priest makes when he blesses water are: "O God, . . . grant that this creature of Thine (water) may be endowed with divine grace to drive away devils and to cast out diseases, that whatever in the houses or possession of the faithful may be sprinkled by this water, may be freed from everything unclean and delivered from what is hurtful . . . Let everything that threatens the safety or peace of the dwellers therein be banished by the sprinkling of this water, so that the health which they seek by calling upon Thy Holy Name may be guarded from all assault."

Another sacramental for use in our homes is the palm blessed and distributed on Palm Sunday. Usually, this palm is placed at a crucifix, a picture or statue, and kept in the home until the next Palm Sunday. At that time the "old palm" should be burned. If this is done in the backyard, the ashes may be buried in the ground. (Sacramentals are not to be thrown away. When discarded, they should be destroyed by fire, water or soil.)

Other sacramentals include the crucifix and various scapulars, badges and medals. A crucifix which we venerate as the symbol of Christ's great love for us — His sufferings and death — should be in all our homes, not only to remind us that we must live as God wishes, but also to have on hand at the time of anyone's death. (Many crucifixes are blessed with the grace of a "happy death", a plenary indulgence imparted to the dying who contritely kiss the crucifix.)

Among the scapulars are the *Brown Scapular*[3], given to us by Our Lady of Mt. Carmel through St. Simon Stock, which offers assurance of salvation and prompt deliverance from Purgatory for its faithful, devout use; and the *Green Scapular,* given to us by Our Blessed Mother, through Sister Justine Bisqueyburu of the Daughters of Charity, to be a special means of conversions and a happy death for those who have no faith. It is, therefore, very useful for distribution to fallen-aways and non-Catholics since others may say, for them, the recommended invocation: *Immaculate Heart of Mary, pray for us now and at the hour of our death.*

Among the badges is the *Badge of the Sacred Hearts,* whose purpose is to remind us of the great love which Jesus and Mary have for us; that we must love them in return; and that graces come from the Heart of Jesus through the Immaculate Heart of Mary. This devotion has been practiced for centuries. Its greatest promoters have been St. John Eudes, St. Margaret Mary, Blessed Claude de la Colombiere and Father Mary-Joseph Coudrin, founder of the Congregation of the Sacred Hearts.

Among the medals are the *Miraculous Medal,* the *Medal of St. Benedict,* and the *St. Joseph Medal.* Our Blessed Mother gave us the *Miraculous Medal* through St. Catherine Laboure', promising that those who wore this medal with confidence and devotion would receive great graces, spiritual and physical. In fact, its use spread so rapidly and obtained so many graces and favors that it quickly became popularly known as the *Miraculous Medal.*

The *Medal of St. Benedict* is one of the oldest and one of the most highly indulgenced. St. Benedict taught his followers to have great reverence for the Sign of the Cross and wrought many miracles through its power. In time a medal bearing the Sign of the Cross was made in his honor. *St. Benedict's Medal* is known throughout the world and is highly regarded as being powerful against the devil, especially in temptations against purity, as a potent power to destroy witchcraft and other diabolical influence, as an efficacious consolation in pregnancy, an aid in mental and bodily suffering, as a means of bringing about conversions, and as a protection against tempests, storms, accidents and contagious diseases.

The *St. Joseph Medal* honors the saint as the universal patron of the Church. It is cast in gold, purple and white colors indicative of St. Joseph's justice, humility and purity. A touch of red symbolizes the Holy Spirit and the redeeming, suffering love of Christ. St. Joseph is depicted in a protective attitude towards the Child Jesus and the circular position of Jesus, Mary and Joseph, attentive to one another, convey unity. The medal's petition reads: *That all may be one; St. Joseph, our protector, pray for us.*

The reverse side reminds us to invoke St. Joseph as protector of the Church, on behalf of the Holy Father, Christ's Chief Shepherd. The dove indicates the Holy Spirit's guidance in teaching divine truth. And the shepherd's staff, the grazing lamb, and the keys are scriptural symbols of the papacy.

Thus, the medal honors St. Joseph as patron of the Church, fosters family and Church unity, and encourages loyalty to the Holy Father. The medal (with a chain or as a bracelet, brooch or key chain) together with a pertinent pamphlet, *St. Joseph Today,* are available from the Capuchin Fathers, 2913 Locust Street, St. Louis, Missouri 63103.

Truly, the Church has given us a treasury of many useful sacramentals designed to obtain for us actual graces, forgiveness of venial sins, the remission of temporal punishment, health of body, material blessings, and protection from evil spirits.

But, we may ask, aren't sacramentals now outmoded? Since Vatican II aren't we supposed to ignore the sacramentals?

No indeed.

In fact, the *Constitution on the Sacred Liturgy,* chapter 3, articles 60, 61 clearly restates approval of sacramentals and acknowledges the efficacy of their proper use.

Of themselves, the sacramentals have no power. To place absolute trust in medals or in any blessed object, as if they had some power of themselves to protect us from carelessness or for "good luck" is a form of superstition, a sin against the true worship which we owe to God and the reverence which we owe to our Blessed Mother and the saints.

Rather, the prayers of the Church upon the sacramentals convey efficacious power and the value, to us, depends upon the faith and the devotion with which we make use of them.

Couldn't we, therefore, appreciate the sacramentals a little more and use them more prudently, more devoutly?

[1] A beautiful home shrine of the Sacred Heart which is a replica of the National Shrine of the Enthronement of the Sacred Heart, priced at $5.50, is available from the shrine at 4900 Tenth Street, N.E., Washington, D.C. 20017; also available are various pictures of the Sacred Heart.

[2] A simple and private blessing which parents may give their children, at any time, is the making of the Sign of the Cross on their foreheads while praying: "God bless and protect you" or "God bless you, and bring you back safely" or some similar phrase, as the occasion requires.

[3] See Index

SACRIFICES

Sacrifice is necessary for us all. Our Lord, His Blessed Mother and His Church have often told us so.

The world, however, teaches us just the opposite. It holds out pleasures, conveniences and self-will, telling us to enjoy ourselves, to take it easy, to do as we please. And so, sacrifice is pushed into the background, away from us. Even the word, sacrifice, seems to have a harsh sound and a harsh meaning. And the very thought of sacrifice rubs the wrong way.

We often think of sacrifice as something difficult, something that we don't want to do, something inconvenient, something which means giving-up. That is partly true but it is only the negative side. The positive side is the motive: the love of God and the love of neighbor.

St. Paul tells us that without this love our greatest sacrifice — even though it be of life, itself — profits nothing. And St. Therese of Liseuix teaches that with this love, our smallest sacrifice acquires immense value; gives great glory to God; and becomes a powerful sanctifying aid for self and others.

Sacrifice assumes many different forms. The greatest sacrifices — those which God demands of us — are the sacrifices necessary in order to obey the Commandments and fulfill the duties of our state in life. *All* the Commandments and *all* the duties. Not just those which we feel like performing, but all of them. For instance: the sacrifice it takes to hold our tongues and our tempers when we are provoked to anger. These and other occasions for sacrificing our own wills to God's Will occur many times each day — sometimes in small matters, sometimes in serious things.

In our daily lives there are many involuntary sacrifices. These are the sufferings and disappointments of the day: the nagging headache, the broken date, the difficult employer, etc. These, borne with patience and resignation, become gifts of our love, our faith and our trust.

There are voluntary sacrifices, too. These are the small mortifications which we willingly seek out and perform, such as giving up cokes for the day, turning off the TV for awhile, etc. Little sacrifices, but they are gifts of love which strengthen our wills and bring God's blessings.

Then there are the sacrifices of our worldly goods — money and materials offered for the Church, the poor, charities and missions. These may be large or small, according to our means and inclinations. There are certainly many opportunities for such offerings and sacrifices.

Added to material sacrifices are the offerings of our time and energy in furthering works of charity and of service, in private or in the parish: visiting someone who is ill when we would much rather stay at home; serving at a church supper when we would much rather see a movie; etc.

Speaking of time, there is the sacrifice of our time in attending daily Mass, in praying the Rosary or the Stations, in making Holy Hours, in attending missions, Bible services, novenas and retreats. And yet, if we look at time as a gift from God, twenty-four hours in each day, then a half-hour for Mass, fifteen minutes for a Rosary, etc., do not seem like very much.

Added to all these sacrifices, is the sacrifice of our human respect and feelings. This is one of the most difficult of sacrifices. For instance: someone in our party suggests going to a popular but sexy movie. We are startled at the suggestion and would prefer not to make an issue of the matter but we sacrifice human respect and object to the movie. Or, the occasion of shady stories arises and we again sacrifice our human respect, saying that we would rather talk about something else; etc.

There are also many occasions for the sacrifice of our human respect and feelings in helping the spiritual lives of our families and our friends. It is far easier to close our eyes to the evils which we might be in a position to help correct. It is much, much easier to turn away, thinking: "What do I care? It's none of my business; let him worry about it!" Yet, we know that we actually are our brother's keeper and when occasions arise where we can prudently and kindly correct an idea or situation, then we are called upon to sacrifice our feelings and our human respect to the teachings of God and His Church — for the good of our neighbor.

In our efforts to serve God sacrifices are necessarily a definite part of our daily lives. But such sacrifices can be — should be — gifts and offerings of love. For in the final analysis, *love is sacrifice and sacrifice is love.* For this, we have Our Lord's own example and His own words: *"Greater love than this no man has — that a man lay down his life for his friends."*[1]

AN OFFERING OF SACRIFICE

Most Sacred Heart of Jesus, it is for love of You, in reparation for the outrages committed against You and the Immaculate Heart of Mary, and for the conversion of sinners.

[1]St. John, 15:13

THE SAINTS

So often we are ardent baseball fans, movie fans, boxing fans, etc. We also honor and imitate our national stars quite readily. But what about our love and appreciation of our spiritual stars — the saints?

We, Catholics, have a magnificent assembly of spiritual stars. Some of these saints were great leaders. Some were heroic martyrs. Some were zealous missionaries. And some were the little, hidden ones. They are our stars — to be honored, loved and imitated. From these heroes and heroines we may obtain, just for the asking, not autographs soon lost or forgotten, but prayers and favors never to be lost.

In other times, in other countries, when the Faith was strong and fervent, people honored their national heroes but they also loved and honored the saints as their heroes.

Almost invariably, besides the names of Mary and Joseph, children were given the names of the saints on whose feast days they were born or baptized. Stories about the lives of the saints were told and re-told within the family circle. And the feast days were joyously celebrated in churches, homes and plazas. A person's patron saint became a treasured friend — one to be honored, loved and imitated. One to turn to through life and at death.

How different things are today. How many of us regard our patron saints as real friends? How much do we know about them? How often do we think of them, pray to them, seek their help in difficulties, and remember them in joys?

There are ever so many books and pamphlets designed to help us to know and love the saints. Among the recent books is *Lives of the Saints* which contains short reports on feasts of Our Lord, Our Blessed Mother and the Saints, together with a short prayer to each. It is easy to read and beautifully illustrated; available from the Lourdes Bureau, 698 Beacon Street, Boston, Massachusetts 02215; $2.95. Among the popular booklets are *God's Heroes,* available from Our Sunday Visitor Press, Huntington, Indiana 46750, 25¢ per copy; and *Is It A Saint's Name?,* containing Christian names for girls and boys, a list of patron saints, and a pertinent section on "What Parents Should Know About the Baptism of Their Children", "What God-Parents Say and Do At Baptism", and the formula for Emergency Baptism, including the formula for baptizing a fetus; available from the Lourdes Bureau, 25¢ per copy.

God has given us the saints for our veneration, our edification and our assistance. They are His heroes. They are our stars.

But, we may wonder, isn't devotion to the saints old-fashioned? Didn't the Second Vatican Council discourage devotion to the saints?

No, indeed.

The saints are still very much a part of the Church Triumphant and so, devotion to them is certainly not old-fashioned. In fact, the Vatican II document, the *Dogmatic Constitution on the Church* (50, 51) clearly states: "It is supremely fitting that we love those friends and fellow heirs of Jesus Christ, who are also our brothers and extraordinary benefactors, and that we render due thanks to God for them and suppliantly invoke them and have recourse to their prayers, their power and help in obtaining benefits from God, through His Son, Jesus Christ, Our Lord, Who is our sole redeemer and savior . . . We seek from the saints example in their way of life, fellowship in their communion and aid by their intercession."

But, we may object, we seldom have sermons about the saints or novenas in their honor anymore, so why should we pray to the saints?

Regarding sermons, these usually are pertinent to the Gospel of each Sunday's Mass, and because the feasts of saints are observed on week days, there are, indeed, few sermons about the saints.

But, many ask, since we lay people are so bombarded by the enticements of the world, couldn't we have at least an occasional sermon about a saint whose feast occurs during the coming week? We need to be encouraged and inspired by the lives, virtues and accomplishments of people who loved God and neighbor so much that they became saints. And if the names of the saints of the week were to be listed in our Sunday parish bulletins, along with the other announcements, this might be an effective incentive to encourage attendance at daily Mass, at least on an occasional feast day.

As to novenas, these are certainly being offered less and less these days but wouldn't our pastors be glad to conduct such devotions if we evidenced our cooperation by a willingness to attend in large numbers?

As some have suggested, since evening Masses are now permissible, couldn't there be occasional novenas consisting of the Mass followed by a very short — five to ten minutes — talk on a virtue or a cross endured, or an accomplishment of the saint; and then a closing prayer to him or her?

But why, many ask, are the statues being removed from more and more of our churches? Did the Second Vatican Council forbid the use of statues? If not, what started this trend and is it a good one?

Vatican II did not forbid the use of statues. Rather, its documents on this subject state: "The saints have been traditionally honored in the Church and their authentic relics and images held in veneration." *(Constitution of Sacred Liturgy,* No. 111); ". . . those decrees issued in earlier times, regarding the veneration of images of Christ, the Blessed Virgin and the Saints, are to be religiously observed." *(Dogmatic Constitution on the Church,* No. 67) "The practice of placing sacred images in churches, so that they may be venerated by the faithful, is to be firmly maintained. Nevertheless, their number should be moderate and their relative positions should reflect right order. Otherwise they may create confusion among Christian people and foster devotion of doubtful orthodoxy." *(Constitution on Sacred Liturgy,* No. 125).

The trend towards removing statues started because of several reasons. One reason is that since the Mass is the greatest prayer, the infinite sacrifice, some pastors, in their zeal to do all that they can to emphasize the center of our worship, decided to remove everything from the church, excepting that which pertains to the Mass and the Blessed Sacrament.

Whether or not this judgment is the wisest is debatable. Some pastors think not. They prefer to keep the statues in their churches. They agree that certainly the churches should not be overstocked with statues but they believe that every Catholic Church should at least honor Mary, Christ's Mother, and St. Joseph, His foster-father, as well as the parish's patron saint.

They also say that having the statue of at least one "guest" saint — especially one that is pertinent to the times or the locale — is a good idea. There are so many from which to choose.

Wouldn't, they point out, a statue of St. Martin de Porres, who spent his life assisting both Blacks and Whites, remind us of the necessity of tolerance, justice and kindness? or a statue of St. Maria Goretti be a reminder that, no matter what the devil or the world promote, the fact remains that purity is a virtue to be fostered and defended at all costs? or a statue of St. Therese remind us that God doesn't demand great accomplishments from us but, rather, that we spend each day in doing the best that we can to please Him, to obey Him? And wouldn't a statue of one of our American saints — St. Frances Cabrini who established many hospitals and orphanages and who expended her fragile strength in loving service to the sick, the old, and the poor in the slums of New York, Chicago and other cities; or St. Isaac Jogues who worked so tirelessly for the spiritual and physical welfare of the Indians in the upper New York area, and who endured terrible sufferings which finally ended in his heroic martyrdom; or St. Elizabeth Seton, the courageous widow who became an exemplary Religious, foundress of the first native community of nuns, the American Sisters of Charity, at Emmitsburg, Maryland, of the first American parish school, and of the first American Catholic orphanage — be a reminder of the zeal, love, courage and sacrifice with which they served God and neighbor?

And, some suggest, along with the "guest" statue, perhaps it might be helpful to have available leaflets or cards relating a short sketch of the saint's life, as well as a prayer to him or her — so that the purpose of the statues would become more meaningful.

A second reason for removing statues is because their presence sometimes causes distractions during the celebration of the Mass. That is, in some places while Mass is being offered, some people completely ignore the Holy Sacrifice and "go-bobbing" along the sides of the church, lighting candles before the statues. And so, thinking to avoid this problem, some pastors remove all statues.

Again, the wisdom of this decision is debatable. Many argue that it is up to local pastors to educate their people regarding the meaning and the importance of the Mass, explaining to them the difference between the Mass and other devotions, so that their people will appreciate and love the Mass and will no longer "go running around" the church during the time of Mass.

A third reason why some pastors remove the statues is in order to appease non-Catholics who may disapprove the presence of statues.

Again, the wisdom of this decision is questionable. Some pastors refute this, saying that any non-Catholic who has ever attended a Catholic funeral or wedding or a novena, mission or retreat, has seen for himself that Catholics adore no one but God. Other non-Catholics who are interested enough to ask questions or read Catholic publications, also learn this truth for themselves. And as to those who are stubbornly opinionated, these, they say, will still think whatever they wish about our devotion to the saints — regardless of whether or not there are statues in our churches.

Some also remark that since both Catholics and non-Catholics honor national heroes and world renowned artists, authors and scientists by having pictures or statues of Washington, Lincoln, Kennedy, Shakespeare, Pasteur, Michaelangelo, etc. in our schools and institutions — often placing plants and flowers before these objects — then surely, non-Catholics can understand why Catholic churches honor God's heroes by statues.

Actually, whether our churches have statues or do not have statues, the fact remains that the saints are a part of the Catholic Church, the Church Triumphant. They are people who loved and served God to a heroic degree — so much so, that they have been given the highest tribute by Christ's Church. And so, they are our "heavenly stars" — saints for us to imitate and to have as special friends who graciously pray to God in our behalf.

Recommended Leaflets:

GO TO JOSEPH! God predestined Joseph to be the head of the Holy Family, the protector of Jesus and Mary. The Church honors him as patron of the universal Church, of the family, of the worker, and of the dying. Next to Our Blessed Mother, there is no greater saint.

GO TO JOSEPH! is an interesting leaflet, designed to help us understand and appreciate this wonderful saint. Copies are available from the Sacred Heart Center, 6026 West Harwood Avenue, Orlando, Florida 32811; 20 copies for $1.00.

"*Saint of the Month Letter*" — a short, easily read life of a selected saint, sent out each month; available from Father Mario, O. Carm., Carmelite Missions, Darien, Illinois 60559; no fee is expected although, if possible, a donation for the foreign missions is appreciated.

SATAN vs. CHRIST

Satan is the avowed enemy of the Sacred Heart of Jesus. Christ taught love; Satan teaches hatred. Christ preached truth; Satan teaches deceit. Christ's way of life brings joy and peace; Satan's way brings evil, despair and destruction.

Since Satan is such a formidable enemy of Our Lord, he is also the enemy of all Christians. And so, our spiritual advisors warn us, we should recognize the malice of the Devil and be alert to his deceitful treachery.

Time was when one of Satan's most clever tricks was to keep us unaware of the fact that he is a real, existing demon. So effective was this strategy that modern paganism laughingly pushed aside the truth about Lucifer's existence and banished him into the realm of myths and old-wives' tales.

The failure to recognize the existence of Satan and the malice of sin led to the intensification of evil to such an extent that we are now inundated not only with the widespread and flagrant breaking of God's laws but also with *direct* attacks against God Himself: Satanism.

Satanism and witchcraft are now practiced in many large cities and small communities, in Satanic clubs, on campuses, and even among teens. The prevalence of Satanic bibles, books, records and films is appalling. And it is public knowledge that the theft of consecrated Hosts, for use in the worship of Satan through the celebration of horrible "Black Masses" occurs frequently.

It is noteworthy that on June 29, 1972, the Holy Father, Pope Paul VI, stated something that many have suspected, namely, that Satan is greatly responsible for the widespread confusion, uncertainty, doubt and dissatisfaction that followed the Second Vatican Council. Here are his words: "It was believed that after the Council there would be a day of sunshine in the history of the Church. There came instead a day of clouds, storm and darkness, of search and uncertainty.

"This came about through an adverse power; his name is the Devil . . . We believe it is some preternatural thing which has come into the world precisely to disturb, to suffocate the fruits of the ecumenical council." He also said that he had the feeling that "by means of some fissure, the smoke of Satan has entered the temple of God."

On November 15, 1972, Pope Paul gave his second talk on Satan and his influence on "individual persons, communities, whole societies and events." The Holy Father began by asking this question: "What are the greatest needs of the Church today? Do not let our answer surprise you as being over simple or unreal; one of the greatest needs is defense from the evil that is called the Devil . . . it is not a question of one Devil, but of many . . . But the principal one is Satan, which means the adversary, the enemy . . ."

Satan's mission is one of hatred — hatred for God, souls and all that is sacred, pure and holy. Christ's mission, on the contrary, is one of love for all souls — tender, merciful, overwhelming love. To St. Margaret Mary and to other chosen souls, Jesus promised that the love of His Most Sacred Heart will triumph over the hatred of Satan.

Our Blessed Lord knew that the hatred which would be rampant in these evil days could best be conquered by a practical form of spirituality which would inspire a return of solid love manifested by trust, sacrifice, reparation, Eucharistic piety and apostolic zeal — a spirituality that could be practiced by everyone in all walks of life, from little children to the most learned theologians.

Such a form of spirituality is to be found in the practice of devotion to the Most Sacred Heart of Jesus, as He Himself requested and taught it, and as it is approved and strongly encouraged by the Church.

In apparitions to St. Margaret Mary in 1673, 1674, 1675, in the convent of the Visitation Sisters at Paray-le-Monial, France, Our Divine Saviour revealed *His* program of sanctification and salvation: *Eucharestic practices in honor of, and in reparation to His Sacred Heart.*

On June 16, 1675 as St. Margaret Mary knelt in prayer before the exposed Blessed Sacrament, Our Lord showed her His Heart and said: *"Behold this Heart so deeply in love with men that It spared no means of proof — wearing Itself out until It was utterly spent! This meets with scant appreciation from most men; all that I receive in return is ingratitude. Witness their irreverence, their sacrileges, their coldness and contempt for Me in this Sacrement of Love. What hurts Me most is that hearts dedicated to My service behave in this way.*

"That is why I am asking you to have the Friday after the Octave of Corpus Christi set apart as a special Feast in honor of My Sacred Heart — a day on which to receive Me in Holy Communion, and make a solemn act of reparation for the indignities I have received in the Blessed Sacrament while exposed on the altars of the world. I promise you, too, that I shall open My Heart to all who honor Me in this way, and who get others to do the same. They will feel in all its fullness the power of My love."

In other apparitions Our Lord asked for reparation, including the practice of the First Friday Devotion and He promised very great favors to those who complied with His requests.

The reason for these extraordinary revelations was given to us by Our Lord, Himself, when He told the saint — and us — that this devotion is as a final effort of His love which wishes to favor men in these last centuries with this loving redemption, in order to withdraw them from the empire of Satan which He intends to destroy, and to replace it with the reign of His love and thus, through His grace, to bring many souls to eternal salvation.

The revelations were officially approved by the Church after thorough and exhaustive study. The favored nun lived to see devotion to the Sacred

Heart practiced throughout the world and, as Our Lord had foretold, those who first opposed it became its most zealous promoters. The feast of the Sacred Heart, specifically requested by Our Lord, was authorized for the universal Church on August 23, 1856. And Sister Margaret Mary Alcoque, to whom the revelations were made, was canonized on May 13, 1920.

Succeeding pontiffs encouraged devotion to the Sacred Heart and various pertinent encyclicals have been issued, including the magnificient *Haurietis Aquas* which traces the devotion from its roots in the Old Testament to its development in the New Testament. And on February 6, 1965 Pope Paul VI issued his apostolic letter *The Unfathomable Riches of Christ,* commemorating the 200th anniversary of the feast of the Sacred Heart and encouraging the spread of devotion "to the Heart wounded for love of us."

The Devil has a most intense fear of this devotion because of the salvation of the multitude of souls which it affects. And so he strives to downgrade and block the Sacred Heart devotion, because he knows something that many Catholics ignore, namely, that *Jesus' plan in revealing this devotion was to destroy the reign of Satan and to replace it with His reign of love.*

Why, then, are we — priests, religious, laity — not more alert, more zealous in carrying out the requests of the Sacred Heart and the recommendations of His Vicars?

One of the reasons may be because too many of us have such a superficial knowledge of what Christ actually said and requested in His revelations to St. Margaret Mary. We could increase our knowledge by reading such pertinent books as the *Autobiography of St. Margaret Mary* ($2.00); *Jesus King of Love* ($3.00); the *Enthronement of the Sacred Heart* ($3.00); *Honestly, Have You Tried Everything?* ($1.25); and *Shields Against Satan* ($1.00); all available from the Sacred Heart Center, 6026 West Harwood Avenue, Orlando, Florida 32811.

At the time of our Baptism, our sponsors, speaking for us, renounced "Satan and all his pomps and works." Then, at the time of our First Communion, we renewed this renunication. Today, when it seems that Satan is winning on all sides, in his efforts to destroy souls, we have the distinct challenge to combat Satan and his works by fulfilling — and getting others to fulfill — the requests of the loving, merciful Sacred Heart.

There may be difficulties, contradictions and opposition in promoting doctrinal devotion to the Heart of Jesus; but in the letters and writings of St. Margaret Mary, there are many and repeated statements of encouragement for us all: to priests that they would be able to convert even the most hardened hearts; to religious, that He would protect their communities so that they would not fail; and to families, that He would protect them in all their necessities and unite broken families.

We also have the magnificent assurance of Our Lord's promise: *"Fear nothing, I will reign despite all opposition, I will reign despite Satan, despite my enemies."*

PROMISES OF THE SACRED HEART OF JESUS TO SAINT MARGARET MARY ALACOQUE

I will give them all the graces necessary for their state of life.

I will establish peace in their families.

I will bless every house in which the picture of My Heart shall be exposed and honored.

I will console them in all their difficulties.

I will be their refuge during life and especially at the hour of death.

I will shed abundant blessings upon all their undertakings.

Sinners shall find in My Heart a fountain and boundless ocean of mercy.

Tepid souls shall become fervent.

Fervent souls shall rise speedily to great perfection.

I will give to priests the power of touching the hardest hearts.

I will grant My charity to all those religious communities in which My image is honored; I will turn away from them My just anger and will restore them to My grace if they should have the misfortune to fall into sin.

I promise, in the excessive mercy of My Heart, that My all-powerful love will grant to all who communicate on the first Friday of the month for nine consecutive months, the grace of final penitence; they shall not die in My displeasure nor without their sacrament; My Divine Heart shall be their safe refuge in this last moment.

SENSITIVITY TRAINING PROGRAMS

The *Sensitivity Training Programs* widely in use these days are causing great havoc, especially to children and youth. This is the judgment of many competent clergymen, educators and medical leaders. Among those who have written sharp disapproval of the program is the late, distinguished Most Rev. William L. Adrian, D.D. His critique, originally published in *The Wanderer*, states in part:

". . . *Sensitivity Training* is a vast subject and goes under many names — such as group dynamics, human relations, touch groups, encounter groups — and is participated in under all sorts of circumstances: interracial, nude, marathon, sensory, meditative; by people from all walks of life: hippies, business, professional and government men and women, the socially elite, club men and women, priests, religious, church groups, and in these last years increasingly by school groups from kindergarten through college. The purpose of it, as stated by its proponents, is to make people become *more aware* of each other and of one's self — to change undesirable attitudes and behavior, and become conformed to members of the group.

"But the adversaries of *Sensitivity Training* don't see it that way. Even granted that some good effects result from it, the dangers and harm connected with it are so great that the practice cannot be justified.

"In general, one may describe *Sensitivity Training* as a form of induced hysteria or a type of brainwashing such as the North Koreans and Red Chinese used on allied prisoners captured during the Korean War. It is meant to break down norms, manners and traditional civility. But some eminent psychologists and psychiatrists have emphatically stated that *Sensitivity Training* can do infinite harm to certain people, both mentally and morally . . . As the *Chicago Tribune* critically stated: 'It can easily become, and often does, a form of group pressure and brainwashing that makes the subjects accept the lowest common denominator in morals, be vulnerable to anti-church and anti-family beliefs, destroys individuality, could lead to sexual promiscuity, creates neurotics, and reduces people to vegetables, unable to do anything but accept the group's orders.'

". . . *POPE Publications* states that 'hardly a Catholic school or youth group has remained free from the contamination of this latest devil-craft. Many priests, religious and lay teachers have absorbed it, usually at some institute — and have become transmitters, passing it along to our children and young adults, within and outside of school hours.'

"In some schools — mostly public — the superintendent recommends that all teachers take *Sensitivity Training*: sometimes it is compulsory, or a part of the parent-teacher program. Sometimes, too, the teacher gives the training unknowingly; more often it is disguised under the cloak of the regular curriculum — music, reading program, sociology, etc., so the parents won't know. Because it is often hard to detect, some parents call it 'sneaky'.

"From a Catholic viewpoint, the program is not only filled with doctrinal errors — like those in *Situation Ethics* — but it distorts the very reason for man's existence, namely, that man is immortal and created for the next world. God and the moral law are never mentioned. Man is considered only as an animal seeking to satisfy his social and sense instincts. That is why it is said to be 'non-intellectual', only 'emotional', because of the objective it seeks to achieve.

". . . Here is the principal reason why the Church condemns *Sensitivity Training:* it is opposed to almost everything that the Church stands for in youth behavior. It teaches the domination of the emotions — the passions — over right reason; self-indulgence over self-denial and self-restraint; indecision for certainty; permissiveness over obedience to authority — parental, civic and ecclesiastic — and hence, tends to lawlessness and disruption of family life.

". . . Even more pernicious is the rejection by *Sensitivity Training* of the supernatural; it recognizes no fixed moral law, no immortal soul; it is all animal. For example, the Church following Christ's command, insists that the virtue of chastity be taught our youth — that they be trained to be 'clean of heart', to be chaste in thought, in dress and act, that even in looking upon one of the opposite sex with evil desire, one commits adultery in his heart.

"*Sensitivity Training* encourages all sorts of thoughts and words and dress (un-dress) and touches and acts against the virtue of chastity. It is repellant to read of some of the 'encounters' that take place.

". . . So we have a program which tends to ruin, or seriously endanger, our youth — physically, mentally, morally, spiritually, and perhaps eternally.

"It makes one wonder whether the prediction made by a Chinese psychologist to an American general after the Korean War is being realized: 'Communists are going to destroy the moral character of a generation of you Americans so that your country will have nothing with which to defend itself against the Communists.'

"We know that the Communist cause is being served in many ways by groups in America — knowingly and unknowingly. So, parents, teachers, be alert! Don't be enticed into the deadly snares of *Sensitivity Training!* Fight back, as many are already doing! The salvation of our youth is worth fighting for!"

Among the pamphlets evaluating the *Sensitivity Training* program is one written by Dr. Dietrich von Hildebrand, entitled *The Superstition of Sensitivity Training,* available from *Catholics United For The Faith,* 222 North Avenue, New Rochelle, New York 10801; 25¢ per copy. This is a masterful expose' of the purpose and evils in this program. The author cautions its promoters, stating: "We can no longer overlook the grave fault of those Catholics who rave about *Sensitivity Training* and who want to introduce it into the Church. Of them, we must say either that they are so blind that they do not realize how they would thereby undermine the very foundation of Christian faith and true Christian life, or else, willingly or unwilling, they are members of a conspiracy aiming to destroy the Church from within . . ."

Dr. von Hildebrand concludes with the admonition: "Let us not be fooled . . . *Sensitivity Training* is a diabolical attack on man's nature and dignity, and especially on his vocation as a Catholic . . . It destroys dignity, spiritual freedom, veracity and moral responsibility, and it thereby undermines our life as Christians, our relation to Christ and the sanctification to which we are called . . .

"Let us fight with all our means to insure that *Sensitivity Training* never becomes a part of the education in our schools or in any religious community . . . Let us recall the words of St. Peter in his first letter (5:8-9): 'Be sober, be watchful, for your adversary the Devil, as a roaring lion, goes about seeking someone to devour. Resist him steadfast in the faith!' "

SEX EDUCATION

Do we try to counteract modern glorification of sex so continuously rammed upon our children — and us — via the pen, the airwaves and the entertainment media? Do we take the trouble to teach our children Christian attitudes toward sex, telling them that although we are children of our parents still, we are also children of God; that our bodies are precious temples of the Holy Spirit, and that immodesty and impurity defile; that the gift of sex is to be used *only* in valid marriage, and that God demands that the gift never be abused.

Do we talk to our youngsters, candidly telling them that contrary to modern promotion, the truth is that sex is not the end-all of life, the prime achievement; that in reality, although sex is an important part of marriage, still, kindness, respect, consideration, concern for one another are major ingredients for any happy marriage; and that people do not "fall in love, get married and live happily ever after", but that happiness in marriage must be worked at — often in struggles, disappointments, tears and sorrows?

Do we take the time to teach our children a little common sense, pointing out to them that if sex were the claimed end-all of life, why is it that there are so many unhappy marriages, so many divorces? Why is it that those who wander in-and-out of "marriages" or affairs are admittedly among the most unhappy of people — their lives often so miserable that they become suicides?

Do we give our children sex instructions according to the teachings of God and His Church, and adequate for their age?

Parents have the serious duty of imparting proper sex-information to their children. Concerning this, Vatican II in its document, *Declaration on Christian Education,* stated: "As they advance in years let youth be trained by a prudent and positive sexual education."

Directives regarding "prudent" education may be found in various recommendations of the Holy See issued in both writings and exhortations. Pope Pius XII, for example, in his *Allocution to Italian Mothers,* stated: ". . . Mothers, you will not fail to watch for and discern the moment in which certain unspoken questions occur to your children's minds and are troubling them. It will then be your duty to your daughters, the father's duty to your sons, carefully and delicately to unveil the truth as far as it appears necessary to give a prudent, true and Christian answer to those questions and set their minds at rest.

"If imparted by Christian parents at the proper time, in the proper measure and with proper precautions, the revelation of the mysterious and marvelous laws of life will be received by the children with reverence and gratitude. Your words, if they are wise and discreet, will prove a safeguard and a warning in the midst of temptations and corruptions which surround them."

Among recent very helpful books for this purpose is *Charity, Morality, Sex and Young People* authored by the Rev. Robert J. Fox; available at $1.95 from Our Sunday Visitor Press, Huntington, Indiana 46750; and *Sex and the Mysteries* written by John Haffert; $.95 per copy, available from the Ave Maria Institute, Washington, New Jersey 07882.

Among the popular cassettes on this subject are the *Talking Catechisms*[1] prepared by the Rev. Robert J. Fox, produced by *Parents for Orthodoxy in Parochial Education* (POPE), P.O. Box 6161, San Rafael, California 94903. These include *Christian Youth and Sex-Education* especially designed for unmarried young people, parents and teachers. The cassette is priced at $5.50 and the reel is $6.50. *The Christian Youth and Education for Marriage* cassette is directed toward young people looking forward to marriage and for couples already married and in their child-bearing years. The cassette is priced at $5.50 and the reel is $6.50. Also available is a companion book, *Looking Toward Marriage* authored by the Rev. John L. Thomas, S.J.; priced at $2.50.

Parents also have the serious duty of checking on the sex-education programs now being presented in some parishes and schools. In fact, because of today's immoral environment and recent questionable developments in this field, Pope Paul VI, in his allocution of March 31, 1971 cautioned: "There is talk of sexual education with praiseworthy pedagogical intent. But people sometimes forget some aspects of human reality, no less objective than those offered by immediate naturalistic observation, such as the necessity of modesty, the regard due to the differentiation of the two sexes, male and female, and above all, the delicacy required by the disorder of the passions introduced into every human being by original sin. All these things do indeed call for sexual education, but also for many, delicate precautions, particularly in the education of the young, and we recommend to parents and teachers a wise and timely intervention, in gradual, limpid and pure language."

The allocution ended with a discussion of the virtue of purity which should characterize every Catholic approach to this subject. Also noteworthy is the Holy Father's warning contained in a previous address, January 14, 1971, regarding the entire area of education: "It must be remembered that there are at stake moral norms which cannot be jettisoned. The Church has her own tradition from which the new guidelines for the schools and the new pedagogical experience may not depart."

The important questions therefore are: Do we give our children sex instructions according to the teachings of God and His Church, and adequate for their age? Do we permit our children to attend sex-instruction programs in school, when we know nothing about such programs? Some of these are presented with far from proper Christian attitudes. In fact, they are decidedly paganistic, using deplorable pictures and texts, and slides so despicable as to be unmentionable.

Among these is the devastating program, *SIECUS* (Sexual Information and Education Council of the United States). One of the first of the hierarchy to recognize and condemn the *SIECUS* program was the late, revered Most Rev. William Adrian, D.D. who repeatedly warned that it is "capable of destroying the moral fibre of children and purports to dignify man's sexuality but, in fact, exploits it."

In an article entitled, *Awake, Our Children Are In Danger,* he cautioned parents to be alert to the fact that "superintendents and school boards are trying to force the *SIECUS* program into schools, from kindergarten through high school. Under the guise of Family Life Education and other like programs, these school boards get the money from the Federal Government to purchase from *SIECUS* the material needed — books, slides, recordings — to put on this sex-education program. So you are now helping to pay with your Federal tax money the most abominable program in the public schools.

"In the higher grades of the school, the students are taught methods of birth-prevention, of abortion, of behavior in pre-marital relations".

The Becoming A Person sex-education program is also judged to be objectionable by many people, both of the clergy and the laity. Among the priests who have publicly denounced this program is the Rev. Robert J. Fox. In his critique, published on April 22, 1973 in the *National Catholic Register,* Father Fox states: ". . . a demoralizing instrument which will greatly disturb our children at a very young age, and will divorce Christian doctrine and morality from the development of the authentic Christian person . . . We are headed for real trouble if this series continues to be used and spread to more schools." This critique has been reprinted in leaflet form and is available (5¢ per copy) from *POPE Publications,* P.O. Box 6161, San Rafael, California 94903.

Among the laity who have prepared a critical analysis of the *Becoming A Person Program* is Professor James Likoudis whose report states: "In its capital disregard of the theology of sexual concupiscence, this program of sex instruction is a moral danger to children . . ." The analysis, entitled *Fashioning Persons For A New Age?,* is available in pamphlet form (75¢ per copy) from Catholics United For the Faith, 222 North Avenue, New Rochelle, New York 10801.

It is noteworthy that in February, 1975 Cardinal John J. Carberry of St. Louis ruled that the *Becoming A Person* series is "theologically deficient" and ordered its withdrawal from the archdiocese's school system.

The Education in Love Program (formerly titled the Rochester Plan) is also denounced by many as being extremely objectionable. Among the authoritative statements decrying this program is that of Dr. Rhoda Lorand, PH.D., psychologist and associate professor at Long Island University and a member of the staff of the Vanderbilt Clinic of Child Psychiatry at Presbyterian Hospital in New York. Dr. Lorand warns that this program is "fundamentally the same as many others and contains dangerous errors. If this material were presented to the children by a saint, it would still overstimulate them and arouse anxiety . . . Religiously educated children suffer incomparably more than others because of the irreverent nature of the thoughts and fantasies aroused in them by this type of instruction . . . The material is grossly inappropriate at every level and shows the pervasive effect of the atmosphere created by SIECUS . . ."

Many pastors, physicians and educators repeatedly encourage parents to take a look at the sex-education programs conducted in the schools and CCD classes which their children attend. Among these forthright directives is that of Dr. Frank J. Ayd, Jr., entitled *Sex Education in School,* published in *The Catholic News,* in which he urges "parents who are interested in their child's welfare to investigate what sex instruction is being given in school.

"Ask to see the literature being used and the films being shown," he states. "Question the qualifications of sex educators. Demand to know what the true objectives of the courses are. If at all possible, attend and evaluate some of the classes on sex education. See for yourself how your child's attitudes toward human sexuality are being formed before it is too late."

Among the organizations fighting the inclusion of sex-education programs in schools, and endeavoring to enlighten parents about the dangers involved — this, on the basis of the information which they have collected on the great psychological harm being done to children by these programs — is an organization of medical men called SIECOP (Scientific Information and Educational Council of Physicians).

Since promoters of sex-education programs in schools state that the need for these courses is because children are not getting adequate instructions from their parents, then isn't the logical conclusion: *parents should be taught how to give sex instructions?* This, after all, is primarily the responsibility of the parents, not of the school.

Just as we have diocesan Pre-Marriage Courses, couldn't there also be a program especially designed to teach parents how to give their children proper sexual information?

Couldn't the talents and efforts of our educators be channeled into developing such a program, set up as a *Parents' Guidance Program?* Perhaps such a course could also include instructive help relating to other parent-children problems.

It is encouraging to note that the archdiocese of Los Angeles has established a *Christian Family Life Education Program* for parents of pupils in its Catholic School and CCD units. The objectives of this program are: 1) to assist parents in instructing their children in the Christian dimension of human sexuality: and 2) to assist in promoting communication within the family.

The program, consisting of a series of six evening sessions, is presented in centers by teams of parents selected and prepared under the direction of the archdiocese's Department of Education.

And in the archdiocese of St. Louis *Guidelines for Catholic Education in Human Sexuality* were written by a committee of teachers and parents, under the direction of the archdiocesan school department. These guidelines, issued in 1975, are used in Catholic elementary schools and in elementary parish schools of religion. Each program is determined by the individual school in consultation with parents, pastors and teachers. The *Guidelines* are not distributed for the personal use of students.

Guidelines for Catholic Education in Human Sexuality were approved by Cardinal John J. Carberry. In his Foreword the Cardinal states: "Affirmed here is the value of wisely planned education of our children in human sexuality in a context of God's law, Catholic morality and the sacredness of the power of sex.

"The guidelines present a summary of the basic concepts for a program dealing with human sexuality as well as the moral principles which are a part of all Catholic approaches to this subject.

"The greatest prudence and understanding is expected in their use. I have the fullest confidence that the guidelines will be of help to our parents, pastors and teachers in explaining human sexuality in the light of respect for human life and human relationships; of moral teaching in right and wrong; of virtue and sin; of our need for prayer, avoidance of temptation, and the need for mortification.

"Care must be taken not to develop a false or scrupulous conscience in children. Yet, one must ever remember the effects of original sin, as well as the fact that human sexuality, while a great gift of God for a noble purpose, can be misused and abused."

Lectures to help parents in understanding the *Guidelines* are conducted. The archdiocesan center also sponsors courses for teachers.

In its *Pastoral Constitution on the Church in the Modern World,* Vatican II clearly stated that the ideal place for sex-instructions is within the family: "Especially in the heart of their own families, young people should be aptly and seasonably instructed in the dignity and duty and work of married love. Trained thus in the cultivation of chastity, they will be able at a suitable age to enter a marriage of their own after an honorable courtship."

This reaffirms directives contained in various encyclicals, beginning with the *Education of the Redeemed Man* issued by Pope Pius XI in 1929, followed by a *Decree of the Holy Office,* dated March 21, 1931, forbidding sex-education programs.

The admoniton contained in the encyclical, *On Christian Education of Youth,* is of particular significance to our world today. "A very grave danger is naturalism which nowadays invades the field of education in the most delicate matter of purity of morals. Far too common is the error of those who with dangerous assurance propagate a so-called sex education, falsely imagining they can forearm youths against the dangers of sensuality by means purely natural, such as foolhardy initiation and precautionary instruction for all indiscriminately, even in public; and worse still, by exposing them at an early age to the occasions, in order to accustom them against such dangers. Such persons grievously err in refusing to recognize the inborn weakness of human nature . . ."

Proponents of sex-education programs sometimes say that such programs are necessary because "times have changed." Times have indeed changed but as Pope Paul VI delcared on September 13, 1972 in a general audience entitled *Chastity is Desired in Today's World,* we still have the same old problems. And in enumerating and condemning today's errors, he mentioned improper sex-education.

Contrary to some opinions, Vatican II made no new rules in this matter. Rather, in its *Declaration on Christian Education,* it solemnly cautioned parents to give their children "a positive and prudent sex-education". And in its *Declaration of Religious Freedom* the council stated: ". . . the rights of parents are violated if their children are forced to attend lessons or instructions which are not in agreement with their religious beliefs."

The all-important questions to be faced at this time therefore are: Can the present type of classroom sex-education programs, often presented in classes attended by girls and boys together, be regarded as in compliance with the directives of the *Magisterium?* Can they be regarded as being the recommended "positive and prudent" instructions?

Parents can prevent the introduction of immoral sex-education programs in local schools — and even obtain their abolishment — if they care enough to get together and send courteous but firm protests to their school boards, mayors, governors, senators, and even to the president.

Proper, persevering action, backed by prayers, brings the desired results; apathy brings disaster.

Recommended Reading:

Classroom Sex Education, pamphlet available from *Catholics United for the Faith,* 222 North Avenue, New Rochelle, New York 10801; 25¢ per copy.

[1]POPE also presents other *Talking Cathechisms* such as one which prepares children for the reception of Holy Communion; another which prepares young people for the reception of the Sacrament of Confirmation; one about Our Lady of the Rosary, The Mass, The Fatima Message and others.

SIN

At Fatima Our Blessed Mother said: "I have come to warn the faithful to amend their lives and to ask pardon for their sins." She also said that wars are a punishment due to sin and that we must stop offending God "already too much offended."

Unfortunately, Mary's warnings are lost to so many because the devil and the world are doing such an excellent job of destroying the very concept of sin. In fact, the idea of sin, responsibility and guilt is laughed off as non-existent and of no consequence. Evils, even the most hideous, are rationalized away and defended as being imaginary.

But, we may say, such diabolical, worldly thinking does not affect us.

Doesn't it? Are we sure that some of this thinking isn't rubbing off on us? At least somewhat?

Do we, for example, think that it doesn't matter too much if, now and then, we miss Sunday Mass or spend the day in unnecessary servile work?

Do we read salacious books or see suggestive movies, TV or plays, excusing ourselves by saying that the journalistic style is excellent, the photography magnificent, the acting superb — that modern literature and entertainment are different, that times have changed? Do we allow our children to read such books — in or out of school — and see such movies, plays or TV programs, erroneously thinking that they might as well learn "what's going-on" in the world? Do we wear immodest fashions, thinking: what's the difference, everyone is wearing them? Do we allow our children to dress immodestly?

Do we think that "getting high" on alcohol or drugs is alright as long as we don't get in too deep? After all, we say, life is a drudge and we are entitled to a few kicks, aren't we?

Do we lie or cheat or steal small items from the factory or store, telling ourselves that this is expected and everybody knows that this is going on? Do we gamble away our paycheck, knowing that our landlord, our doctor, the grocer and others will not be paid? After all, we say, they can wait; they have enough money.

Do we date the married or divorced? Is our courtship sinful? Is our married life contrary to God's commands? And do we quiet conscience with the fallacy that purity is now outmoded?

Do we disobey our parents, pastors or teachers, thinking that they are old-fashioned squares? Do we fail to teach and discipline children, saying that "they won't listen anyway"?

Is our speech irreverant or unkind? Do we spread gossip, thinking: well, it's the truth, isn't it?

Are we angry, quarrelsome, uncharitable, unforgiving — proudly judging ourselves as better than others?

The devil and the world shrug off these and other sins as nothing to be concerned about. Nothing, they say, is anyone's fault because we are the products of our heredity and our environment — of an unhappy childhood or unfair poverty or unkind discrimination. But the truth of the matter is that sin, responsibility and guilt cannot be rationalized away. In fact, when we sin we choose self-will in preference to God's Will, and so we actually are to blame for our own sins.

Regardless of the devil's and the world's attempts to hide the reality and the enormity of sin from us, we know that sin does exist and that it is the most terrible of all evils. Our sins cost Our Blessed Lord the agony of a horrible crucifixion. Our sins cost Our Blessed Mother the crushing pain of interior martyrdom. And our sins can cost us the devastating loss of God and heaven.

FORGIVE ME

Forgive me my sins, O Lord, forgive me my sins; the sins of my youth, the sins of my age; the sins of my soul; the sins of my body; my idle sins, my serious voluntary sins; the sins I know, the sins I do not know; the sins I have concealed so long and which are now hidden from my memory. I am truly sorry for every sin, mortal and venial, for all the sins of my childhood up to the present hour. I know that my sins have wounded Your Sacred Heart. O my Saviour, let me be freed from the bonds of evil through Your most bitter sufferings and death. O my Jesus, forgive and forget what I have been. Amen.

THE TEN COMMANDMENTS

(Laws given by Almighty God to guide man to happiness in this life and in the next.)

1) I AM THE LORD THY GOD: THOU SHALT NOT HAVE STRANGE GODS BEFORE ME.
   Commands: faith, hope, love and worship of God; reverence for holy things; prayer.
   Forbids: idolatry, superstition, spiritism, tempting God, sacrilege, attendance at false worship.
2) THOU SHALT NOT TAKE THE NAME OF THE LORD, THY GOD IN VAIN.
   Commands: reverence in speaking about God and holy things; the keeping of oaths and vows.
   Forbids: blasphemy, the irreverent use of God's name, speaking disrespectfully of holy things, false oaths, and the breaking of vows.
3) REMEMBER THOU KEEP HOLY THE SABBATH DAY.
   Commands: worship of God.
   Forbids: unnecessary servile work; public buying and selling.

4) HONOR THY FATHER AND MOTHER.

Commands: love, respect, obedience on the part of children; care on the part of parents for the spiritual and temporal welfare of their children; obedience to lawful civil and religious superiors.

Forbids: hatred of parents and superiors; disrespect, disobedience.

5) THOU SHALT NOT KILL.

Commands: safeguarding of one's own life and the bodily welfare of self and that of others.

Forbids: unjust killing, suicide, abortion, sterilization for the direct purpose of preventing procreation, dueling, endangering life and limb of self or others excepting for a legitimate reason, such as attempting to save one's life or that of another.

6) THOU SHALL NOT COMMIT ADULTERY.

Commands: chastity in word and deed.

Forbids: obscene speech, reading and entertainment; impure actions alone or with others, whether single or married; artificial contraception.

7) THOU SHALT NOT STEAL.

Commands: respect for the property and rights of others; the paying of just debts; paying just wages to employees; integrity in public officials.

Forbids: theft, damage to the property of others; not paying just debts; not returning found or borrowed articles; giving unjust measure or weight in selling; not paying just wages; bribery; graft; cheating; fraud; accepting stolen property; not giving an honest day's work for wages received; violation of contract.

8) THOU SHALT NOT BEAR FALSE WITNESS AGAINST THY NEIGHBOR

Commands: truthfulness, respect for the good name of others; the observance of secrecy when required.

Forbids: lying; injury to the good name of others; slander; talebearing; rash judgment; contemptuous speech; and the violation of secrecy.

9) THOU SHALL NOT COVET THY NEIGHBOR'S WIFE.

Commands: purity in thought.

Forbids: willful impure thoughts and desires.

10) THOU SHALT NOT COVET THY NEIGHBOR'S GOODS.

Commands: respect for the rights of others.

Forbids: the desire to take, to keep, or to damage the property of others.

SOULS IN PURGATORY, THE

Most of us are a kindly sort. When we hear the distressing news that someone's home has burned, we hurry over to help with food, clothing and household goods. When an accident has taken the life of a neighbor, we take care of the children and do all that we can to help those who grieve. When someone is stricken ill, we call the priest, the doctor and the ambulance.

How generous and how heroic we so often are with the living. How many sacrifices and hardships we endure for them. But how very forgetful and unconcerned we can be about the dead, even our nearest and dearest, our benefactors, our priests and religious, our teachers and doctors. How quickly we forget that some of them may be detained in Purgatory, anxiously hoping for our prayers and penances.

Purgatory, we know, is a state or process of purification for departed, repentant but imperfect souls. These souls are in Purgatory because of Divine Justice — because nothing defiled can enter heaven. They are helpless but God, in His Infinite Mercy, has ordained that we can obtain many indulgences for them through the Mass and the Sacraments; through acts of charity, prayers, penances, alms, and through the *Heroic Act*.

The Church encourages us to remember our departed ones. In fact, Vatican II in its document, the Dogmatic Constitution on the Church (#50) states: ". . . The Pilgrim Church from the first ages of the Christian religion has cultivated with great piety the memory of the dead. Because it is 'a holy and wholesome thought to pray for the dead that they may be loosed from sins', the Church has also offered prayers for them."

Saints Augustine, Vincent Ferrar, Francis de Sales, Bridgit and other saints have also reminded us of the sufferings in Purgatory and of the importance of our prayers for the Poor Souls.

Knowing this, how very strange it is that we can be so forgetful of the Souls in Purgatory, especially when there is so very much that we can do for them.

Of course, the very best that we can do for them is to have the Holy Sacrifice of the Mass celebrated for them and to assist at Masses for the relief and release of suffering souls. We may also make the same daily intention for all the Masses to be celebrated through the world each day.

Among the recommended "little" prayers which we — even the most busy — may offer each day, and often each day, are:

PRAYER FOR THE POOR SOULS

Eternal rest grant to the Poor Souls in Purgatory, O Lord; and let perpetual light shine upon them. May the souls of all the faithful departed, through the mercy of God, rest in peace.
May Jesus have mercy on all dying sinners, Amen.

PRAYER TO THE POOR SOULS

O Holy Souls, which have passed from this world into Purgatory, and who are awaited in heaven, pray for us and ask for all the graces which we need, and which we beg of the Divine Majesty.

Other prayers may be found in various leaflets, including *Prayers for the Dead,* available from the Apostolate of Christian Action, P.O. Box 24, Fresno, California 93707; 5¢ each; $4.00 per 100 copies; $30.00 per 1,000 copies.

And, if we wish, we could offer the *Heroic Act for the Souls in Purgatory.* This is a completely unselfish offering to God of the satisfactory value of one's prayers and good works, as well as the prayers and good works which will be offered for us after our own death, for the benefit of the Poor Souls. This is not a vow, but rather, a simple personal act which does *not* oblige under pain of mortal sin and which can be revoked at will. Its actual ratification depends on the will of God. This *Heroic Act* has been blessed by many popes who have granted special indulgences to those who make it. For example, by it, priests may gain a plenary indulgence each time that they offer Mass for a deceased; and by it, lay people may gain a plenary indulgence for the Souls in Purgatory at every Holy Communion received.

The *Heroic Act* may be made without using any particular formula. It is sufficient to have the intention and to make it from the heart. However, a formula of offering which can be repeated occasionally is useful, especially because it increases zeal for the relief of the souls in Purgatory by prayer, penance and good works. Such a formula is as follows:

Holy and Adorable Trinity! Desiring to cooperate in the deliverance of the souls in purgatory, and to testify my devotion to the Blessed Virgin Mary, I cede and renounce in behalf of those holy souls all the satisfactory part of my works, and all the suffrages which may be given to me after my death, consigning them entirely into the hands of the most Blessed Virgin, that she may apply them according to her good pleasure to those souls of the faithful departed whom she desires to deliver from their sufferings. Deign, O my God, to accept and bless this offering which I make to you at this moment. Amen.

The *Heroic Act* does not subject us to the consequences of having to undergo a long Purgatory ourselves. Rather, it allows us to rely with greater assurance and confidence on the mercy of God in our own regard, for God is never outdone in generosity.

Prayers for the dead are an excellent form of charity especially since the Souls in Purgatory are not in a position to help themselves. Throughout the ages saints and pontiffs have often encouraged the clergy and the laity to pray for the dead. And many of our contemporary spiritual directors now caution us not to forget such prayers, particularly because all too often little emphasis is placed upon the need to remember the dead by our prayers and sacrifices.

The Rev. John M. Dougherty, S.S., for example, in his column, *Thoughts from Sunday's Mass,* recently stated: ". . . The beautiful Masses for the faithful departed underscore two fundamental characteristics: one is the happy message of the bodily resurrection of those who have died in Christ; one day they will rise from the grave, with their risen bodies glorified and made like the glorified Risen Body of Christ. The other is this: the Masses are filled with deep compassion and concern for the Poor Souls, and they contain numerous magnificent prayers for their liberation from their sufferings and for their entrance into heaven. Perhaps, the latter is being neglected in our liturgy and our funeral homilies, in our times, and the former unduly emphasized. Those who have departed in the friendship and grace of Christ are assured of a glorious resurrection on the Last Day. So why overstress this in the liturgy? Is it for the consolation and comfort of the bereaved? Certainly, such emphasis will not help the souls in Purgatory, or the one or ones whose funeral Mass is being offered. What they need is our prayers, and more prayers of petition should be said for them, and more appeals for prayers made for them in the pulpit during their funeral Mass and at the cemetery following the Mass."

Of concern to a great many people is the fact that in many places, the Rosary is no longer prayed at wakes. Although the Psalm Card now being used — sometimes exclusively — certainly presents meritorious prayers, still countless people prefer that the Rosary be prayed.

They base their preference on the fact that the Rosary was treasured by the deceased during life and it should therefore be prayed for him or her in death; that the Rosary is an officially approved and highly recommended devotion; and that a plenary indulgence is granted upon praying the Rosary in *common.*

People further state that the sympathetic atmosphere of a wake is conducive for non-Catholics to follow along with the prayers of the Rosary; also, that more non-Catholics are beginning to understand and appreciate the Rosary, especially since they have learned about this devotion from the recent Rosary book, *Five for Sorrow: Ten for Joy,* written by a Methodist minister and theologian, the Rev. J. Neville Ward.

Many Catholics therefore see no reason why the Rosary should be dropped from prayers at wakes and they are happy to hear that there is now available a beautiful *Rosary Card for Wakes* which presents a courteous invitation to non-Catholics to join us in the prayers of the Rosary offered for the deceased. (see chapter on the Rosary). Anyone or any group interested in the use of this special card at their local mortuaries may obtain further information by contacting the Sacred Heart Center, 6026 West Harwood Avenue, Orlando, Florida 32811.

The Souls in Purgatory implore our charitable assistance. We, the *Church Militant,* through our prayers, penances and alms, can lessen their sufferings. By responding to their need, we are privileged to gain their grateful, reciprocal prayers.

We are indeed blessed and fortunate to belong to the *Communion of the Saints.*

Recommended Reading:

The Church Suffering: Theology and Visions on Purgatory. This presents as good an idea as possible in this life of what Purgatory is and how it should affect our lives. This booklet's presentation is one of hope and resolution, not of depression. Available from the Rev. Charles Kovari, S.J., 6765 State Road, Parma, Ohio 44134; $1.00 per copy.

SPEECH

Everyone is talking about Ed. So he finally left Margie . . . Well!

We just can't wait to tell the bridge club about it. Why not? After all, it is true, isn't it?

Even so, Ed and Margie have a right to their good name and their reputation and we have no business spreading the gossip — true or false.

The other day while we were at the garage, Jack came in. And after he left, the mechanic said: "He is quite a guy."

But we do not particularly like Jack so instead of agreeing or saying nothing, we can't resist answering: "Yes, but he drinks too much."

That little word, but, — it can be quite devastating. Couldn't we watch it and let it ring a warning stop signal to our thoughts and our words?

This morning Evelyn stopped by. Dejected and in tears, she confided a crushing mother-in-law problem. Then before she left, she asked that we please keep the matter secret.

We agreed and we intended to keep the secret but this afternoon at the neighborly get-together, Evelyn did not show up. And when the others remarked about her absence, we just could not keep still.

Couldn't we?

At the office coffee-break someone runs down an absent employee. Do we join in? Do we agree by our silence? (Willing listeners share in a speaker's guilt). Or do we say something in the man's defense and then steer the conversation to other things?

And what about our telephone chats? Are they friendly calls or just occasions for idle talk, groundless rumor, inneundos, insinuations, gossip?

A pertinent question: what would we have done in circumstances similar to those which we are chatting about? Better? Worse? Much worse? . . . We are reminded of Our Lord's warning: "Judge not, lest you be judged!"

Even though we may not be guilty of grave detraction or calumny, still our petty criticism and gossip chip away at the person's integrity and destroy friendship. And if the "facts" that we relate are actually *not* facts, then we must repair the injustice done, we must restore the person's good name.

Unfortunately, this is not always possible since the few to whom we spoke may have spread "the facts" to a few more, and more, and more. Therefore, wouldn't it be far better, far easier, far safer to have kept silence in the first place?

And what about our careless remarks, often made in the presence of children, detracting from the esteem which should be given to relatives, pastors, teachers, policemen and other authorities? Such remarks tend to destroy children's confidence in their advice and proferred assistance, thus often resulting in serious loss of good.

Bla, bla, bla — — so it goes, day after day. Why? Have we become so callous, so blase', that we no longer care whom we hurt?

Have we forgotten the virtue: say something good or nothing at all?

And have we forgotten that telling lies is also sinful, an offense against God's eighth commandment? It is interesting to note that not only have saints — St. James[1], for example — cautioned us in this matter, but so have such distinguished Americans as President Thomas Jefferson who on August 19, 1785 stated: "He who permits himself to tell a lie once finds it much easier to do it a second and third time, till at length it becomes habitual; he tells lies without intending to do it, and truths without the world's believing him. This falsehood of the tongue leads to that of the heart, and in time depraves all its good dispositions."

And what about God's second commandment; "*Thou shalt not take the Name of the Lord thy God in vain*"? Taking the Holy Name of God in vain has become shockingly universal these days, even among young children. Too often we hear such expressions as God, but I'm tired; God, it's hot; by God, you will do your homework or else, etc. And the use of God's name in vain on TV and radio programs — to say nothing of its use in books and magazines — is commonplace.

Defenders of this flagrant offense sometimes claim that the seriousness of the matter is minimized because the practice has become a habit. But the truth of the matter is that whether the offense is by habit, deliberation, ignorance or stupidity, the end result is the same: the Lord's Name is taken in vain and the majesty of God is outraged.

The gravity of this offense was emphasized by Our Lady of La Salette in 1846 in France. At the time, when the two shepherd children, Melanie and Maximin, witnessed Mary weeping, she told them that her tears were caused by the sins of cursing, swearing and of working on Sundays. She also warned of the punishments that would come upon France and upon the world, if these practices continued.

Corrections of the abuse of God's Name should, of course, begin with self and family. And we could certainly voice our objections to radio and TV officials. And, if we wish, we could also cooperate in the efforts of the *Apostolate to Honor God's Name,* originated by Peter Chilelli and sponsored by the *Fatima Chapter of Lay Carmilites,* 63 Garland Drive, Eggertsville, New York 14226. This apostolate encourages people to offer reparation, especially through the Mass, Holy Hours, Visits, and Rosaries. It advocates praying "*Blessed be the Name of God; Blessed be the Name of Jesus*!" — either silently or loud enough to attract the attention of the speaker — each time that a person hears God's Name used in vain. It also distributes small, attractively printed cards stating, "*You Should Not Use God's Name in Vain*", and "*Love and Respect the Holy Name of God,* please!" The cards are suitable for placing in stores, restaurants, taverns, plants, garages, etc. — always with the permission of the owner or manager, of course. Experience has indicated that about ninety-five percent of these officials are willing to cooperate and do keep the cards on display.

Through this simple program, attention is drawn to the plea which Christ Himself offered in His prayer: *"Our Father, Who art in heaven, hallowed be Thy Name . . ."*

And we Catholics are reminded to ask ourselves: how can idle gossip, malicious gossip, unkind remarks, uncharitable insinuations, angry, bitter words, harsh judgments, lying, half-truths giving distorted or biased interpretations, impure conversations, the use of God's Name in vain, blasphemy, cursing, swearing be such a common part of our speech, especially since they are uttered by the same tongue upon which Our Blessed Lord rests when we receive Him in Holy Communion?

[1]Epistle of St. James, the Apostle, Chapters 1, 2, 3.

SPIRITUAL READING

Too often, spiritual reading is not a part of our daily life. Yet, such reading is very important. In fact, many spiritual advisors tell us that there is little chance of living spiritually without spiritual reading.

What, then, shall we read?

The most important of all spiritual reading is the Bible. In these sacred writings we become acquainted with Our Blessed Lord. We hear His words. We see His sanctity. His love and His compassion shine forth from the inspired pages. The more we read the Bible, the more we learn to know Christ.

Our spiritual directors recommend that we read the Bible regularly. Vatican II directives repeat this recommendation. Its document, *Revelations* (25) clearly states:

". . . This sacred Synod earnestly and specifically urges all the Christian faithful, especially religious, to learn by frequent reading of Sacred Scriptures the 'excelling knowledge of Jesus Christ.' (Phil. 3:8). 'For ignorance of the Scriptures is ignorance of Christ.' (St. Jerome)."

It is also noteworthy that the revised *Raccolta* — an official compendium of indulgenced prayers and good works — gives significant mention to the reading of the Bible, stating that a plenary indulgence may be gained, *daily,* for at least a half-hour's reading.

A unique, beautiful Bible is *The Bible in Pictures: Great Masters Edition,* particularly suitable for children and for parents who wish to explain the New and Old Testaments to their children. Its text is noteworthy for its clarity and simplicity and its 1,000-plus illustrations and colored prints make the Bible live. Teachers will also find it fascinating and helpful. This exceptional Bible, 300 pages, has a lovely white and gold hardback binding and is available at $13.80 postpaid from the National Catholic Register Book Dept., 86 Riverside Drive, New York, New York 10024.

We are also reminded that if we are to gain from our reading of the Scriptures or other spiritual books, we should read with a desire to grow in the love of God and of our neighbor. And so, before we begin our reading we should offer a prayer to the Holy Spirit for His guidance and His blessing.

Besides the Bible there are a great many interesting books which bring inspiration, tranquillity and a deepening of the love of God and of neighbor.

There are the classics such as the *Imitation of Christ* by Thomas A. Kempis; *Jesus, King of Love* by the Rev. Mateo Boevey-Crawley, SS. C.C.; and the *Introduction to a Devout Life* by St. Francis de Sales; and the various books about the life of Christ. Among the books relating to the life of Our Blessed Mother is *The City of God,* a complete history of her life, as told by Mary, herself, to a Franciscan nun, Mother Mary of

Jesus. (The author has been declared Venerabilis by the Church and her writings have been declared free from error. Her body is preserved incorrupt at Agreda, Spain.) On April 29, 1929 Pope Pius XI granted the Apostolic Benediction to all its readers and promoters. *The City of God* is available in a complete edition of four volumes at $27.00, an abridged edition at $8.00, and as Daily Rosary Meditations (a three volume set) at $3.50, through Catholic bookstores and from various apostolates such as the *Apostolate of Christian Action,* P.O. Box 24, Fresno, California 93707.

There are also many interesting books about Our Lady's apparitions at Guadalupe, Lourdes, La Salette, Fatima and Beauraing; about the lives of the saints, the Mass, the Sacraments, prayer, liturgical works, the encyclicals, theology for the laity, the spiritual life and the apostolic life; and books about various Catholic subjects, efforts, autobiographies, biographies, conversions, family life, religious life and mission life.

Our pastors and spiritual directors are willing to help us plan a program of spiritual reading. Book lists from our Catholic book clubs, schools and information centers are readily available, also.

Of course, we say, there are certainly many and varied Catholic books but we just do not have the time for spiritual reading.

Really? Isn't it a fact that we have the time, or take the time, to read whatever we want to read — the popular magazines, the digests and the current best-sellers?

It is interesting to note that besides our spiritual advisors, many distinguished statesmen and scholars have alerted us to the importance of, and the necessity of, spiritual reading. Daniel Webster, for example, cautioned:

> "If religious books are not widely circulated among the masses in this country, and the people do not become religious, I do not know what is to become of us as a nation. And the thought is one to cause solemn reflections on the part of every patriot and Christian. *If truth be not diffused, error will be; if God and His Word are not known and received, the devil and his works will gain the ascendancy;* if the evangelical volume does not reach every hamlet, the pages of a corrupt and licentious literature will; if the power of the Gospel is not felt through the length and breadth of the land, then anarchy and misrule, degradation and misery, corruption and darkness, will reign without mitigation or end."

Sadly, we now see that his warning is all too applicable in our times.

Our Catholicity is not just something to be practiced in Church. Rather, it is a complete way of life. Daily spiritual reading helps us to learn, to appreciate and to practice our Faith so that we may really come to "know God, love Him and serve Him in this life, and then to be happy with Him forever in Heaven."

STEALING

We would be appalled and highly insulted if we were ever accused of stealing. The very idea, we would think.

Granted that we may not be thieves or robbers, but what about shoplifting? Are we among the thousands of self-styled "respectable" people who regard store-pilfering as something to which we are entitled, defending this vice by such specious excuses as: this store sometimes gives me short weight; or this shop's prices are too high; or this chain of supermarkets makes millions; or everybody picks up some "little" things?

If we indulge in this something-for-nothing policy or brag about padding expense accounts or cheating on income taxes, etc., is it any wonder that our youth caught stealing fail to show regret or even an awareness that they have committed a sin, a criminal act? Our own good example and sound religious training could do much to fortify youth from joining the expanding "pilfering crowd".

Reliable sources indicate that about eighty percent of all apprehended shoplifters are under eighteen and of these, only ten percent are from families on relief or suffering from unemployment. Youths, fifteen through seventeen, have the highest arrest rate and one out of every six are referred to a juvenile court before their eighteenth birthday.

Although the need to obtain alcohol or drugs is recognized as an increasing motive for stealing, still much of the shoplifting occurs because youth simply do not realize that it is a crime. Many, who would not dream of stealing money, will take merchandise without giving it a second thought. Often they steal just because they are restless and bored. And sometimes they admit that shoplifting is just a game between themselves and clerks — "just for kicks."

According to F.B.I. information, shoplifting is the fastest growing form of larceny in the United States, occurring every forty-five seconds, and resulting in an estimated nationwide loss of ten million dollars a day.

Parents are advised: "If your son or daughter has stolen merchandise, see to it that he returns it. Do not close your eyes to shoplifting because if you do, you consent to the theft."

To avoid this problem, the *National Retail Merchants Association* offers this *advice to parents:*

1. Be sure children understand that shoplifting is a crime which can result in criminal records, jail sentences, and the impairment of future education and careers.

2. Do not let a child hang around shopping centers or department stores.

3. Know how much money your children have and how they spend it. Know where their belongings and any additional clothes come from.

4. Emphasize that it is more "chicken" to go along with the crowd than to refuse to pilfer.

5. Set a good example by respecting the property rights and the privacy of others — including those of your children.

6. If charges should be pressed against a juvenile shoplifter, get a lawyer before entering a plea.

Perhaps neither we nor our children are shoplifters but are we always perfectly honest and fair in our dealings with others, about the rights and the property of others? For example, when a clerk gives us too much change, do we acknowledge it and give the money back?

Are we careful to return library books or anything else which we may borrow? And in good condition?

Are we always late in paying our bills, thus inconveniencing our creditors?

Do we cheat in exams? At school or at work do we dishonestly blame others for mistakes, causing them to lose honors, promotions or raises? Do we take credit for accomplishments which are not due us?

Do we start or spread gossip, thus robbing someone of his good name and reputation?

During vacation or business trips, do we "collect" souvenirs: spoons, towels, Bibles, etc. (If we want these things, we are supposed to ask for them and pay for them. The loss of such items to hotels, cafes, etc. runs into thousands of dollars, annually.)

As employees, do we give a good day's work for a good day's pay? Do we take unfair advantage of sick-leave benefits, lunch hours or coffee breaks? Do we pad expense accounts? Do we help ourselves to stamps, pencils, etc. from the office or bring home something from the store or business?

As employers, do we pay an honest wage — what our workers deserve and need? Do we go along with unfair trade practices or do we promote integrity? If we need sound advice about the morality of a transaction, do we seek it?

Do we apply for relief or accept it when we do not need it?

Do we overstate losses or expenses on tax returns, insurance claims, etc.?

Have we made restitution in full for past infractions of justice?

Do we prefer to be honest, even to the point of losing a gain or taking a loss? Or do we go along with the crowd, excusing ourselves by saying: everybody is doing it?

Maybe they are. Even so, God expects us to be honest and just. His command, *Thou shalt not steal,* applies to us all, at all times, in all things.

SUFFERING

We live within the shadow of the cross, for suffering and sorrow are always close by in our own lives or in the lives of our dear ones. Sickness, misfortunes, failures, mental troubles and anguish of the heart — how they darken our lives.

Of course, we may — and should — do whatever is possible to alleviate physical pain, to correct frustrating situations, and to eliminate mental suffering. However, our spiritual directors remind us that it is impossible to avoid *all* suffering and so it is of utmost importance that we — and our youth — learn to accept suffering and other trials with patience, with serenity, and with trust in God's love and mercy.

This may be a difficult lesson to learn — and teach — but it is worth the effort because impatience, complaint and/or revolt simply irritate suffering and increase it immeasurably. Spiritual advisers tell us that probably the best way to learn how to suffer is to gaze upon the crucifix. A minute a day, spent in contemplating the crucified Christ often leads to understanding and peaceful acceptance of trials.

The help of God is available to anyone, at anytime, through humble, persevering prayer. When God gives, or permits, suffering He either grants a cure at the right time or He gives the strength necessary to bear pain, of whatever kind, if only we trustfully ask Him.

But, we may question, why does God allow us to suffer? Because, our spiritual fathers point out, God asks us to share in His sufferings and in the sacrifice of His life for us.

We know that suffering and sorrow were present in the lives of Jesus, Mary and Joseph. In fact, Their lives were lives of *voluntary* suffering — lives of loving sacrifice for us. And so, in our own sufferings and sorrows we can turn to Them for guidance and comfort.

They know what it is like to be poor and to be forced to flee from Their own country. They know how it feels to be insulted, betrayed, hated and persecuted. They know the sadness of ingratitude, the agony of physical and mental pain, and the sorrows of bereavement. Suffering was certainly no stranger to the Holy Family. Neither can it be for any of us.

Pain and sorrow can be a loss or a profit, depending upon our attitude. We can give way to discouragement and self-pity, becoming so aware of our own personal problems that nothing else seems to matter. Or we can accept suffering in patience and humility, rise above it, and make it a gift of love and confidence — an offering, united with Christ's sufferings, for the salvation of souls, for the needs of the Church, and for the welfare of all mankind.

Of inestimable assistance in this regard is membership — open to both the clergy and laity — in any of the Church's fine apostolates for the sick, the handicapped and the infirm. Among these are the *Apostolate of Suffering* and the *Catholic Union of the Sick in America*.

The purpose of both organizations is to assist the sick and the afflicted by helping them to understand that their lives are very important: *that God has chosen them for a special vocation — that their sufferings, prayers, and resignation ascend to God as powerful weapons needed to back up the work of priests and religious, to obtain conversions, to aid the dying, to relieve the Souls in Purgatory, and to make reparation for their own sins and the sins of all mankind.* Thus, in the acceptance and offering of pain, illness is not looked upon as a misfortune, but rather, as a true vocation.

The *Apostolate of Suffering* (1501 South Layton Blvd., Milwaukee, Wisconsin 53215) was founded in 1926 by the late Cardinal Aloysius Muench and Clara M. Tiry. The Rev. Msgr. Alphonse S. Popek, M.A., J.C.D., serves as its spiritual director. It is a Pious Union placed under the protection of the Sacred Heart of Jesus and Our Lady, Health of the Sick. Its patroness is St. Lidwina of Schiedam, Holland, who suffered excruciating pain for thirty-eight years.

Membership is open to the sick, the physically handicapped, the mentally defective, invalids, incurables, and those, who though able to work, are afflicted with some disease, ailment or infirmity which causes suffering. Men and women, priests and religious, young and old, are eligible as members.

Enrollment is made by sending name and address to the apostolate's headquarters. Obligations consist of resolving to accept all suffering in harmony with the holy designs of God and in bearing them in a spirit of Christian resignation; offering all suffering for the intentions of the apostolate (this does not exclude personal intentions); and praying the apostolate's *Daily Prayer* with fervor and love.

The apostolate sends its quarterly, *Our Good Samaritan,* which contains articles of interest to the sick and which promotes their spiritual welfare, to both members and patrons (annual subscription, $1.00).

Also available is the book, *Comfort for the Sick,* authored by Clara M. Tiry. The book is aptly titled for it is, indeed, a comfort for the sick, as well as inspiring reading for their families and for those who serve the sick. Chaplains and hospital personnel also find it to be a useful means of encouraging the sick. It is a welcome addition to any home or parish library. *Comfort for the Sick* may be ordered at $1.25 per copy, postpaid, from the apostolate's center.

The *Catholic Union of the Sick in America* developed through the efforts of the late Louis Peyrot. While he was a patient in a sanatarium in Switzerland he organized a group of suffering Catholics whose purpose was to help and encourage each other through friendly group letters, but essentially as brothers and sisters in Christ, sharing in His redemptive suffering.

The plan spread quickly through Europe, Canada and the United States. In America the apostolate was inaugurated in 1947 and was placed under the patronage of the Immaculate Heart of Mary. Its foundress was the late Mrs. Robert Brunner, assisted by Jerry Filan. The Rev. Josph Lamontagne, S.S.S., serves as its administrative leader. Headquarters are at 184 East 76th Street, New York, New York 10021.

Requirements for membership are that a person must be a practicing Catholic and must be in a state of health which offers the occasion for sacrifice.

To apply for membership it is necessary to send the apostolate a letter giving name, address, age, condition of health, and special interest, if any. Because the *Catholic Union of the Sick in America* issues a magazine, circulars, bulletins and mailing envelopes, etc., yearly dues are placed at five dollars for those who can take care of this expense. Otherwise, the dues requirement is gladly waived. No one is ever denied membership because of a lack of funds. Membership is also available in a number of special groups such as in an Adolescence Group, a Braille Group and a Tapes Group.

Each group consists of eight members with a leader, a liaison officer and a chaplain. Members correspond with one another through a group letter, a little booklet in which each one writes, according to the order on the mailing list. The leader begins the letter, the liaison officer writes in the middle, and the chaplain ends the letter so that he can answer everyone. Then the group letter goes back to the leader and another round is started.

In these group letters the members tell each other about their interests, their problems, anxieties, disappointments, etc. They give each other their prayers and encouragement. They compassionate each other's sufferings and they rejoice with each other's joys. They discuss things of general interest, too, such as a new book, a point of Faith, etc.

No special writing talent is needed. The group letters are just simple letters in which members talk to each other about "this and that". When the letter is answered, it is mailed to the next person on the list. Special envelopes are provided for mailing the group letters and extra stamps are attached to the mailing list, so as to be available for anyone needing them.

Pope Paul VI has granted his blessing to both apostolates and members share in numerous Masses, in the prayers of the Divine Office, and in other prayers. Members also share in each other's prayers and in the merits of the good works which they perform according to the spirit of the apostolate.

Added to these benefits are the special blessings received from the loving, merciful Heart of Christ, for when these chosen ones bring their tears, prayers and suffering to Him, they are answering His invitation: *"Come to Me, all you who labor or are burdened and I will refresh you."*

The apostles, the saints, our pontiffs and spiritual fathers have always encouraged us to make suffering profitable. Among such teachings is that of St. Peter. In his first epistle from Rome, Christ's chosen Vicar tells us to be positive in our thinking; to remember how much we have been blessed; and to give thanks to God that we are His children, destined for an eternity of happiness with Him in heaven.

And from St. Francis de Sales we have the encouraging reminder:

> "Do not look forward to what might happen tomorrow; the same Everlasting Father who cares for you today will take care of you tomorrow and every day. Either He will shield you from suffering or He will give you unfailing strength to bear it. Be at peace, then, and put aside all anxious thoughts and imaginations."

Pain and sorrow are often God's way of drawing us to Him. And although trials may be hard to accept or understand, still, if we trust in God, believing in His Divine Providence — His loving care for each one of us — then the weight of the cross becomes lighter. In this way our love of God is strengthened and perfected. In this way we surrender our wills to God's Will and we prove that we love Him for His own sake.

And when pain, sorrow and trials are over for us, God, Who is never outdone in generosity, will Himself be the reward of our sufferings. He will be there to lift us from the shadow of the Cross.

JESUS, HELP ME[1]

In every need let me come to You with humble trust, saying,

Jesus, help me!

In all my doubts, perplexities and temptations,

Jesus, help me!

In hours of loneliness, weariness and trials,

Jesus, help me!

In the failure of my plans and hopes; in disappointments, troubles and sorrows,

Jesus, help me!

When my heart is cast down by failure, at seeing no good come from my efforts,

Jesus, help me!

When others fail me, and Your grace alone can assist me,

Jesus, help me!

When I throw myself on Your tender love as Father and Savior,

Jesus, help me!

When I feel impatient and my cross irritates me,

Jesus, help me!

When sickness and loneliness overcome me,

Jesus, help me!

Always, in weakness, falls and shortcomings of every kind,

Jesus, help me!

[1]Copies of this prayer are available from the Benedictine Convent of Perpetual Adoration at Clyde, Missouri, 64432; 1¢ each; $1.00 per hundred, plus postage.

SUNDAY

It is Sunday afternoon. In our community and in thousands of similar places, most of us seem to be very busy. We have just finished painting the garage. Our neighbor is hanging a large wash. Across the street, Bill is washing and polishing his car. And a few doors down, Ed and Dorothy are digging and planting a garden.

So this is Sunday? What has happened to the reverent observance of Sunday and our obedience to the Third Commandment?

True, we have been to Mass this morning but have we forgotten that the worship of God on Sunday, although the most important part, is not the only part of the Sunday commandment? Have we forgotten that unnecessary servile work is forbidden?

No, we have not forgotten but everybody works on Sunday now-a-days. Besides, we just did not have the time to paint or to wash, etc. during the week.

Really?

Although "everybody" may be abusing the Sunday command, still that does not mean that we are entitled to follow the crowd. And as for time, we did have a day off during the week, we played golf twice, went to a picnic, and just lolled around the house other evenings. Now, on Sunday, we "just have to" paint or wash or clean or work at something.

Do we? Why the compulsion for doing chores on Sunday? Couldn't the work be done tomorrow or the next day or the next?

Isn't it true that we have the duty not only to refrain from unnecessary servile work on Sundays and holy days of obligation, but also to give good example so as to encourage a trend back to the observance of Sunday rest?

And what about unnecessary buying and selling on Sunday? Just because our community supermarket is open all day on Sunday, does this mean that we are allowed to let our shopping slide during the week, knowing that we can get it done on Sunday? Far from it. In fact, we could also try to do something constructive toward eliminating current Sunday buying and selling by registering complaints and withdrawing patronage from firms and stores which insist on Sunday sales, as a matter of policy.

Like all the commandments, the Third Commandment, *Remember to keep holy the Lord's Day . . . thou shalt do no work on it, thou nor thy son, nor thy daughter, nor thy manservant, nor thy maidservant, nor thy beast, nor the stranger that is within thy gates,*[1] is a law of God which everyone is bound to respect and obey.

For Catholics, the worship aspect of this commandment means participation at the Holy Sacrifice of the Mass. Regardless of shadowy rumors to the contrary, attendance at Mass is still mandatory.

A Catholic goes to Mass, first of all, to offer God love, adoration and reparation — to offer Him the most perfect of all prayers the unbloody sacrifice of the Cross.

We also go to Mass to thank God for His manifold graces and favors and to beseech His blessings upon our own needs and intentions, as well as those of others.

There, in the presence of God, the complexities of the world are simplified and brought into proper perspective. There, we receive the grace, strength, courage, love and zeal to live as His faithful sons and daughters.

The Mass is the very heart of Catholic worship. It is the most priceless of all the treasures which have come to us from the Giver of every good and perfect gift.

It is therefore our inestimable privilege to participate at Sunday (and daily) Mass. And it is our duty to refrain from unnecessary servile work so that the day which was sanctified by the Holy Trinity — the Father began creation on this day; the Son arose from the dead on Easter Sunday; and the Holy Spirit descended upon the apostles on Pentecost Sunday — may be a day of joy: to worship God; to rest our minds and bodies; and to strengthen family unity and love.

SUNDAY CODE FOR CATHOLICS[2]

I

I will acknowledge that the essential work of the Lord's Day is the worship of God through the devout offering of the Holy Sacrifice of the Mass. Therefore:

I will spend Saturday evening in a way that will prepare me worthily for the special blessings of the Lord's Day.

I will arrive on time for Sunday Mass.

I will devoutly fulfill my role, co-offering the Mass with the priest, joining the congregation in dialogue or sung Mass.

I will adopt as my general practice the reception of the Holy Eucharist each Sunday.

I will attempt to foster deeper family unity through Sunday family worship.

I will support the Church in every way in which my talents and my resources can advance the cause of Christ.

II

I will seek that rest and relaxation that befits the Lord's Day. Therefore:

I will not perform any unnecessary servile work.

I will not do any unnecessary buying, selling, or shopping on Sunday.

I will use the leisure of this day to deepen my knowledge of my faith through mature Catholic reading and meditation.

I will seek to strengthen, within the family circle, the bonds of Christian family life and love.

III

I will remember that my practice of this code will lead others to a fitting observance of the Lord's Day.

[1]Exodus, 20:10

[2]Compiled by the New York Professional Sodality, 980 Park Avenue, New York, N.Y. 10028. (Reprinted by permission).

SUPERNATURAL CLASSES AND LITERATURE

Are the teens in the high schools or colleges of our locality taking courses on *Literature of the Supernatural?* If so, have we examined the text books covering these courses? If not, we should!

Perhaps we have glanced through the books and they seem to contain an impressive array of sections from the *Bible* and such classics as Dante's *Inferno* or Goethe's *Faust,* or Milton's *Paradise Lost* and/or the works of *Shakespeare,* all quite respectable. However, the terrible fact of the matter is that the study and promotion of *Satanism* is often included in these courses.

Apart from the supernatural aspects involved, these courses are known to be psychologically injurious and pedagogically unsound.

Not too long ago such classes were taught in just a few places. Unfortunately, however, the study has gained rapid momentum and is now offored in many schools and colleges in big cities and small towns.

Clergymen of many faiths, as well as concerned professors, psychiatrists and parents denounce the courses and warn against the dangers involved. Among these is the Rev. John W. Mole, O.M.I., editor of *Christian Communications* and founder of the Institute of Social Communications at St. Paul University, Ottawa, Canada. In a statement made to the editors of *Immaculata* magazine, Father Mole cautions:

". . . The problem in introducing such a course, even though it incudes such beautiful works of literature as Dante's *Inferno,* Shakespeare, etc., is that the originators of the courses are taking their subject matter out of the context in which it was placed, thus making the occult an end in itself.

"The motivation for introducing courses such as *Literature of the Supernatural* at this time seems to be due in no small measure to so much current interest in the occult, such as Satanism, witchcraft, ouija boards, etc. But this interest is obviously obsessive. Our society, and in particular our youth, are obsessively fascinated with these phenomena, just as they are fascinated in an obsessive way with sex and drugs.

". . . The proper context to treat of devils, witches and the supernatural would be in a theological course. But this cannot be, for the teachers and administrators know well that they can not teach theology in the public school system of America, which is a pluralistic and secularistic society.

"So what do they do? They isolate these subjects from their proper theological context and put them into what they call a literature course, not realizing perhaps that by isolating them from their proper context they make them objects of obsession. Any obsession is harmful, as the word implies. Many youth already have an obsessive interest in the occult. Such a course will merely intensify their obsession. Pedagogically, it is an enormous mistake.

". . . The defenders of the course, *Literature of the Supernatural,* say:

'We must trust the integrity of the teachers and the maturity of the students.' But if young people are subject to an obsessive experience, it is not a question of integrity; it is rather a pathological problem.

"In regard to the youth having sufficient maturity to deal with a course on the occult, one can very well ask: 'Who has sufficient maturity to deal with this subject of Satanism without adverse effects?' A great deal of prudence and caution is necessary. Even a trained theologian has to enter into this subject, which exposes one to satanic influence, with a great deal of humility and must be a man of deep faith and prayer. No one is so mature that he can go into such a course without exposing himself to the real danger of diabolic possession or obsession . . ."

What can be done to prevent these courses from being inaugurated and/or continued in the schools in our locality?

Prayer, protest and cooperation — these are the ingredients used by those who care enough to fight for God and youth.

To cite just one example: in Kenosha, Wisconsin the people found, to their great dismay, that a course in occultism had been introduced in one of their public high schools and would soon be started in the other school. Their concern led them to the decision to "fight" for the elimination of this course.

Numerous holy hours of adoration and reparation were offered before Jesus in the Blessed Sacrament, as well as many prayers, especially to the Holy Spirit for guidance; to the Blessed Virgin Mary, she who is destined by God to "crush the head of the Serpent"; to St. Joseph, the head of the Holy Family and patron of the Church; and to St. Michael, the Archangel who led the battle which defeated Satan and the rebellious angels.

A committee of citizens issued a newsletter alerting parents and clergymen. An open meeting was held, well attended by people of various denominations. The majority were opposed to such courses — especially since one of the teachers admitted that the study included an element of witchcraft and occultism. Later, a group known as the *Kenosha County Clergy Association,* comprised of Catholic and non-Catholic clergymen, invited the school administrators to a meeting at which they presented their constructive criticisms and objections.

The current widespread promotion of Satanism and occultism in schools, in literature and by other means, gives very special significance to the admonition made by Blessed Maximilian Kolbe,[1] the priest martyred by the Nazi on August 14, 1941 in the concentration camp at Auschwitz. "Modern times," he warned, "are dominated by Satan and will be more so in the future. The conflict with hell cannot be engaged by men, even the most clever. The Immaculata alone has from God the promise of victory over Satan. However, assumed into heaven, the Mother of God now requires our cooperation. She seeks souls who will consecrate themselves entirely to her, who will become, in her hands, effective instruments for the defeat of Satan and the spreading of God's kingdom upon earth."

PRAYER TO ST. MICHAEL, THE ARCHANGEL

St. Michael, the archangel, defend us in the battle; be our protector against the malice and snares of Satan. May God restrain him, we humbly pray, and do thou, prince of the heavenly host, by the power of God, cast into hell Satan and the other evil spirits who go about in this world, seeking the ruins of souls. Amen.

Recommended Reading:

A Notebook on the Devil and Exorcism; $1.00 per copy; and the *Youth for the Immaculata and Tarcisian Kit;* 50¢; both available from the Marytown Press.

Shields Against Satan by the Rev. Francis Larkin, SS. CC.; emphasizes the fact that the Hearts of Jesus and Mary are our defense against the rise of satanism; our fortress of faith and love; our means of security and peace; $1.00 per copy (discounts on quantity orders); available from the Sacred Heart Center, 6026 West Harwood Ave., Orlando, Florida 32811.

[1] A very interesting and inspiring autobiography of Blessed Kolbe, entitled The Death Camp Proved Him Real; paperback, 95¢; is available from the Marytown Press, 8000 39th Avenue, Kenosha, Wisconsin 53141.

THIRD ORDERS

From the days of childhood most of us have been taught that it is true wisdom to aim high — to reach for the top. Whether the striving is toward success in sports, music, art, business, education or science, we are taught to seek perfection.

And in the spiritual life we are also taught to aim for perfection. This is the perfect wisdom of Christ, Himself, Who said: *"Be perfect, even as your Heavenly Father is perfect."* (Matthew 5:48) And this is the counseling given us through the teachings of the Catholic Church.

Among the means of striving for spiritual perfection is membership in one of the secular branches — the *Third Order* — of the Church's great monastic Orders. Such memberships offer spiritual affiliation with a chosen Order and monastery. Members share, in life and in death, in the spiritual treasures of the Order.

Third Orders began in the early centuries of Christianity when devout lay people associated themselves with their monasteries. They generally lived nearby and as their time and circumstances permitted, they entered into the spirit, the prayer and the work of the monastery. The Church has set her approval on these memberships, and in a certain sense, the affiliation makes one a member of the chosen monastic family. Not only do members share in the prayers and good works of the Order, but they receive inspiration for leading a more perfect life in the world.

Membership in the Third Order of any of the monastic Orders follows, more or less, the same general pattern toward perfection. For example, a person who wishes to affiliate himself with the Carmelite Order strives to live in the spirit of the Order's purpose: "to adhere to God by a continual and loving dwelling in His Presence and to serve Him faithfully with a pure heart and a good conscience in honor of, and out of love for, the Blessed Virgin Mary."

Membership in the Lay Carmelites is open to practicing Catholic lay people and to secular priests.[1] Candidates attend at least four orientation meetings and then upon approval of the unit's chaplain, are received as probationary members for a period of one year. During this time the new members attend regular meetings and study the Carmelite Rule. At the completion of this period, candidates make their profession accepting the Carmelite way of life, and the Order thereby accepts their spiritual commitment.

The purpose of the Lay Carmelite is to live the spirit of the Gospel in the world. His life is therefore aimed at witnessing Christian values in his temporal affairs: to seek God's Will in every event; to see Christ in everyone, friend or stranger; and to make correct judgments about temporal things.

The success of this living union with Christ evolves from an intensified spiritual life and so Lay Carmelites are encouraged to be faithful to the following practices:

a) daily Mass and Holy Communion, whenever possible;
b) the practice of the Presence of God;
c) daily reflective prayer according to individual choice, such as the Little Office of the Blessed Virgin, the Short Breviary, the Divine Office or the meditative Rosary;
d) frequent reading of Sacred Scripture and the study of Catholic doctrine, the encyclicals and the documents of Vatican II;
e) the Morning Offering and the evening examination of conscience;
f) attendance at Lay Carmelite meetings;
g) a yearly retreat or suitable substitution such as a parish mission.

Since the Carmelite Order has always been especially dedicated to the Blessed Virgin Mary, Lay Carmelites honor Mary particularly by:

a) devoutly wearing the Brown Scapular[2] and distributing and explaining it;
b) placing in their home a blessed image of Our Lady of Mt. Carmel;
c) celebrating the chief feasts of Mary, especially the solemn commemoration of the feast of Our Lady of Mt. Carmel on July 16th; also the feasts of the major protectors of the Order: St. Joseph, and Archangel Gabriel, St. Joachim and St. Anne;
d) praying at least five decades of the Rosary daily, while meditating on its mysteries;
e) promoting Communions of Reparation and Consecration to the Immaculate Heart of Mary on the First Saturdays of each month;
f) including in the monthly meeting a special Marian form of prayer such as a Marian Bible Service, the Litany of Loreto, etc.;
g) practicing the apostolate of Aylesford with the prayer: *Mary, use me this day.*

The Lay Carmelite's endeavors to sanctify self leads him to the Church's apostolic aim: the evangelization and sanctification of mankind. And so, cooperating with the hierarchy, he involves himself in spiritual and corporal works of mercy in parish, civic, cultural, ecumenical, economic and social activities in order to penetrate these spheres with truly Christian principles.

Lay Carmelites realize that the perfect example of this type of spiritual and apostolic life is the Blessed Virgin Mary, Queen of Apostles. And so, following the directives of Vatican II as particularly expressed in the *Decree on the Apostolate of the Laity,* Chapter I, No. 4, they "devoutly venerate Mary and commend their life and their apostolate to her motherly care."

A cordial invitation to membership in the Lay Carmelites or in any of the Church's Third Orders is open to any practicing Catholic. Would we care to become affiliated?

[1]Detailed information for membership and/or establishing local units may be obtained by contacting the Aylesford Carmelite Center at Cass Avenue North at Rt. 66, Westmont, Illinois 60559

[2]See the Index

THE TRUTH

These days we hear and read so many disturbing and confusing statements falsely attributed as advocated by the *aggiornamento.* However, if we stop, look and listen to what Pope John XXIII and Pope Paul VI and the Fathers of Vatican II actually said, we will see that the tenets of our Faith are still on the solid rock of Peter.

Christ's Vicars and the Council Fathers of Christ's Church have explicitly and repeatedly stated that the purpose of Vatican II was — and is — self renewal (each one of us); the safeguarding of the Deposit of Faith; and the carrying out of Christ's command to bring this Faith to all nations.

This renewal is not found in, nor carried out, by the dissenters, the downgraders and the rebellious, nor by turbulent publicity, nor by the spread of misconceptions and false teachings. Rather, these impede the renewal, obstruct true ecumenism, and weaken the good effects of *bona fide* changes.

Pope Paul VI has repeatedly warned us about this danger. On September 1, 1971, for example, in a discourse given to a general audience, he stated: ". . . He who thinks he can remain a Christian by his own efforts, deserting the institutional bonds of the visible and hierarchical Church, or who imagines he can remain faithful to the mind of Christ by fashioning for himself a Church conceived according to his own ideas, is on the wrong track, and deceives himself. He compromises and perhaps ruptures, and makes others rupture, real communion with the People of God, losing the pledge of its promises."

The official changes — those authorized by the *magisterium* of the Church — in the structure of the Mass, in the use of the vernacular, in the simplified form of the Sacraments, etc., are all designed to help us more fully understand and take part in the liturgy of the Church; to increase our faith, hope and charity; and to encourage us to strive for greater holiness and a greater concern for the needs of others and the problems of the missions.

These official changes are all within the authority and the competence of the Church. However, the all-important point — the point too often obscured and misrepresented — is that *nothing essential in faith or morals has changed.* No new doctrine was defined by Vatican II, nor has any been defined since. So if there is *any new doctrine* in faith or morals promoted today, it is *false doctrine.* The Catholic Church is infallible in its teaching on matters of faith and morals, and indefectible in its duration. So the pre-Vatican II teaching of the Church is just as valid today as it was then.

Pope Paul VI — repeatedly and especially in his *Credo*[2] — has made it perfectly clear that in all matters of doctrine and morality, the Church stands exactly where she has stood for centuries:

> The Church is still the one, true Fold. The Pope is still the infallible Vicar of Christ. Our Lord is still truly present in the Holy Eucharist. He still continues His Sacrifice of Calvary in Holy Mass. The Sacraments are still channels of grace. The Church still loves and honors Mary and wishes her to be loved and honored. We still believe in Purgatory and pray for the dead. We still honor and pray to the Angels and the Saints. Private prayer, the Rosary, and other approved devotions and sacramentals are still highly recommended. The moral law is still summarized in the Ten Commandments. And we still dread hell and look forward to heaven.

Commemorating the fifth anniversary of the close of the Second Vatican Council, Pope Paul VI issued an exhortation dated December 8, 1970, calling upon the bishops of the world to reaffirm authentic Catholic teaching.

Reminding them of their "grave and urgent duty" to transmit the Faith in its entirety and to proclaim the essential doctrines of Catholicism, the Holy Father specifically mentioned "the Trinitarian and Christological dogmas, the mystery of the Holy Eucharist and the Real Presence, the Church as the institution of salvation, the priestly ministry in the midst of the People of God, the value of the Sacraments and prayer, and the moral requirements concerning, for instance, the indissolubility of marriage and the respect for life."

The papal message noted two trends adversely affecting the contemporary Church: silence in the matter of attacks on traditional teaching and a tendency to reconstruct religion from science rather than from revelation.

The Holy Father called upon each bishop, synod, and episcopal conference to be careful that their teaching never betray "the truth and continuity of the teaching of the Faith."

In spite of this exhortation and the clear teachings of the Church, loud and strident voices of the dissenters, the rebellious and the downgraders continue to beat against us insisting that there is a new way, an easy way, an individual way to Christ's peace and love. They insist that we are living in a new era with a "new morality" which permits anything in the name of "love" and expediency.

The truth is that the "new morality" is neither new nor morality.

It is not new because it is a mode of living already experienced in past centuries, recorded in the Bible and by history, and often severely punished by God. It is the same way of life which caused the downfall of the Roman Empire and most certainly can cause the ruin of any nation, including our own. Therefore, it is *not* new.

Neither is it morality. In fact, it is not morality at all because morality is a code of ethics or duties by which man controls his thoughts, his words and his actions; but in the advocated "new morality" there is no control, no duties, no responsibility. There is nothing except one's own desires, as one wishes, how one wishes, and when one wishes. And so, the "new morality" is actually no morality.

Above the clamoring din of the dissenters, the rebellious, the downgraders and the prophets of the "new morality", we hear the kind and authoritative voice of Christ's divinely appointed Vicar telling us, over and over again, to renew our personal lives, to stand firm with the teachings of Christ and His Church. And we hear the loving compassionate voice of Christ's Mother warning us — at Fatima just a few months before the rise of communism and the spread of worldwide evil — that the formula for true love and peace is the same as that taught by Christ Himself: obedience to God's commandments attained, not in any new, easy, popular way, but only through daily prayer, sacrifice and the practice of humility, charity, justice, purity, patience, prudence and temperance.

Countless voices may continue to loudly cry: peace, peace, love, love; but the only voices which can teach us the true way to enduring peace and love are the voices of Christ, His Blessed Mother and His Vicar on earth.

Recommended Reading:

Renewal for All God's People by Rev. Robert J. Fox; available from Our Sunday Visitor Press, Noll Plaza, Huntington, Indiana 46750; paperback $2.50. This important book offers hope, renewed Faith, and a balanced view of doctrines and disciplines of the Catholic Church.

[1]*The Credo of the People of God* by Pope Paul VI is available in booklet form at 15¢ per copy, (discounts for quantity orders) from Our Sunday Visitor Press, Huntington, Indiana 46750.

THE VIRTUES

Getting-by in school, at work, and in various other circumstances seems to be such a prevalent attitude these days. Unfortunately, the same attitude sometimes affects our spiritual life, also. So much so, that we think that aiming for perfection is for the saints — not for us, ordinary people.

Yet we know that our Blessed Lord asked that we be perfect and in His moving Sermon on the Mountain[1] He stressed the importance of the practice of virtue.

The *Beatitudes* He spoke of teach us about the virtues necessary for the happiness of our minds, hearts and souls. They are the power which bring us to serenity and holiness. Among these virtues are:

Humility — which forgets self and self-interest in the interests of God and neighbor;

Obedience — which helps us place first things first and to bow to the Commandments and to the duties of our particular state in life;

Purity — which brings tranquility, self-respect and reverence for our bodies, the temples of the Holy Spirit.

Faith and Confidence — which teach us that we are all God's children whom He loves and in whom He is vitally interested;

Fortitude — which gives us the courage to stand up for God and the things of God, even though we may have to stand alone, against the crowd.

Charity — which makes us kind, patient, tolerant, understanding and forgiving. *Charity* — which makes us love God above all things and our neighbors as ourselves, so that everything else falls into its proper place — into the happiness of inner peace, contentment and joy even in adversity.

To achieve virtue — to grow daily in holiness — is not easy. We know very well that of ourselves, it cannot be done. But with the help of God, it can be done. It must be done.

An effective means of assisting us in striving for this holiness is the virtue of *Fear of the Lord.* In fact, the Book of Proverbs (1:7) says: "the fear of the Lord is the beginning of wisdom." And our spiritual fathers often remind us that in these times of secular humanism, this virtue is of special importance. It serves as a warning against the sophisticated fallacy, advanced by the devil and the world, that sin does not exist and that "anything goes". It helps us realize that we cannot deny the reality of the future life and the responsibility for our transgressions.

But, we may object, in these post-Vatican II times, isn't fear of the Lord supposed to be replaced by love?

No. Actually, fear of the Lord is a most efficacious means of developing true and enduring love of God and neighbor.

Although — primarily and ideally — we should certainly try to please and serve God because God loves us and desires our good and our eternal happiness, still a healthy fear of eternal punishment is often a very effective means of restraining from sin and of obtaining conversion. And so, the virtue of fear of the Lord is not to be belittled.

Saints and popes have often spoken forcibly about the necessity of recognizing the existence of hell. Pope Pius XII, for example, cogently reminded preachers that "sermons on the primary truths of the Faith and on our last ends, far from ceasing to be opportune, have become more than ever necessary and urgent, even sermons on hell. Certainly, the subject should be treated in a dignified and prudent manner; but as regards the substance of this truth, the Church is under a solemn obligation, before God and before men, to preach it and to teach it, without attempts to water it down, in just the way that it was revealed by Christ. No present-day circumstances can lessen the force of this obligation. It binds in conscience every priest to whom, in the ordinary or extraordinary ministry, has been entrusted the task of instructing, warning, and guiding the faithful."

In the years since the reign of Pope Pius XII secularism has made deeper and deeper inroads into our culture — so much so that his successors, John XXIII and Paul VI, have often found it necessary to repeatedly warn us of the reality of sin, its malice, its disastrous consequences, the existence of Satan and hell, and the necessity for the cultivation of virtue.

Fear of the Lord leads to a deeper awareness that the Holy Spirit — ever present in our souls unless we cast Him out by mortal sin — gives us the necessary graces to conquer our faults and imperfections, to balance and strengthen our vacillating wills.

His sevenfold gifts — wisdom, knowledge, understanding, counsel, fortitude, piety and fear of the Lord — strengthen our faith, hope and charity. They direct and guide us in our decisions, vocations and endeavors. They fortify us in our daily struggles against the world, the flesh and the devil. They assist us to withstand misunderstandings, unjust criticisms, sufferings and sorrows. And they help us to become loving, adoring, prayerful, obedient, trusting children of Our Father in heaven.

During long, hard working days; during weeks, months and years of trials and sufferings; and during the endless monotony of daily duty, what a grace it is to know that a simple turning of our minds to the presence of the Holy Spirit within us can lift us from the depths of discouragement, failure, sadness and despair. God within us is the Light which brings joy to our spirits and the courage, wisdom and understanding to go forward along the way to heaven — not dully and listlessly — but with hope, vigor and zeal.

And so, as the Church teaches, we should give the Holy Spirit an honored place in our daily lives. We should remember that our bodies are

His living temples and we should turn to Him often, praying:

> Holy Spirit, beloved of my soul, I adore You. Enlighten me, guide me, strengthen me, console me. Tell me what I should do. Give me Your orders. I promise to submit myself to all that You desire of me, and I accept all that You permit to happen to me. Let me only know Your Will.[2]

If we do this, our lives will be serene, even in problems, crosses and suffering, and we will advance in the practice of virtue.

Then, though the devil and the world put up a tremendous fight to make us forget the purpose of life, though confusion and error are spread all around us, we will remain steadfast to Christ's unchanging teaching: *"Thou shall love the Lord, thy God, with thy whole heart and with thy whole soul and with thy whole mind and with thy whole strength . . . Thou shall love thy neighbor as thyself."*[3]

PRAYER FOR CHARITY

Grant, O Lord, that every moment of this day in all my dealings with others, I may keep in mind Your words: "Whatsoever you do to one of them, you do it unto Me."

Grant that I may regulate all my dealings with others according to your command: "Love one another as I have loved You."

Grant that I may think of them as You think of them and of me;

Grant that I may feel towards them as You feel towards them and me;

Grant that I may speak to them and of them as You would, were You in my place;

Grant that I may consider it a privilege not to be ministered unto, but to minister;

Grant that I may seek opportunities of doing for others in a kindly, humble way — seeing You and serving You in them.

Place in my mind Your thoughts; in my heart Your love; on my lips Your words that I may learn to love others as you love me.

Recommended Reading:

The Way: this book is called the modern *Imitation of Christ;* over a million copies have been printed in 28 languages; it has also been brailled; (available from the Franciscan Marytown Press, 8000 39th Ave., Kenosha, Wisconsin; 53141; $3.50 hardcover; 95¢ paperback.)

[1]St. Matthew, 5,6,7

[2]From the *Book of Devotions to the Holy Spirit published by the Pious Union in Honor of the Holy Spirit,* 262 Blackstone Boulevard, Providence, Rhode Island 02906. (The purpose of this society is to foster and spread devotion to the Holy Spirit. There are no annual dues. One dollar covers life membership and the Book of Devotions.)

[3]St. Matthew 22: 37-39

VISITS AND HOLY HOURS

Now and then as we read or hear the gospels, perhaps we may think how wonderful it would have been to have lived during the time of Christ's Presence on earth.

Surely, when we heard that Our Lord was on His way to our city, we would have hurried to the gates of the town to meet and welcome Him. We would have brought our little ones to Him for His blessing, our suffering ones to be healed. And we would have followed Him to other towns, too — eager to be with Him and to hear His words.

So we think. And yet, it is a startling truth that all too often we forget that Our Lord is truly in our midst, here and now. The Christ Who lived in Palestine is the same Christ Who lives in the Blessed Sacrament in the tabernacles of our Catholic churches. He is always there, day and night, waiting for our visits, ready to listen to our troubles, to bless and guide us, to give us His graces. And yet, how often we forget this.

Christ tolerates the indifferent ones who pass Him by without a greeting; the tepid ones who come to Him without love; and the sacrilegious ones who profane Him. Couldn't we take a little time, every now and then — or even daily — to visit Him, to offer reparation for these ungrateful ones? And couldn't we interest our families and others in praying holy hours?

Among the popular books and booklets designed to help us pray fruitful Holy Hours are the following items:

Twenty Holy Hours by Father Mateo Crawley-Boevey, S.S. C.C.; contains one for each First Friday and others for special occasions; paperback, $3.00; available from the Sacred Heart Center, 6026 West Harwood Avenue, Orlando, Florida 32811; *Could You Watch One Hour With Me?*, published by the Soul Assurance Apostolate, P.O. Box 1632, Chicago, Illinois 60690; 75¢ per copy; *Holy Hour With Mary*, available from Montfort Publications, 40 South Saxon Ave., Bay Shore, New York 11706; 25¢ each; and *Jesus and I* (Prayers for use at Youth Holy Hours) obtainable from Precious Blood Monastery, 135 Keyes Avenue, Watertown, New York 13601; 25¢ each.

Together, couldn't we start an adoration program in our parish? At least for First Fridays and First Saturdays? An adoration program is not a difficult task to set in motion. All that is necessary are prayers asking for God's blessing upon the project and cooperation between priests and people. (A free kit of instructions for starting parish adoration programs is available from the Adoration Apostolate, Marytown, 8000 — 39th Avenue, Kenosha, Wisconsin 53141).

Many parishes which started with First Friday and First Saturday adoration programs have since extended their adoration to every day; and some parishes, to every day and night.

The graces and blessings received from such programs are remarkable.

Besides personal favors which people report, pastors relate an increase in attendance at daily Mass, in conversions, in vocations, and in a far better spirit of cooperation within the parish.

Perhaps our parish might also be interested in All-Night Vigils of Adoration and Reparation, such as those conducted at St. Peter' Church in downtown Chicago by the *Ambassadors of Mary* with the co-operation of the *Men of the Sacred Heart*, the *Blue Army of Our Lady of Fatima*, the *Legion of Mary* and other apostolates. These are held on the vigils of special feast days such as the Kingship of Christ, the Queenship of Mary, New Year's Eve, etc. The attendance at each vigil ranges between 500 and 800 people from all walks in life.

These nights of prayer begin at 8 P.M. with the Holy Sacrifice of the Mass and Exposition of the Blessed Sacrament. The Holy Hours are interspersed, in an orderly manner, with Scripture services, homilies, hymns, the Rosary and other prayers prayed in common. Benediction ends the Holy Hours and the All-Night Vigil concludes at 6 A.M. with the celebration of another Mass.

Further information, including a detailed schedule of the program, may be obtained by writing to the *Ambassadors of Mary* at 5851 West Madison Street, Chicago, Illinois 60644. Also available is an inspiring story of people who participate in all-night vigils of loving prayer before Our Lord in the Blessed Sacrament. The book, which also contains meditations, is entitled *Night of Love* and may be ordered from the Ave Maria Institute at Washington, New Jersey 07882; $2.50 per copy.

But, we may ask, shouldn't we be more concerned about stressing the liturgy rather than promoting adoration programs? Isn't the Mass more important?

The Mass is most certainly the center of Catholic worship — the greatest, the infinite sacrifice. The changes in the liturgy, especially the celebration of the Mass in the vernacular, with the priest facing the people, are designed to help us to a better understanding, appreciation and love of the Mass — to greater participation in its offering.

But this does not mean that adoration of Our Lord in the Blessed Sacrament, present in our tabernacles, is to be ignored or downgraded.

On the contrary. In fact, throughout the centuries the Church has encouraged adoration of the Blessed Sacrament not only in private devotion but also publicly through monastic and parish adoration programs, through the Forty Hours devotion, through national and international Eucharistic Congresses; and through the celebration of the feast of Corpus Christi which universally honors Christ in the Blessed Sacrament.

Our pontiffs have also issued various documents relating to the Blessed Sacrament. For example, the encyclical, *Mystery of Faith,* relates:

"The Catholic Church has always offered and still offers divine worship to the Sacrament of the Eucharist, not only during Mass, but also outside of it, reserving Consecrated Hosts with the utmost care, exposing them to solemn veneration of the faithful and carrying them in processions to the joy of great crowds of the faithful.

"In the course of the day the faithful should not omit to visit the Blessed Sacrament, which according to liturgical laws must be kept in the churches with great reverence in a most honorable location. Such visits are a proof of gratitude, an expression of love to Christ the Lord present in the Sacrament, and the duty of the adoration which we owe.

"Not only while the Holy Sacrifice is offered and the Sacrament is confected, but also after the Sacrifice has been offered and the Sacrament has been received, as long as the Eucharist is kept in our churches and oratories, Christ is truly the *Emmanuel,* that is 'God with us'. Day and night He is in our midst. He dwells with us full of grace and truth. He restores morality, nourishes virtues, consoles the afflicted, strengthens the weak."

And the Instruction on Eucharistic Worship, *The Eucharistic Mystery,* issued by the Sacred Congregation of Rites on May 25, 1967, states:

"Abiding with Christ the Lord, the faithful enjoy His intimate companionship; before Him they pour out their hearts for themselves and for others; and they pray for the peace and salvation of the world. Let the faithful according to their station in life strive to worship Christ the Lord in His Sacrament, and in this let pastors exhort by word and lead by example."

It is also noteworthy that the revised *Raccolta* — an official compendium of indulgenced prayers and good works — gives significant mention to adoration, stating that a plenary indulgence may be gained *daily* for adoration of the Blessed Sacrament for at least one-half hour.

The Church, therefore, invites and encourages us to make frequent visits and holy hours. Our Blessed Lord invites us also. His sorrowful reproach at Gethsemane echoes down through the ages to our own times:

"Could you not watch one hour with me?"[1]

ADORATION PRAYER[2]

Most Holy Trinity, Father, Son and Holy Spirit, I adore You profundly and I offer You the most precious Body, Blood, Soul and Divinity of Jesus Christ, present in all the tabernacles of the world, in reparation for the outrages, sacrileges and indifference by which He Himself is offended. Through the infinite merits of His Most Sacred Heart and those of the Immaculate Heart of Mary, I beg of You the conversion of poor sinners.

Recommended reading:

Mystery of Faith (Mysterium Fidei) — Pope Paul VI's inspiring encyclical on the Holy Eucharist; (Daughters of St. Paul Press, 50 St. Paul Avenue, Boston, Mass. 02130; 25¢ per copy).

The World's Greatest Secret by John Haffert — portrays the role of the Holy Eucharist from the Last Supper to our own times; emphasizes the importance of the Blessed Sacrament to everyone, pointing out that the Holy Eucharist is actually the Real Presence of Our Lord; (Ave Maria institute, Washington, New Jersey 07882; 95¢ per copy).

[1] St. Matthew, 26:40

[2] Prayer taught by the Angel to Lucia, Jacinta and Francisco at Fatima, Portugal in 1916.

VOCATIONS: RELIGIOUS

There are millions of people in the world and millions who have gone before us. And yet, it is strange and wonderful thing that, excepting for rare cases of identical twins, no one looks exactly like another, has exactly the same personality or has exactly the same likes and dislikes. Only a Divine Creator could have fashioned a world of such distinct individuals.

Each of these distinct individuals has a specific role in life for God calls everyone to a definite vocation, whether it be in the religious, married or single state. And it is vitally important that every individual recognize and follow his God-given vocation for therein lies happiness and holiness.

The highest vocation is that of a priest, brother or nun. Such a vocation is the greatest of gifts for Christ Himself gives this special calling: "You have not chosen me: I have chosen you."[1] A religious vocation is a family's very special "medal of honor." A boy or a girl chosen for the religious life ministers directly to Our Lord, just as Our Blessed Mother and St. Joseph did. And to these privileged ones, God has promised a special reward — a "hundredfold" not only in eternity, but in this life as well.

Yet, sad to say, many are the religious vocations lost to God, to the individual and to mankind.

Why must this be so? Is it because we do not understand, do not appreciate, a religious vocation? Just what is a vocation? How can it be recognized? What can be done to encourage and promote vocations?

A religious vocation is that of a life spent with God, in the service of God. When God invites someone to this life, He says, "Come, follow Me."[2] But, as our spiritual directors point out, God does not send His invitation in Person, with a tap on one's shoulder. Rather, the call comes softly, quietly, though insistently. It is made known, simply, in a sincere desire to live a life dedicated to the service of God. Now and then the call may come suddenly and dramatically but to most people it is just a gathering conviction that Christ wants them in His service. The conviction may be serene or troubled, clear or vague, but still it is there. To each one called there is the conviction that *the religious life is the best life for me.*

Unfortunately in the noise, the hurry and the excitement of the world the call is often lost. The conviction is stilled. Why? Who is to blame?

Some of our spiritual leaders have been clear in answering these two questions for us. Generally, they attest that in our times there are two very outstanding reasons: *parental attitudes and modern, easy living.*

There is the parental objection: *too young.* Granted that a teen may not be able to make such an important decision, *still parents sometimes forget that the final decision is not made at that age, nor at that time.* Ordination or religious profession comes only after years of living, studying and training in a seminary or convent.

If a boy or girl has a desire to serve God, has normal physical and mental health, and if there are no hindering obstacles, *then the logical thing is to try.* As time goes by, the novitiate will surely discover whether or not a candidate's vocation is a genuine one.

If there is a vocation, so much the better. If not, then there is the abiding satisfaction that an attempt to serve God was made, and that in the attempt God has been glorified, and the candidate and his family blessed. Incidentally, *there is no stigma attached to candidates who leave seminary or convent if they find that they do not have a vocation.* On the contrary. Among the former candidates are some of the Church's most outstanding lay men and women.

Sometimes parents think that their children should "wait until they have had a chance to see how the world is" before entering religion. Such parents forget that "seeing the world" may stifle a real vocation.

Besides, as one holy priest recently remarked: "What is there to see? What does the world contain which the monastery or convent does not have? God? Peace? Beauty? Inner happiness? Contentment? Education? Satisfying work? Proper recreation? No; not these. What, then? What more does the world have to offer? Noise, taverns and night clubs, speed, public sin, disillusionment, heartbreak, despair. These the world has but the monastery does not have."

And can any parent truthfully say that a teen-ager needs to "see how the world is?" No. Not really. Not in these days of magazines, radio, movies, television. Not in these days of so many divorces and of so much public crime. In these days are there any normal teen-agers who do not have a good idea of "how the world is?" Hardly.

Let us face it: *"too young" and "wait and see how the world is"* are really the devil's clever tricks causing procrastination. Satan knows the dangers of delay. He knows that "the world" is eager to take youth as its own.

Then there is the objection that *in a religious vocation a boy or girl leaves the family* — breaks it up. This is true, but only in a sense. The parents of any priest, brother or nun are the first to state that as the years go by it is their child in religion who is their greatest comfort and consolation.

The other children? They, too, have left the family, but in a far greater sense. Married and often living far away, their husbands, or wives, and children have first claim on their affections and time — as is only right and natural. And so, as time goes by the parents find that it is their child in religion who is their greatest consolation.

Another objection commonly raised is: *the life of a priest or religious is too hard.* Too hard? What of the life of a father or mother? Or of a single man or woman? Are their lives easy? Far from it. The truth is: no one's life is entirely easy.

Sometimes life in the world brings hardships and struggles with very little balance. On the other hand, a religious life has both balance and serenity for the days are composed of prayer, work and innocent recreation. Too hard? Perhaps hard, but never too hard for the blessings of God and the help of fellow religious are always available.

Then there is the objection which comes in the form of a question: *How can I be sure that my son or daughter will be happy as a priest or a religious?* The answer: Because Christ promised this — not only in eternity but in this life as well.

And if we are to apply the same question to the married or single state: How can any parent be sure of a child's happiness in either of these states? The answer can only be: parents can not be sure. Unfortunately, there is always the possibility of unhappiness, loneliness, disappointment, separation and divorce. A boy or girl may leave monastery or convent before ordination or profession if he or she finds that this vocation is not for him or her. But a boy or girl married is married for life — there is no turning back.

We need a positive approach to the matter of religious vocations. With prayer and thoughtful consideration, parents and families will come to understand that a religious vocation is a priceless thing, something to be handled carefully. Something to be accepted in humility and in joyous thanksgiving.

In Catholic circles there is a well known axim: Remember, no one goes to heaven alone. And one of the best ways of helping others to heaven is to help others to the religious life, for these, in turn, help so many others.

How can we foster religious vocations? In so many ways.

First of all, and best of all, we can pray for religious vocations.

Then we can work for vocations by helping the young, and the not-so-young, who may have vocations: by encouraging them and helping them make proper contacts; by helping their parents to understand the great favor being conferred upon them; and by inviting them to attend vocational institutes, etc.

And what about spreading vocational prayers and vocational literature? Perhaps one of our parish organizations might be interested in such a project. Another means of aiding vocations is to contribute towards a burse for some deserving boy or girl in a seminary or convent. Another way is to pay for advertisements in Catholic publications about various religious orders, their work and their opportunities for aspirants.

And then besides the *Serra International,* (22 West Monroe Street, Chicago, Illinois 60603) and the *Theresians* (330 Lake Avenue, Pueblo, Colorado 81005) apostolates, there are vocational clubs to join or to organize. There are a number of such clubs, such as *Mary Immaculate's Sponsors of Seminarians* (M.I.S.S.)[3] organized by lay people, under a spiritual director. These are doing excellent work towards fostering vocations and helping belated vocations; acquainting aspirants with the purpose and work of various Orders; and helping them to find the one most suited to their interest and capabilities. The importance of these clubs is unquestioned for there have been hundreds of priestly and religious vocations resulting from their work.

No sincere Catholic needs to be told about the tremendous worth of God's priests, nuns and brothers, or of the great debt we, and the world, owe to these apostles and handmaids of the Lord.

Thrice blessed are they who receive the gift of a vocation, for God sends His special blessing to them, to their family and to all those who may have helped them in realizing or following their vocation.

PRAYER FOR AN INCREASE IN RELIGIOUS VOCATIONS

O Dearest Jesus, Son of the Eternal Father and Mary Immaculate, grant to our boys and girls the generosity necessary to follow Thy call, and the courage required to overcome all obstacles to their vocation. Give to parents that faith, love, and spirit of sacrifice which will inspire them to offer their children to God's service, and cause them to rejoice exceedingly whenever one of their children is called to the Religious Life. Let Thy example, and that of Thy Blessed Mother and St. Joseph encourage both children and parents, and let Thy grace sustain them. Amen.

[1]St. John 15:16

[2]Mark 1:17

[3]Headquarters of M.I.S.S. are at 1070 Parkside Avenue, Buffalo, New York 14214. This apostolate is open to single women, 21 and over. It is dedicated to praying for peace and providing for the education of worthy young men to the priesthood and for the erection of chapels in mission areas.

VOCATIONS: MARRIAGE

And then there is the great and wonderful sacrament of matrimony. Catholics know that marriage is for life. And yet, so many marriages are not happy nor holy.

There comes the question: Why? Why must this be so? Why can there not be an increase in holy and happy marriages, rather than an increase in broken, fallen marriages? Who is to blame? What can we do about it?

Our spiritual directors and our Catholic marriage counsellors have studied and worked to help us achieve holy and happy marriages. Among the things which they tell us are to pray and to develop a spirit of self-sacrifice.

Parents should pray for their children's vocation, whatever it may be, as soon as children are on the way; and children should begin vocational prayers as soon as there is understanding.

Prayer is most important — especially to the Holy Spirit that He may bless and direct us to God's choice of a partner for us; to Mary and Joseph, the Perfect Couple; to our own particular Guardian Angel and Patron Saints; and to the Angel Raphael,[1] the patron of love, light, and happy meetings.

Self-sacrifice is necessary for any successful marriage. The ability to try and see the other's point of view, to consider the other's preferences and to gracefully surrender one's will to the other's leads to mutual efforts towards pleasing one another. This, in turn, reduces little grievances and the danger of harboring resentments.

Our priests and our Catholic marriage counsellors also tell us that so many marriages fail because they are based on romantic love, only. To this many a person asks: "Well, what is real love? How can I recognize it? Am I really in love?"

The answer lies in simplicity: romantic love is the enchanting state of "being in love." Romantic love is the love which naturally develops from the sharing of beauty and joy. It comes from steady dating, from the enjoyment of movies, dances, picnics, symphonies, football games, etc. But "being in love" is an effervescent thing. The glow fades in the reality, hardships and struggles of daily living.

And so they tell us that for an ideal marriage, a truly holy and happy marriage, there must also be "the other love."

What about this "other" love? How can we recognize it? Perhaps one of the best answers lies in the series of questions which we can ask ourselves:

Do I really like him (her)? Do I like his mental and spiritual interests? his ambitions, plans, hopes? Can I depend on him? Am I proud of him? Can I talk to him about almost anything? Do I understand him? Do I know his faults and shortcomings, and like him anyway? Am I really sympathetic towards his problems? Would I like him even if there should be no parties, picnics, etc.? Would I like him even if we will never have much money? Or what if he should be sick or crippled, would I still like him? If he needed help would I be willing to go out of my way to help him, no matter what? Am I willing to consider his preferences, even at the cost of giving up my own? Am I willing to sacrifice and forego things for him?

Then there is that all-important question: Would he (she) be the kind to help me grow in the love of God and neighbor? This is a very vital question. Contrary to what the stories say, in real life people do not get "married and live happily ever after." Happiness in marriage is achieved only through God's blessings upon mutual effort.

A positive answer to these questions adds up to real, abiding love — the kind which grows and lasts until death. Romantic love plus abiding love make the ideal marriage. But the counsellors say: "Be warned; do not marry for romantic love alone."

Another recognized cause of marriage failures is the lack of preparation. Knowing that marriage is for life, how is it that we spend so little thought and time towards preparing for a happy marriage? Do we understand and are we willing to accept God's laws regarding contraception, sterilization and abortion? And although it is so very important to pray and to be careful about our choice of a partner, do we also prepare ourselves for the work of this vocation?

For example: do you (a female) know how to cook, to clean, to make a real home? Do you know the value of money and how it should be spent? Etc., etc. And are you (a male) willing to assume the responsibilities of marriage? Do you have a steady job and like to work? Etc., etc.

If not, why not? The time to get ready for marriage is now. In real life, jokes about indigestible food or a selfish husband are not jokes at all. Character training and occupational training are both very necessary ingredients for any happy marriage.

Nowadays we are so fortunate in having so many fine Catholic marriage-preparation books. They are really helpful if read with prayer and thought. Also available in most cities are the invaluable services of Pre-Cana Conferences and/or Marriage Preparation Courses. (If there is none where we live, is there anything we could do, with our pastor's permission, toward getting such a conference course started? If we can, it is really very much worth the effort. And the good we will be starting will bring God's blessings not only on self but on countless others, too.)

And for those who live in remote areas, or those who really cannot get to the meetings, there is a pre-marriage course available by correspondence for engaged couples. Pastors are glad to help couples get started with this course.

And why not have our engagements blessed with the Church's beautiful Engagement Ceremony? More and more couples are seeking this blessing, and daily they privately consecrate their engagement to Our Blessed Mother.

Then there is the unhappiness caused by mixed-marriages. Generally speaking, mixed-marriages are not ideal marriages. How can they be? If a couple cannot pray together, if they cannot obey God's laws together, how can there be harmony and joy?

How can we avoid the dangers and unhappiness of mixed-marriage? Many marriage counsellors advise: "The time to stop mixed-marriage is *before it starts.* If you want to save yourself from future heartaches, do not date a non-Catholic."

And what about teen-age marriages? So many of these turn out sadly. How is it that there are so many of these? Is it because we are doing so little about discouraging teen-age "going steady?"

Regardless of current trends, the truth is that "going steady" among teens is *definitely wrong.* Why? Without getting into ethics, dating normally leads to courtship, and courtship to marriage. The problem is as basic as that. Teens are not ready for marriage. Therefore, they are not ready for "going steady."

No matter what others say or do, Catholics must take Christ's stand in this — even though we stand alone. Our pastors and spiritual leaders warn and beg us to do all that we can to stop teen courtships. It is up to the parents and to the Sisters and Brothers in our schools to take up the challenge. *If enough Catholic adults can get behind a movement to discourage teens from "going steady," the trend will turn, even in non-Catholic circles.* And the blessings of God will descend on all concerned. Is there anything we can do about this? Could we interest our local Parent-Teachers Association in this?

What about couples who are not happily married? Should they give up, and seek separation or divorce? Is their plight hopeless?

A couple's marriage is hopeless only if they want to leave it so. God gives His blessings to anyone who seeks it. But there must be cooperation, too. Sometimes, sad to say, we forget that happiness must be earned. To have happiness, we must give happiness.

Are you an unhappy husband or wife? Why? Is the fault yours or your partner's or both? Our spiritual directors say: "Take time out to look into yourself — to find out where you are to blame. If you need outside help, go and see your pastor, *together.* He will be glad to help in any way possible. And if he thinks that your marriage needs some very special help, no doubt he will suggest a competent Catholic marriage counsellor or psychiatrist." Most parishes have *Cana Conferences* to aid in such troubles, also. And there are a number of pertinent Catholic books designed to help.

Any valid marriage is worth saving. The process may be difficult and painful, but the resulting happiness far outweighs the efforts. Happy marriages may be "made in heaven" but they are achieved on earth only by prayer, effort and sacrifice. These are the things which make love in marriage grow and last throughout the years "for better or worse, for richer or poorer, in sickness and in health, until death do us part."

PRAYER FOR CHOOSING A PARTNER

O my Saviour, Who died for my redemption, I beseech You by the infinite merits of Your Precious Blood, to grant me the necessary light and grace to choose the partner with whom I can best work out my eternal salvation.

Mary, my Mother, obtain for me this grace by your most powerful intercession.

St. Joseph, patron of Christian families, pray for me. Amen.

BLESS OUR MARRIAGE[1]

We thank You, O God, for the love You have implanted in our hearts.

May it always inspire us to be kind in our words, considerate of feelings, and concerned for each other's needs and wishes.

Help us to be understanding and forgiving of human weaknesses and failings.

Increase our faith and trust in You and may Your prudence guide our life and love.

Bless our marriage, O God, with peace and happiness, and make our love fruitful for Your glory and our joy both here and in eternity. Amen.

[1]This prayer was composed by the Rev. Joseph E. Keller.

(Copies are now available in card form in quantities of 10 for 50¢; 25 for $1; 100 for $3 and 500 for $10 from the Miller Printing Co., Box 1206, Springfield, Ohio 45501).

[1]The *Book of Tobias* in the Old Testament relates how God sent the Angel Raphael to help Tobias and Sara to a happy, holy marriage.

VOCATIONS: THE SINGLE LIFE

So many of us seem to forget that the single state is a vocation, too. Singleness a vocation? Definitely.

There are hundreds of thousands of people whom God calls neither to the religious or the married life. For them He wills another purpose in life — sometimes a very special purpose.

Some of these single ones are called to their vocation as shut-ins, invalids or handicapped ones to be Christ's crossbearers to the end. Others are destined to a serving love, caring for a family, the sick or aged. And still others are called to be lay apostles, sometimes as members of a dedicated lay institute; sometimes, working privately for God; and sometimes as lay missionaries.

Such work is a vital, distinct calling. Lay missionaries are Catholics who understand Christ's desire that all nations and peoples be brought to Him. And so they leave home, personal ambitions and worldly interests for a few years or for life and they go off to the "market places" in the home and foreign missions.

They mingle with lay people, becoming co-workers with them as doctors, engineers, teachers, farmers, craftsmen, technicians, social workers, nurses, laborers, office workers, accountants, etc. By their personal lives, by their teaching and work, they bring the love of God and His Church to "the others". And through their daily contacts, they win confidence and are able to develop local lay apostles.

Special training is needed for this important vocation. Here in America we are privileged to have a number of fine apostolates which offer lay missionary training and opportunities for service. Among these are the *Lay Mission Helpers* and *M.D.: Mission Doctors,* both headquartered at 1531 West Ninth St., Los Angeles, California 90015. A listing of lay missionary groups, of general apostolates and of secular institutes may be found in the *Catholic Almanac;* also in such publications as the paperback, *Total Dedication for the Laity,* available from the Daughters of St. Paul Press, 50 St. Paul Avenue, Boston, Mass. 02130; $1.00 per copy.

Whatever the reason, whatever the purpose, we Catholics can be justly proud of our thousands of single people living honorably in the world. They are doing untold good and their reward will one day be great.

Life in the single state can be happy, holy and thoroughly satisfying. How tragic it is that this vocation is so little understood. The world so often belittles, ridicules and scorns the single life. Even parents, relatives and "those who should know better" sometimes join in the attack. How often they will say: "Well, what is the matter with you? Why don't you get married?"

How often such words lead to tragedy. So common is this critical nagging, this interfering pushing, that many have found themselves thrust into an unhappy marriage just because marriage was expected of them, or because of an unreasoning fear of being left alone, out of the crowd. Fear of criticism and ridicule has made them vulnerable to an unwise marriage. And the resulting misery has often ended in divorce and broken lives.

An unfortunate state of affairs. And the tragedy goes on repeating itself, daily, in city and in hamlet. The situation could be improved. An enlightened Catholic laity could do much to give the single man or woman recognition instead of ridicule, praise instead of scorn. We could face facts: the single state is God's Will for some of us and for some of our relatives, friends and neighbors. They are happy that way and holy that way.

Is the single life for you? If so, our spiritual advisors say: "Recognize your vocation. Glorify God in it. Be proud of it. And be happy in it. Happiness in the single state, as well as in the other states, is achieved in the love of God and in the desire to serve Him as He sees fit."

The good being accomplished by thousands of our fine single people cannot be measured. It may be in the hidden, uncomplaining kindness of the one who shoulders the family's cross of need or illness. It may be in service outside the family, as that of a teacher who relieves a nun or brother. It may be in being the parish sacristan or "right-hand man." Or it may be in the service of the lay apostolates, lay missions or secular institutes.

(Secular Institutes are associations wherein members — clerical or lay — seek Christian perfection by observing the evangelical counsels of obedience, poverty and chastity, and who dedicate themselves to the apostolate of the world. They remain in the world, are not obliged to live in community, and do not wear distinctive habits. Their apostolate is devoted to works of charity, the spread of the Faith, and the Christianizing of society in the environment in which they live and work.)

Who can measure the value of a vocation to the single life? As one zealous priest recently remarked: "Our single ones — whatever would we do without them? — God bless them!"

PRAYER FOR CHOOSING A STATE IN LIFE

O my God, Thou Who art the God of wisdom and good counsel, Thou Who readest in my heart a sincere desire to please Thee alone and to direct myself in regard to my choice of a state of life, in conformity with Thy holy will in all things, by the intercession of the most holy Virgin, my Mother, and of my Patron Saints; grant me the grace to know what state in life I ought to choose, and to embrace it when known, in order that thus I may seek Thy glory and increase it, work out my own salvation, and deserve the heavenly reward which Thou hast promised to those who do Thy holy will. Amen.

Recommended Reading:

Choose Your Tomorrow: this book presents interesting, thoughtful information designed to help young people choose the vocation which is "right for me"; (Daughters of St. Paul, 50 St. Paul's Avenue, Boston, Mass. 02130; cloth $2.00 paperback $1.00).

Total Dedication for the Laity: a guidebook to the aims and the activities of twenty secular institutes; (Daughters of St. Paul; cloth $2.00; paperback $1.00).

Looking Ahead to Marriage: this book is intended for teens of senior high school age and is useful for discussion within the family as well as in religion classes; it is objective and practical and is based on the solid teachings of Christ and His Church; it covers such subjects as choice of a partner, the engagement and wedding, family harmony, in-laws, children, divorce and birth control. (Daughters of St. Paul; cloth $3.50; paperback $2.50).

The Truth About Mixed Marriages: this booklet indicates that mixed marriages are not the ideal since disparity of religions can be a sword of division; it presents the findings of trained investigators of every faith and shows that every study leads to one conclusion: mixed marriages have so many inherent difficulties and disadvantages that young people who wish to achieve deep and lasting happiness should avoid them; the book's aim is to safeguard and promote the happiness of both Catholics and non-Catholics contemplating marriage; (Our Sunday Visitor Press, Huntington, Indiana, 47650; paperback 50¢).

Lifetime of Love: this book is a "way of life" for the married — young and old; it is filled with wisdom and offers sound solutions to daily problems; its facts and examples are written in an interesting style; highly recommended for Pre-Cana and Cana Conferences; (Daughters of St. Paul; cloth $5.00; paperback $4.00).

THE WAY OF THE CROSS

It seems strange that so many of us would not think of missing the "Stations" during Lent yet we forget all about this devotion as soon as the season is over. How unfortunate this is and what a loss this is.

The Church recommends that we pray the Stations often — so much so, that no other devotion is more highly indulgenced. And yet we often forget that the Stations are erected for our use, today and every day.

The *Way of the Cross* is an ancient devotion. From the earliest days of the Church many pilgrims journeyed to Palestine to visit the sacred places of Our Lord's sufferings and death. They prayed and meditated as they walked along the way from Pilate's palace to the hill of Calvary, a distance of about a half-mile.

The Way begins here at the court where Pilate washed his hands of the responsibility for Christ and delivered Our Blessed Lord into the hands of His enemies. And there is the courtyard where the rough soldiers and the frenzied mob mockingly made Christ, King; crowned Him with thorns; and spat upon Him. From there the heavy cross was placed upon His shoulders.

A short distance away is the point where Jesus fell the first time and so here the third station is marked. And there, a little farther along, is the scene of the sorrowful meeting between God and Mother. Then the walk extends to the place where Simon was forced to help Jesus carry His cross.

Still farther along the way are the markers placed where Veronica offered her veil to Christ; where Jesus fell the second time; where the holy women wept in sympathy; and a little farther on, the place of the third fall.

And finally, the journey's end at Calvary. Here are marked the terrible scenes of the stripping of garments, the crucifixion, the death and the burial.

To these holy places, there came great throngs of pilgrims. No hardship or peril of travel was considered too great. But as time went by, Jerusalem became a Mohammedan city barred to the Christians.

However, the places of Our Lord's sufferings were not forgotten. Tradition tells us that one day while Blessed Alvarez, a Dominican of Cordova, Spain, was thinking about the former pilgrimages, he was inspired with the idea of having paintings made picturing each scene of Our Lord's suffering. This was soon accomplished. And to his joy and that of the other monks, they could now make daily spiritual pilgrimages to Calvary. About the same time Blessed Eustachia, a Poor Clare, is said to have constructed a similar set of Stations in her convent at Messina. St. Leonard of Port Maurice, a Franciscan, also spread the devotion on his missionary journeys. Thus began the "Stations" as we know them today.

In the meantime, in 1342, the Franciscans had been assigned to the guardianship of the Holy Places. Then in 1686 Pope Innocent XI granted this Order the right to erect stations in all their churches, attaching to this devotion *all the indulgences that could be gained by devoutly visiting the actual scenes of Christ's sufferings and death,* including a plenary indulgence applicable to the souls in Purgatory. And in 1731 Pope Clement XII extended this privilege by permitting the indulgenced Stations to be erected in all churches of the world.

The *Way of the Cross is a* simple devotion suitable for any time. There are no specific prayers to be said although, if we prefer, we may use our prayerbooks or a "Stations" pamphlet. Among the newest of these is *The Stations of the Cross for Captive People.*[1] This unusual booklet combines the traditional meditations and prayers of the *Way of the Cross* with prayers for particular groups of people who live in captive countries and are deprived of freedom of worship — people who must live without the counsel and consolation of their religion, and who die without the assistance and comfort of the sacraments.

Another recent Stations pamphlet is the one entitled, *With Christ to Calvary.*[2] This, too, is unusual in that its meditations emphasize Christ's love for the Father and His overwhelming and constant desire that His Father's Will be done ever and always in all things. The meditations then follow through with pertinent applications regarding the necessity for our own faithful adherence to God's Will.

It is not necessary to kneel at each Station, though we may do so if we wish. In fact, the only requirements for gaining the indulgences are to be in the state of grace;[3] to meditate on the sufferings and death of Our Blessed Savior; and to move from Station to Station (unless the priest or a leader is making the *Way of the Cross* in public for the congregation). We may spend a few seconds or many minutes at each Station, according to time and desire.

Shut-ins and others who cannot get to church are privileged to be able to pray the "Stations" simply by holding a specially indulgenced Stations Crucifix — available free of charge to shut-ins, from the *Apostolate of the Way of the Cross* at 174 Ramsey St., Paterson, New Jersey 07501 — while praying twenty *Our Fathers, Hail Marys* and *Glorys.* Fourteen of these *Paters, Aves* and *Glorias* are to be said in memory of the fourteen Stations, five in memory of Our Lord's Sacred Wounds, and one for the intentions of the Holy Father. Those who are too ill to say the prayers may kiss the crucifix and offer a brief ejaculation in memory of Our Blessed Lord's Wounds.

Over 500,000 Stations Crucifixes have been distributed to shut-ins throughout the world. Typical of their appreciative response are the following excerpts from their letters:

"I am a cancer patient, soon to die. Your crucifix has brought me comfort and courage and I thank God." (Mrs. R. — Kansas)

"Your apostolate is my only contact with the outside world, and a great consolation that God has not forsaken me in my loneliness." (M. — Russia)

"All the Catholic lepers at Molakai now have your Stations crucifix and they use it, daily." (Sacred Heart Father-Kalaupapa, Molokai)

"I distributed your Station Crucifixes to my First Friday sick calls. The response has been tremendous." (Diocesan Priest — Kansas)

"All my novices received your Station Crucifixes on their profession day. I have tried to make the Stations of the Cross a vital part of their religious life." (Salesian Father, Master of Novices — South India)

"We give patients your Station-Crucifix and it is edifying to see it at the bed of Catholic Soldiers. (Chaplain — Army Hospital)

"Our children in this school for over a year have been faithful in making the Stations of the Cross each day." (Franciscan Sisters — Jamaica)

But, we may wonder, in these post-Vatican II times, isn't the *Way of the Cross* an old-fashioned devotion to be discouraged?

On the contrary. Speaking of devotions, Vatican II documents *(Constitution on the Sacred Liturgy,* No. 13) clearly state: "Popular devotions of Christian people are to be highly recommended, provided that they accord with the laws and norms of the Church, above all when they are ordered by the Apostolic See."

It is also noteworthy that the revised *Raccolta* — an official compendium of indulgenced prayers and good works — gives significant mention to the Stations of the Cross.

The center of our religion is Christ's redemption and the renewal of His Sacrifice on the cross through the Holy Sacrifice of the Mass.

Meditation on Our Lord's sufferings and death — especially through devoutly praying the Stations — is, therefore, *not* pious sentimentality but, rather, an effective means of strengthing our faith; of realizing the malice of sin and the necessity of observing God's commandments; of consoling resignation in the acceptance of our own particular crosses; of gaining graces to help us withstand the onslaughts of the world, the flesh and the devil; and of assisting our beloved ones and others who may be in Purgatory.

Most certainly, the *Way of the Cross* is a highly approved, traditional devotion. In fact, the Stations are a part of our churches and chapels everywhere. They are there for our use not only during the times of Lent but for today and every day.

To help us realize this and to help us understand the value of this devotion, the *Guild of the Cross,* headquartered at the Franciscan Monastery, 110 West Madison Street, Chicago, Illinois 60602, distributes a pertinent leaflet (with the same title) and invites anyone who wishes to pray the "Stations" daily or frequently to become members of this apostolate. Enrollment does not involve meetings or dues but postage to cover mailing of a certificate of membership and the leaflet would be appreciated.

Long ago Our Savior made His painful Way to Calvary. His beloved Mother and a few faithful friends prayerfully and sorrowfully followed Him along the way. Since that time countless people — saints and sinners — have spiritually joined Them in Their journey to Golgotha, offering love and reparation for their own sins and for the sins of others.

When there is a little time before or after Mass, during a visit or while making a Holy Hour, couldn't we pray along the *Way of the Cross?*

[1]Available from the Rev. Cletus Healy, S.J., 3400 West Michigan Street, Milwaukee, Wisconsin 53208; 50¢ per copy; discounts on quantity orders.

[2]Authored by the Rev. A. H. Goldschmidt, S.A.C.; 25¢ per copy; C/O St. Mary's Hospital, Huntington, West Virginia 25701.

[3]Even a person in the state of mortal sin who prays and makes the *Way of Cross* will gain the indulgences when he goes to Confession. The *Way of Cross* is especially beneficial for sinners.

WHICH WAY?

Recognizing our faults and accepting responsibility for them is a forward step towards personal amendment. The importance of this cannot be over-estimated. It is a necessary requirement for personal renewal.

In fact, the Council Fathers of Vatican II clearly defined the importance of personal renewal in their *Message to Humanity,* dated October 20, 1962: "In this assembly, under the guidance of the Holy Spirit, we wish to inquire how we ought to renew ourselves, so that we may be found increasingly faithful to the gospel of Christ."

Subsequent deliberations of Vatican II reaffirmed the importance and the necessity for interior renewal. This is stated in numerous passages of the Council's documents, including the following excerpts: "This Sacred Synod summons all to a deep interior renewal . . . Let all realize that their first and most important obligation toward the spread of the Faith is this: to lead a profoundly Christian life . . ." (*Decree on the Church's Missionary Activity,* Nos. 11, 35-36) Wherever they live, all Christians are bound to show forth by the example of their lives and by the witness of their speech, that New Man which they put on at Baptism and that power of the Holy Spirit by whom they were strengthened at Confirmation." (*Decree on the Apostolate of the Laity,* Nos. 4, 12, 13, 16).

Since the close of the Council various leaders of the clergy and the laity have been trying to help us understand and accept this responsibility. To quote just one member of the laity and one recent pontiff, we have the following admonitions:

Catherine de Hueck Doherty, the distinguished foundress of Madonna House, writing in *Restoration* frankly and courageously says: "Christians of the world, including Catholics, must face themselves first of all. This facing must be done by Christian men, at long last face to face with God, in whom they profess to believe. This encounter can result only in two decisions. Either the Christian will live the Gospel henceforth, preaching it with his life *without any compromise, without any effort of rationalizing it* . . . or he will tell Christ silently, but truthfully, as some early disciples have already done, *'Your sayings are too hard, Lord, and we shall walk with You no more!'*

"There is no room now for in-between Christian life. We have to realize that to be a Christian, a follower of Christ, means *all, or nothing at all.* We are either brothers of Christ, heirs of the Father; or we reject Him, the Father, and the Holy Spirit.

"We have played at being Christians. Chesterton was right when he said, *'Christianity has not failed. It has not yet been tried.'* . . .

"It is time that men faced a simple fact of this total commitment, this total surrender to Christ and His Gospel — *by ourselves we cannot live that Gospel.* Christ said, 'Without me, you can do nothing.'

"Because of the word of Christ and because of man's dependence upon

God, a Christian will become a man of prayer . . . of *being* before God, and, concurrently, *doing* for God. Then he will be able to live by the Gospel and preach it with his life on all the modern fronts of the Christian apostolate — political, economic, social, personal, Unless Christians do this, we will be like men battling the wind or like chaff in the wind.

"The greatest temptation presented to the Christian and his apostolate today is that he will forget this dependence and make himself the God whom he will adore. The feverish activities of so many well-meaning Christians; the restlessness of the priests, religious and the laity; the confusion that exists everywhere, are witnessing to the fact that the majority of us have not yet tried to have this encounter with God . . . do this deep examination of conscience . . . make that painful journey inward.

"We are still 'playing at being Christians.' This time our Christian masks bear the many faces of what each one of us thinks is the *aggiornamento.* Those of us who studied the documents of Vatican II often continue the game of adaptation and rationalization, instead of praying to the Holy Spirit to enlighten our intellects to understand and implement the luminous decisions of the Council.

"We bear a grave responsibility before the world — each one of us who professes to be Christ's followers. If Christ, the Living, Resurrected Christ, Who truly dwells among us, is to be understood and presented to this secular world of ours, we had better stop wasting our time in arguments and rationalizations, and begin to prove His existence by witnessing to His Reality in our midst, by being His Witnesses with our lives."

And from Pope Paul VI the reigning pontiff of Vatican II, we have the explicit reminder: ". . . We must all examine our consciences. Let us try to be true Catholics. Convinced Catholics. Firm Catholics. Good Catholics. There cannot be a watered-down, approximate and camouflaged Catholicism . . .

"A religious and moral aping of easier and questionable forms of the Christian life will not help our witness or apostleship, nor will it gain anything by way of esteem, example and trust. It will serve only to depreciate the cause of Christ and His Church . . .

"All Catholics ought to strive for Christian perfection."[1]

Above these and other admonitions, we have the teachings of our Divine Master: *"Be perfect, as your heavenly Father is perfect."* (Matthew, 5:48)

Not be fairly perfect, not be sometimes perfect, but: *be perfect!*

But, we may protest, perfection is for saints. I am just an ordinary person. How could I ever become a saint?

Anyone can become a saint. In fact, the saints attained perfection but *they were not born saints. They acquired sanctity.*

Like each of us, the saints were "ordinary" people of various ages, circumstances and vocations. They, too, had to sustain relentless struggles in the difficulties, temptations, problems, sorrows and sufferings common to us all — often much greater than ours.

However, they achieved sanctity *little by little, step by step,* through complete confidence in God, heroic fidelity to His commandments, unflinching faith and trust in His love and mercy, and willing cooperation with His Grace. In a word, they became saints by serving God in love, prayer and sacrifice, according to the vocations and circumstances of their daily lives.

The same way[2] is open to each of us, whether we are single, married or religious, whether we are rich or poor, healthy or sick, famous or unknown. To be a saint, the Church repeatedly reminds us, is the work of God's grace, together with the *free, faithful and heroic co-operation of our will.*

Sanctity is, therefore, within the reach of us all. It can be, it must be, acquired. In fact, we know that the primary and entire purpose of life is *to know God, to love Him, and to serve Him faithfully in this life so that one day we may be happy, with Him, forever in heaven.*

If God's loving providence places us in the position of being saintly popes, heroic martyrs, holy founders of great monastic orders or apostolates, or staunch defenders of the Faith, this is fine and wonderful. But God does not expect the impossible from anyone. For most of us, sanctity simply consists in loving and faithfully serving God, *day by day,* in sickness and in health, in sorrow and in joy, and in the monotony, difficulties, temptations and problems encountered by the teacher, the student, the housewife, the clerk, the business man, the laborer, the factory worker, the salesman, the professional, political and artistic ones.

Whatever the vocation and the circumstances of our lives, God calls us all to love Him above all things and to love our neighbors as ourselves. And so, facing ourselves and facing truth, there comes the piercing challenge:

Shall we continue along our way, mediocre and lukewarm in our love of God and of neighbor? Or shall we put forth valiant, even heroic, efforts so that moving forward in the footsteps of Christ, we may truly answer Our Savior's plea: *"If you love Me, keep My commandments!"*

[1]Excerpts from an address entitled *Unity Among Catholics is First Essential for Christian Unity,* given to a general audience on January 21, 1970.

[2]Among the books pertaining to this "daily way to perfection", is the simple but eloquent book, *Story of a Soul* (Autobiography of St. Therese of Liseux); available from the Apostolate of Christian Action, P.O. Box 24, Fresno, California 93707; $1.50 paperback.

Recommended Reading:

Renewal for All God's People by Rev. Robert J. Fox; available from Our Sunday Visitor Press, Noll Plaza, Huntington, Indiana 46750; paperback, $2.50. This important book offers hope, renewed faith, and a balanced view of doctrines and disciplines of the Catholic Church.

A CHALLENGE

Everyone who walks with Christ understands the words: if you will go with Me, you must go against the wind and the tide; you must follow Me in My rags as well as in My silver slippers; you must stand by Me when I am bound in irons as well as when I walk with applause.

Adversity will lose its power to discourage when your life has for its purpose the Christ Who was crucified. So, too, in the good things that you do, you are made better by identity with Christ.

(Excerpts from The Purpose of Living by Richard Cardinal Cushing; published by the Daughters of St. Paul Press, 50 St. Paul Avenue, Boston, Mass. 02130.)

PRAYER

O Christ Jesus, I acknowledge You as Universal King. All that has been made was created for You. Exercise over me all the rights that You have.

I renew my baptismal promises, renouncing Satan, his pomps and his works, and I promise to live as a good Christian. Especially do I pledge myself by all the means in my power to bring about the triumph of the rights of God and of Your Church.

Divine Heart of Jesus, I offer You my own poor actions to the end that all hearts may recognize Your consecrated Kingship and that thus the Kingdom of Your peace may be established in the whole world. Amen.

INDEX

Page

Page

Page

Page

Page

INDEX TO BOOKS, CASSETTES, LEAFLETS, MOVIES, PAMPHLETS, RECORDS, AND TAPES

Page

Page

Page

INDEX TO PRAYERS

RECENT POPULAR PAPERBACKS BY THIS AUTHOR:

DEAR ALCOHOLIC

($1.25); this very special paperback offers hope and encouragement to potential alcoholics, alcoholics and their families; relates positive suggestions for gaining sobriety and achieving personal and family happiness.

ARE WE SHORT-CHANGING OUR YOUTH?

Foreword by Bishop Vincent Waters

Highly recommended as a valuable help for parents, pastors and teachers in assisting youth with their problems; $1.25 postpaid.

LET'S SAVE THE UNBORN!

Foreword by Rev. Msgr. Alphonse Popek, J.C.D.

A very important, interesting digest; answers questions which are being asked about abortion; classed as "a must" for anyone who cares about the safety of the unborn; $1.25 postpaid.

HONESTLY, HAVE YOU TRIED EVERYTHING?

Foreword by Rev. Francis Larkin, SS. CC.

The foreword states: "Sometimes people beset with suffering or frustrations will say: 'What shall I do? I have tried everything.' But, HONESTLY, HAVE YOU TRIED EVERYTHING? . . .

"This exceptional paperback shows that any problem can be solved or endured with God's help." $1.25 postpaid.

FATIMA OR MOSCOW?

An interesting, "different" Fatima booklet; takes a candid look at Our Lady's message in relation to self; and reports the necessary means for attaining the true and lasting peace promised by Our Blessed Mother; 50¢ postpaid.

Discounts on bulk orders of each of these items is available.

Order from: Sacred Heart Center, 6026 West Harwood Avenue, Orlando, Florida 32811.